MW00577589

To:

_____

From:

_____

Date:

_____

Inspire You

Daily
Devotions

You

TERRY WARD
TUCKER

Scripture Quotation Sources Used by Permission:

NIV The Holy Bible, New International Version © 1973, 1978, 1984. International Bible Society. Used by permission of Zondervan Bible Publishers.

KJV King James Version.

MSG The Message © 1993. Used by permission of NavPress Publishing Group.

NKJV New King James Version © 1979, 1980, 1982. Thomas Nelson, Inc..

NASB New American Standard Bible © 1960, 1962, 1963, 1968, 1971, 1972, 1973, 1975, 1977, 1988, 1995. The Lockman Foundation.

AMP Amplified ® Bible © 1954, 1958, 1962, 1964, 1965, 1987. The Lockman Foundation.

AMPC Amplified Bible, Classic Edition © 1965, 1987. The Lockman Foundation.

NLT The New Living Translation © 1996, 2004, 2007, 2013, 2015. Tyndale House Foundation. Used by permission of Tyndale House Publishers, Inc., Carol Stream, Illinois, 60188.

TLB The Living Bible © 1971. Used by permission of Tyndale House Publishers, Inc., Carol Stream, Illinois, 60188.

ESV The Holy Bible, English Standard Version ® Copyright © 2001. Crossway, a publishing ministry of Good News Publishers.

CEV Contemporary English Version © 1991, 1992, 1995. American Bible Society. Used by permission.

GNT Good News Translation in Today's English Version, Second Edition © 1992. American Bible Society. Used by permission.

MEV The Holy Bible, Modern English Version © 2014. Charisma House.

WEY Weymouth New Testament (The New Testament in Modern Speech) © 1903.

CEB The Common English Bible © 2011. Church Resources Development Corporation.

NET The NET Bible® © 1996-2003. Biblical Studies Press.

GULLAH TRANSLATION, De Nyew Testament © 2005. Wycliffe (www.gullahbible.com), American Bible Society.

All songs and lyrics are public domain with the exception of "Lord of the Dance." Stainer & Bell Ltd. © 1963. (Admin. Hope Publishing Company, Carol Stream, IL 60188.) All rights reserved. Used by permission.

Copyright © 2020. Terry Ward Tucker.

All rights reserved. No content may be reproduced without the expressed written permission of the author.

Cover and interior design by Rich Carnahan.

ISBN: 1734112204
ISBN-13: 9781734112207
LCCN: 2019917507

January

ASK GOD FOR A FRESHENED BEGINNING. HE WILL PROVIDE IT, BECAUSE HE LOVES YOU.

Launch the new year with your Heavenly Father.
Praise him for the vibrant new thing he is doing in
your life through his Son and Holy Spirit.

Therefore, if anyone is in Christ, he is a new creation.
The old has passed away; behold, the new has come.

2 Corinthians 5:17 ESV

Dear God, thank you for the blessing of a hopeful new start in my Savior Jesus, who saved me by his grace, forgiveness, and gift of faith through his death and resurrection. I am a new creature in him, regenerated by the Holy Spirit into the newness of everlasting life. Heavenly Father, I pray my gratitude in your Son's name for doing this new thing in me. Praise you, Father, Son, and Holy Spirit. Amen.

Since you have heard about Jesus and have learned the truth that comes
from him, throw off your old sinful nature and your former way of life,
which is corrupted by lust and deception. Instead, let the Spirit
renew your thoughts and attitudes. Put on your new nature,
created to be like God – truly righteous and holy.

Ephesians 4:21-24 NLT

NOTES & PRAYERS ....

....

....

....

GOD WILL HELP YOU OVERCOME ANY DIFFICULTY.

Are you depressed about life's trials and troubles? Tell Jesus! Only he can replace your sadness with divine confidence. You will find peace, rest, and hope, if you turn your burdens over to him. But be careful. The last thing you need is to take them back.

Pile your troubles on God's shoulders – he'll carry your load.
He'll help you out. He'll never let good people topple into ruin.
PSALM 55:22 MSG

Father God, I feel overwhelmed by my circumstances more often than I care to admit. I ask you today and every day, help me practice casting my cares on you and leaving them in your divine competence. I do not know why I find myself reaching for them again. In your Word, I hear you reassuring me in loving language to surrender my woes to you, for how can I help others carry their burdens, if I am weighed down by my own? I am comforted you love me enough to remind me I can always give my troubles to you. In Jesus' name, thank you, Father. I feel lighter already! Amen.

[Jesus] Come to me, all you who are weary and burdened,
and I will give you rest.
MATTHEW 11:28 NIV

NOTES & PRAYERS ....

....

....

....

YOUR HEAVENLY FATHER OFFERS YOU TENDER SOLACE IN JESUS. SEEK COMFORT IN THE NEARNESS OF HIS SPIRIT.

Have you discovered your one and only peaceful place is close to God's Son? It is a wonderful thing to learn, for when you grasp that his nearness is a Spiritual reality, you realize suddenly and slowly, joyfully and completely, delightfully, refreshingly, and without reservation, life is worth living in your Savior.

Come close to God, and God will come close to you.
JAMES 4:8A NLT

Lord Jesus, accept my gratitude for your presence in unity with God the Father and Holy Spirit. What a comfort that when you saved me, you fulfilled your promise to make your home with me in Spirit. I will not have to face this day or any other day alone. You are with me through chaos and calm, waking and sleeping, joy and sorrow. As I rest and rejoice in your company, I ask you to put someone who needs you in my path. Please, Lord, let me share your nearness. In your name, thank you, Jesus, for keeping me close. Amen.

Jesus replied, "Anyone who loves me will obey my teaching. My Father will love them, and we will come to them and make our home with them."
JOHN 14:23 NIV

NOTES & PRAYERS ....
....
....
....

GOD IS WITH YOU WHENEVER YOU ENCOUNTER CRUELTY. JUST ASK HIM FOR FAITH TO TRUST HIM THROUGH IT.

What is your first and best response to maltreatment?
If it is loving and praying for your offender,
you have chosen the mindset of Christ.

[Jesus] I say, love your enemies! Do good to those who hate you.
Bless those who curse you. Pray for those who hurt you.
You must be compassionate, just as your Father is compassionate.
LUKE 6:27B-28; 36 NLT

Father, heal me from getting irritated with people who treat me poorly. Give me a softer heart. Remind me to pray most for those who hurt me most. You know me, Lord. I find it easy to pray for those who please me, but difficult to pray for those who do not. And though I am aware of your promise to reward me if I love my enemies, I still fall short. Take self's prickly feelings out of my heart and replace them with Jesus' forgiving attitude. In his name, I pray to meet my adversaries with love, never self's hostility. Amen.

In your relationships with one another,
have the same mindset as Christ Jesus.
PHILIPPIANS 2:5 NIV

NOTES & PRAYERS

DO YOU CONSTANTLY FEEL SHORT OF TIME? IF YOU DO, YOU ARE DEALING IN HUMAN TIME, NOT GOD'S TIME.

God gave you plenty of time to do whatever he has planned for you. If you find yourself always wishing you had more time, you are allowing self's plans get in the way of your Father's plans. If your priority is God, you will have more than enough time to honor his goodness. But if your priority is self, you will never have enough time to honor goodness in anyone or anything.

Father, remind me to stop packing so much busyness dreamed up by self into the time you have given me. Too often I find myself suffering from a case of striving – toiling away long hours on self's projects, instead of respecting the Spiritual intentions of your God-blessed time. I have learned in Scripture all time is yours, even unto infinity. Thank you for prompting me to focus on the Spiritual Truth that to be worthwhile, everything I do in the time you have allotted me must be to your glory. In Jesus' name, thank you, God, for eternity in you. Amen.

With the Lord a day is like a thousand years,
and a thousand years are like a day.

2 PETER 3:8B NIV

NOTES & PRAYERS ....

....

....

....

IF YOU MAKE PRAISING GOD YOUR PRIORITY, EVERYTHING ELSE WILL FALL INTO PLACE.

God created you to glorify him in joyful worship
that pleases him and blesses you. Praise God extravagantly,
and he will bless you more extravagantly.

Bring all who claim me as their God, for I have made them for my glory.
It was I who created them, the people I formed for myself
that they may proclaim my praise.

ISAIAH 43:7 NLT; 43:21 NIV

Father, I am troubled by how much I think of self. I ask you
to empty my heart of egocentric pettiness and fill it, instead,
with reverence for your supernatural glory. You designed
me to worship you, a blessing for which I am grateful. In
Jesus' name, I beg you to accept my love and adoration.
Thank you for the privilege of glorifying you. I am a citizen of your Kingdom in Jesus, sealed eternally by your Holy
Spirit. Thank you, Abba, for the joyful gift of praising your
Holy Trinity forever – Father, Son, and Holy Spirit. Amen.

So we praise God for the glorious grace he has poured
out on us who belong to his dear Son.

EPHESIANS 1:6 NLT

NOTES & PRAYERS ....

....

....

....

GIVE THANKS TO YOUR HEAVENLY FATHER FOR ASSURANCE OF SALVATION IN JESUS.

For his Spirit (God's Holy Spirit) joins with our spirit to affirm that we are God's children.

ROMANS 8:16 NLT

Father, help me when I sink into the dark pit of negative thinking. I pray in Jesus' name my mind will be lifted up by the power of your Spirit, not weighed down by the Enemy's lie that wickedness is out of control. Whenever I fall into thinking iniquity has become all-powerful in the world, – Satan's evil deception, for he and his malevolence have already been defeated – I find myself discouraged, even doubting my salvation at times. I beg you, Mighty Father, in the name of Jesus, Faithful and True, heal me of every faithless thought. Help me remember your Truth, Lord, that no matter how hopeless any situation appears, you are sovereign, good, immutable, and eternal. Praise you for delivering your children from evil, even me. Thank you, Holy Spirit, for hope and asurrance in Jesus. Amen.

Oh! May the God of green hope fill you up with joy, fill you up with peace, so that your believing lives, filled with the life-giving energy of the Holy Spirit, will brim over with hope!

ROMANS 15:13 MSG

NOTES & PRAYERS ....

....

....

....

OBEDIENCE REVEALS YOUR LEVEL OF COMMITMENT TO GOD, AND SO DOES DISOBEDIENCE.

Father, thank you for Truth in your Word that I will find my best life and best blessings through hearing and heeding your Holy Spirit's instruction. In the name of Jesus, remind me to listen, hear, obey, and act in full submission. Amen.

Listen- Then a cloud appeared and covered them, and a voice came from the cloud: "This is my Son, whom I love. Listen to him!"
Mark 9:7 NIV

Hear- [Jesus] My sheep hear my voice, and I know them, and they follow me. I give them eternal life, and they will never perish, and no one will snatch them out of my hand.
John 10:27-28 ESV

Obey- Listen! Obedience is better than sacrifice, and submission is better than offering the fat of rams.
1 Samuel 15:22b NLT

Act- But be ye doers of the word, and not hearers only, deceiving your own selves.
James 1:22 KJV

NOTES & PRAYERS ....

....

....

....

PRAYER IS FRAGRANT PERFUME POURED OUT BEFORE YOUR HEAVENLY FATHER.

Just as God's love is sweet fragrance to you, your love for God expressed in prayer is sweet fragrance to him.

Father, I hope with all my heart you experience my prayer as perfumed incense rising in love. I am grateful to be a vessel for Christ, filled by his Spirit with delightful aromas of prayer, praise, and worship. Holy God, I believe your use of fragrance in Scripture is not merely a metaphor, but literal, that you enjoy pleasant physical and Spiritual bouquets as they float up to you in prayers of believers. In your Son's name, thank you for the privilege of emanating his essence of love in prayer to you, just as he emanates his essence of Truth in salvation for me. Amen.

May my prayer be set before you like incense;
may the lifting up of my hands be like the evening sacrifice.
PSALM 141:2 NIV

Follow God's example, therefore, as dearly loved children and walk in the
way of love, just as Christ loved us and gave himself up for us
as a fragrant offering and sacrifice to God.
EPHESIANS 5:1-2 NIV

NOTES & PRAYERS ....

....

....

....

WHEN LIFE'S WEATHER FORECAST IS SCATTERED SHOWERS AND THUNDERSTORMS, YOUR FAITH IN JESUS LEADS YOU TO SEEK SHELTER IN HIM. HE COVERS AND PROTECTS HIS FAITHFUL ONES WITHOUT FAIL.

Consider it pure joy, my brothers and sisters, whenever you face trials of many kinds, because you know that the testing of your faith produces perseverance. Let perseverance finish its work so you may be mature and complete, not lacking anything.

JAMES 1:2-4 NIV

Thank you, Father, for your counterintuitive teaching on the storms of life. You instruct me in your Word to view troubles as opportunities, not adversities. And though I often falter as tough situations rush toward me, I know in my heart you will never allow a child of yours face difficulties alone. You are with me. In Jesus' name, I ask for help with being as thankful for hard times as easy times. Teach me to count everything for joy in your Son, even life's storms. He is my good portion in all circumstances. Amen.

Many are the afflictions of the righteous, but the Lord delivers him out of them all.

PSALM 34:19 ESV

NOTES & PRAYERS ....

....

....

....

LIVING WATER OF THE HOLY SPIRIT IS JESUS' SUPERNATURAL GIFT TO YOU.

When God saved you in Jesus, the Holy Spirit entered your heart and made his home with you. According to Jesus' divine Truth in God's Word, the Holy Spirit is living water that sustains your Spiritual life, just as physical water sustains your physical life.

[Jesus] "Let anyone who is thirsty come to me and drink. Whoever believes in me, as Scripture has said, rivers of living water will flow from within them." By this he meant the Spirit, whom those who believed in him were later to receive.

JOHN 7:37B-39A NIV

Thank you, Father God, for living water of the Holy Spirit. I am grateful for his everlasting spring of grace that quenches my Spiritual thirst for salvation. In the name of your Son, who is your loving Truth and holy Word, I ask to drink deeply from the Spirit's well of eternal life. Praise you, Father! Praise you, Jesus! Praise you, Spirit! Amen.

For we were all baptized by one Spirit so as to form one body – whether Jews or Gentiles, slave or free – and we were all given the one Spirit to drink.

1 CORINTHIANS 12:13 NIV

NOTES & PRAYERS ....
....
....
....

JESUS IS GOD'S BREAD OF LIFE FOR YOU.

Are you serving your Savior because you want him to perform miracles, the way he fed five thousand from two fish and twelve loaves? Or are you serving him because Jesus himself is the miracle – God's Spiritual and eternal bread of life.

Seek the Kingdom of God above all else, and live righteously, and he will give you everything you need.
MATTHEW 6:33 NLT

Lord Jesus, lead me away from thinking constantly of what you can do for me, and focus my heart on what I can do for you – falling down before you, worshiping you, glorifying you for who you are, beloved Son of Almighty God, His Miracle Word. In your name, I pray my thanks that when I seek you, I find God's entire Kingdom within your Spirit. Loving Savior, I choose you above all others. Amen.

Jesus replied, "I tell you the truth, you want to be with me because I fed you, not because you understood the miraculous signs. But don't be so concerned about perishable things like food. Spend your energy seeking the eternal life that the Son of Man (God's Son himself) can give you. For God the Father has given me the seal of his approval."
JOHN 6:26-27 NLT

NOTES & PRAYERS ....
....
....
....

WHEN YOU ARE EXHAUSTED, JESUS IS YOUR ONLY TRUE REPOSE.

Would you like to trade self's weariness for rest in Jesus?
Then stop, breathe, pray, and relax in the knowledge your Savior
will give you relief the moment you lean on him.

[Jesus] Are you tired? Worn out? Burned out on religion? Come to me.
Get away with me and you'll recover your life. I'll show you how to take a
real rest. Walk with me and work with me – Watch how I do it. Learn the
unforced rhythms of grace. I won't lay anything heavy or ill-fitting on you.
Keep company with me and you'll learn to live freely and lightly.
MATTHEW 11:28-30 MSG

Father, how many times do I have to learn the same lesson –
working too hard and resting too little makes me sick. And
I am not the only one experiencing this debilitating cycle. I
hear others talking about the same result in their own lives.
It is epidemic! Touch me, Lord. Touch all of us with the
wisdom of your true Word, your only begotten Son, Jesus
Christ. For he is your Truth and my repose. In his name, I
pray all gratitude for rest in him, my salvation. Amen.

I look up to the mountains – does my help come from there?
My help comes from the Lord, who made heaven and earth!
PSALM 121:1-2 NLT

NOTES & PRAYERS ....

....

....

....

GOD PROMISES AMAZING BLESSINGS TO CHEERFUL GIVERS. IF YOU WANT TO BE FAVORED MIGHTILY, JOIN THAT GROUP.

Your Heavenly Father, who is generous to you, wants you to be generous to others, and in the process, receive all blessings that will flow to you from kindhearted sharing. You can never out-give or out-share Mighty God. That is his promise, and as you already know, your Father always keeps his promises.

Lord, you have convicted my heart concerning resources and giving. Your expectations are clear in Scripture. Yet, in my own strength, I cannot find the discipline to be generous to others. Self does not want me to share. I pray for help in becoming a responsible steward of every blessing you send my way, which starts with becoming a generous, faithful, loving, cheerful giver. In your charitable name, Jesus, and for your glory, teach me to give. Amen.

You must each decide in your heart how much to give. And don't give reluctantly or in response to pressure. "For God loves a person who gives cheerfully." And God will generously provide all you need. Then you will always have everything you need and plenty left over to share with others. As the Scriptures say, "They share freely and give generously to the poor. Their good deeds will be remembered forever."
2 Corinthians 9:7-9 NLT

NOTES & PRAYERS ....

....

....

....

GOD WANTS YOU TO ENJOY FOOD TO HIS GLORY. WHAT A BLESSING!

Good food is a pleasing gift from your Heavenly Father. The question is: How do you show gratitude for God's nourishing food – by enjoying or overindulging? In God's economy, less consumption often demonstrates more gratitude. And when it comes to health, gratitude always contributes more than greed.

Heavenly Father, I am tempted every day by unhealthy food, and too often I give in to shocking excess. In Jesus' name, help me choose self-control over self-indulgence. Amen.

But Daniel was determined not to defile himself by eating the food and wine given to them by the king. He asked the chief of staff for permission not to eat these unacceptable foods. "Please test us for ten days on a diet of vegetables and water," Daniel said. "At the end of the ten days, see how we look compared to the other young men who are eating the king's food." At the end of the ten days, Daniel and his three friends looked healthier and better nourished than the young men who had been eating the food assigned by the king.
DANIEL 1:8; 12-13; 15 NLT

Whether you eat or drink, or whatever you do,
do all to the glory of God.
1 CORINTHIANS 10:31 ESV

NOTES & PRAYERS ....

....

....

....

DIVINE PATIENCE OVERCOMES WORLDLY IMPATIENCE.

Godly patience with others (or lack thereof) is an accurate measure of the Holy Spirit's supremacy within your heart. Are you meeting your Heavenly Father's gold standard in practicing patience? If not, ask the Holy Spirit to help you get out of your own way and God's way. Look to Jesus as your model for patience.

Dear God, I admit impatience has become a stronghold in my heart as I struggle with navigating modern life. I am impatient even with myself. I already know behaving patiently or impatiently is a choice, and I have fallen into the habit of choosing badly. Let me be patient, not impatient, even as life's pressures conspire to trip me up. I recognize I cannot embody the fruit of the Spirit that is patience without yielding my entire existence over to you. Thus, I yield, Father, beseeching the Holy Spirit to keep my eyes trained on Jesus, for he is my Savior and perfect example of Godly patience. Jesus is the good shepherd who leads me in the paths of righteousness. I pray in his name for divine patience that only he can provide. Amen.

Therefore, as God's chosen people, holy and dearly loved, clothe yourselves with compassion, kindness, humility, gentleness, and patience.
COLOSSIANS 3:12 NIV

NOTES & PRAYERS ....

....

....

....

COMPASSION IS YOUR HEAVENLY FATHER'S KIND WAY. PRAY FOR HELP IN DEVELOPING COMPASSION, WHICH WILL BE GOD'S COMPASSION SHOWN TO OTHERS THROUGH YOU.

Gratitude to God for compassion when you are suffering softens your attitude toward those around you who are also hurting. If you pray, God will turn your gratitude into compassion. Be grateful to Jesus he taught you gratitude, but be more grateful he modeled compassion.

Thank you, God, for divine compassion. You sacrificed Jesus, your Son, to redeem me from sin and guarantee my eternal life through his resurrection. Jesus is my example of what divine compassion looks like, dying to self and living for others. My Savior, you declared that when I am compassionate toward those in need, it is the same as being compassionate toward you. In your name, I pray to have more compassion, knowing if it is genuine, it will be your compassion flowing through me toward those you love. Amen.

Summing up: Be agreeable, be sympathetic, be loving, be compassionate, be humble. That goes for all of you, no exceptions. No retaliation. No sharp-tongued sarcasm. Instead, bless – that's your job, to bless. You'll be a blessing and also get a blessing.

1 Peter 3:8-9 MSG

NOTES & PRAYERS ....

....

....

....

JESUS IS FAITHFUL, NOT FICKLE.
WHICH ARE YOU?

Bless people you care about with the loyalty of Jesus and with the Spiritually nourishing fruit of the Spirit that is faithfulness.

Jesus Christ is the same yesterday and today and forever.

HEBREWS 13:8 NIV

Father, am I faithful or fickle in my relationships? Who can count on me? Savior Jesus, you have made yourself a living example of God's steadfast character, my model for faithfulness. I weep over being fickle at times, but I dry my tears in the knowledge that for the sake of others, your Spirit can change me from fickle to faithful. In Jesus' name – Faithful and True – help me share his faithfulness. Amen.

The faithful love of the Lord never ends! His mercies never cease. Great is his faithfulness; his mercies begin afresh each morning.

LAMENTATIONS 3:22-23 NLT

Never let loyalty and kindness leave you! Tie them around your neck as a reminder. Write them deep within your heart. Then you will find favor with both God and people, and you will earn a good reputation.

PROVERBS 3:3-4 NLT

NOTES & PRAYERS ....

....

....

....

GOD'S LOVINGKINDNESS IS PERFUMED OINTMENT FOR YOUR SOUL.

Welcome to residency in God's kingdom, where saved citizens are characterized by kindness. If you are kind to others by the power of the Holy Spirit in the name of Jesus, your Heavenly Father will do an amazing amount of good work through you, which blesses you more than those whom you bless.

Chosen by God for this new life of love, dress in the wardrobe God picked out for you: compassion, kindness, humility, quiet strength, discipline.
COLOSSIANS 3:12 MSG

Savior Jesus, you demonstrated lovingkindness from the cross as you exercised divine grace by praying for those who were killing you, *Father, forgive them for they know not what they do.* And then, as weak and near death as you were, you exercised more divine grace and kindness by promising the thief suffering crucifixion next to you, *Today you will be with me in paradise.* In your name, Lord and Savior, teach me your lovingkindness. Glorify you! Amen.

Be kind to one another, tender-hearted, forgiving each other, just as God in Christ also has forgiven you.
EPHESIANS 4:32 NASB

NOTES & PRAYERS ....
....
....
....

JESUS' GENTLENESS IS A CURIOUS INDICATOR OF HIS MIRACULOUS STRENGTH.

Do not confuse your Savior's gentleness with weakness.
He is your tender shepherd and
God's Lion of Judah, simultaneously.

[Jesus] I am the good shepherd.
The good shepherd lays down his life for the sheep.
JOHN 10:11 ESV

Look, the lion of the tribe of Judah (Jesus),
the heir to David's throne, has won the victory.
REVELATION 5:5B NLT

My Savior, your custom of reaching out to children becomes more meaningful as I recall you refer to believers as children of God. You are gentle in caring for your children, yet mighty in conquering the cross. I pray in your name to be gentle-and-strong like you. Be glorified, Son of God. Amen.

But Jesus called the children to him and said, "Let the little children come
to me, and do not hinder them, for the kingdom of God belongs to such
as these. Truly I tell you, anyone who will not receive the kingdom
of God like a little child will never enter it."
LUKE 18:16-17 NIV

NOTES & PRAYERS ....

....

....

....

GOD IS THE ONE SOURCE OF TRUE GOODNESS. PRAISE HIS VIRTUOUS NAME.

Have you ever congratulated yourself for being good or
doing good? If you have, stop a moment and consider
the real author of any goodness flowing through you.
It is not you. It never was. It is your Heavenly Father.
He gave you his divine goodness when he gave you Jesus.

*For once you were full of darkness, but now you have light from the Lord.
So live as people of light! For this light within you produces
only what is good and right and true.*

EPHESIANS 5:8-9 NLT

It delights me, Father, that in your Word, you so often connect promises with commands and precepts. You assure me if I walk in goodness, I will find safe pasture in you. Remind me, God, any goodness flowing from my heart toward others is yours, not mine, and any righteousness shining from my soul is the Spirit of your perfect Son, not self. Precious Jesus, in your name, I pray to be a channel for your goodness and purity. Praise you, Righteous Savior. Amen.

You (God) are good, and the source of good; train me in your goodness.

PSALM 119:68 MSG

NOTES & PRAYERS ....

....

....

....

GOD'S DIVINE GRACE GIVEN TO YOU IS HIS GENEROUS BLESSING OF UNDESERVED FAVOR.

Let your Father's willingness to save you by his grace (though you do not deserve it) inspire you to extend grace to others (though they do not deserve it, either). God's grace is a gift of love and favor no one deserves. That is what makes grace amazing.

Heavenly Father, help me throw out all ungracious thoughts that reverberate inside my head whenever I encounter people I view as wicked, particularly those who have hurt me or my loved ones. I remind myself of Jonah, who got angry with you, Father God, for sparing the citizens of Nineveh when they turned away from evil to please you. Jonah thought they should be punished for past wrongdoings, not forgiven. I admit, I have no more right than Jonah to be resentful when you extend grace to undeserving people. After all, you continually extend grace to me, chief of the undeserving. In Jesus' name, I pray to be like him, your graceful Son. Amen.

So we praise God for the glorious grace he has poured out on us who belong to his dear Son (Jesus). He is so rich in kindness and grace that he purchased our freedom with the blood of his Son and forgave our sins. He has showered his kindness on us, along with all wisdom and understanding.
EPHESIANS 1:6-8 NLT

NOTES & PRAYERS ....

....

....

....

YOUR TREASURE IS IN JESUS, NOT POSSESSIONS.

You can depend on the accuracy of God's map to lasting treasure. His map – his Word – leads to Jesus, his beloved Son and ultimate treasure, whom God sacrificed and resurrected to save your soul.

Indeed, I count everything as loss because of the surpassing worth of knowing Christ Jesus my Lord. For his sake, I have suffered the loss of all things and count them as rubbish, in order that I may gain Christ.
PHILIPPIANS 3:8 ESV

I am grateful, Father, you gave me Jesus, your pearl of great price, your sinless gem, your loving treasure, whose sacrifice unto death and subsequent resurrection made him worthy to forgive my sins and ransom my soul. In his name, thank you for salvation grace, your treasure-gift that guarantees life in your presence eternally. Praise the Son. Amen.

[Jesus] Do not lay up for yourselves treasure on earth, where moth and rust destroy and where thieves break in and steal, but lay up for yourselves treasures in heaven, where neither moth nor rust destroys and where thieves do not break in and steal. For where your treasure is, there your heart will be also.
MATTHEW 6:19-21 ESV

NOTES & PRAYERS ....
....
....
....

WHEN YOUR HEART FEELS TROUBLED... WHEN DISQUIET TORMENTS YOUR MIND... WHEN RESTLESSNESS PLAGUES YOUR SOUL... GOD WILL WALK YOU THROUGH EVERY UPSET AND BRING YOU OUT VICTORIOUS.

If you will humble yourselves under the mighty hand of God, in his good time he will lift you up. Let him have all your worries and cares, for he is always thinking about you and watching everything that concerns you.

1 PETER 5:6-7 TLB

Dear God, in Jesus' name, make me grateful for thorns that prick when I do not get my way. Getting my way has been an ongoing ambition, which has often resulted in your blessing me by stopping my efforts. Thank you, Father. Amen.

[Paul] So to keep me from becoming conceited because of the surpassing greatness of the revelations, a thorn was given me in the flesh, a messenger of Satan to harass me, to keep me from becoming conceited. Three times I pleaded with the Lord about this, that it should leave me. But he said to me, "My grace is sufficient for you, for my power is made perfect in weakness."

2 CORINTHIANS 12:7-9A ESV

NOTES & PRAYERS ....

....

....

....

YOU ARE A LIVING STONE OF SERVICE IN JESUS' CHURCH.

On saving your soul, Jesus turned you into a precious living stone
that he shaped into a perfect fit for his church body,
which proved he loved you and wanted you to be an integral
part of his Kingdom, all before you ever loved him.

*You also, like living stones, are being built into a spiritual house to be
a holy priesthood, offering spiritual sacrifices acceptable
to God through Jesus Christ.*

1 PETER 2:5 NIV

Savior Jesus, I am grateful you are the capstone of your one
true church. Make me a living stone in your service. You
are the Truth holding your church together, indeed, holding
everything together. In your name and to your glory, thank
you that all believers are in unity with you and each other.
We are the living stones of your congregation. Let us serve
you by serving one another – and others – inside and outside brick-and-mortar buildings. As living stones in service,
Savior Jesus, we are grateful to be one in you. Amen.

---

*And I tell you, you are Peter, and on this rock I will build my church,
and the gates of hell shall not prevail against it.*

MATTHEW 16:18 ESV

NOTES & PRAYERS ....

....

....

....

NATURE IS EXQUISITE EVIDENCE OF YOUR HEAVENLY FATHER'S MAGNIFICENCE.

Your deep appreciation and respect for the natural world come from knowing nature is one of God's beautiful expressions of his beauty as Creator of everything, seen and unseen.

Worthy are you, our Lord and God, to receive glory
and honor and power, for you created all things,
and by your will they existed and were created.

REVELATION 4:11 ESV

Father, in Jesus' name, thank you all nature proclaims your power, and that Jesus and the Holy Spirit were also present at creation – Jesus, not created, but God's Christ; and the Holy Spirit, not created, but presider over the waters. Amen.

Ask the animals, and they will teach you, or the birds in the sky, and they
will tell you; or speak to the earth, and it will teach you, or let the fish of
the sea inform you. Which of all these does not know
that the hand of the Lord has done this?

JOB 12:7-9 NIV

Everything was created through him (Jesus);
nothing – not one thing! –came into being without him.

JOHN 1:3 MSG

NOTES & PRAYERS ....

....

....

....

WISDOM IS A GIFT FROM GOD TO THOSE WHO SEEK HIM.

When you discovered in your Heavenly Father's Word he is the holy author of true wisdom, you began seeking him to become wise. You stepped out on faith to claim his Scriptural promise that if you put him first in all you do and obey his precepts, he will teach you wisdom. Therefore, you do not have to fret if you stumble, for Jesus, the Son, will pick you up and give you his mind, God's loving Source of wisdom and Truth.

Fear of the Lord is the foundation of true wisdom. All who obey his commandments will grow in wisdom. Praise him forever!

PSALM 111:10 NLT

Father, thank you for revealing in Scripture that believing in Jesus is wisdom and disbelieving is foolishness; therefore, I choose Jesus, obedience, wisdom, love, and life. Remind me to make your Son the heart of my every decision, for he is the perfect imprint of your divine wisdom. In his name, I beg the Spirit to ever guide me toward his Truth. Amen.

If any of you lacks wisdom, you should ask God, who gives generously to all without finding fault, and it will be given to you.

JAMES 1:5 NIV

NOTES & PRAYERS ....

....

....

....

RESPECT IS TO GIVE, NOT CRAVE.

To enjoy respect from others, you must be respectful in the divine manner of Jesus. You do not have to look any farther than God's Son for your model of divine respectfulness and respectability.

[Jesus] Here is a simple, rule-of-thumb guide for behavior: ask yourself what you want people to do for you, then grab the initiative and do it for them. Add up God's law and prophets and this is what you get.

MATTHEW 7:12 MSG

Heavenly Father, when I consider people for whom I have the most respect, I realize they all have one essential characteristic in common. They behave respectfully toward others in the Spirit of Jesus. What does my own behavior look like? Respectful to some? Disrespectful to others? Always acting on the assumption I am entitled to decide who is deserving (or undeserving) of my respect, and then parceling out favor or denial accordingly? In your name, Jesus, I pray you will make my heart like your heart...respectful. Amen.

Do nothing out of selfish ambition or vain conceit. Rather, in humility, value others above yourselves, not looking to your own interests but each of you to the interests of others.

PHILIPPIANS 2:3-4 NIV

NOTES & PRAYERS ....

....

....

....

YOUR HOME IN JESUS IS THE KINGDOM OF GOD. BE THANKFUL TO YOUR LORD AND SAVIOR, FOR HIS SALVATION GUARANTEES YOU ALL RIGHTS AND PRIVILEGES AS A KINGDOM CITIZEN FOREVER.

God welcomed you into his Kingdom at the time of your salvation in Jesus, who sealed your citizenship by the power of the Holy Spirit with his own divine stamp no one can ever revoke.

[Jesus] I give them eternal life, and they will never perish. No one can snatch them from me, for my Father has given them to me, and he is more powerful than anyone else. No one can snatch them from the Father's hand. The Father and I are one.

JOHN 10:28-30 NLT

Heavenly Father, thank you for establishing my citizenship in your Kingdom by your grace and gift of faith through the death and resurrection of Jesus. In his name, I pray to be an obedient Kingdom citizen pleasing to you. Amen.

We're citizens of high heaven! We're waiting the arrival of the Savior, the Master, Jesus Christ, who will transform our earthly bodies into glorious bodies like his own.

PHILIPPIANS 3:20B MSG

NOTES & PRAYERS ....

....

....

....

ONLY JESUS CAN GIVE YOU A PEACEFUL MIND.

Have you considered your thought life can progress to becoming your real life? Ask Jesus to make your mind pure and peaceful, which will make your life pure and peaceful.

We demolish arguments and every pretension that
sets itself up against the knowledge of God,
and we take captive every thought to make it obedient to Christ.

2 Corinthians 10:5 NIV

Father God, thank you for soothing my mind with divine peace in your Son, Jesus, who calms me with reassurance he provides in Scripture. Sometimes, I think I might wear out Psalm 23 and the Lord's Prayer, reciting them over and over as I prepare to pray. At first, I find myself repeating them fast and rote to disrupt and redirect my racing thoughts. And then, by your grace and mercy, I am able to relax and contemplate the beauty and meaning of each phrase, which helps me pray in the name of my loving Savior. Amen.

Think about the things of heaven, not the things of earth. For you died
to this life, and your real life is hidden with Christ in God.
And when Christ, who is your life, is revealed to the whole world,
you will share in all his glory.

Colossians 3:2-4 NLT

NOTES & PRAYERS ....

....

....

....

YOUR TRUST IN JESUS IS A MARVELOUS GIFT FROM GOD.

Thank your Heavenly Father for his blessing of calming trust in his Son.

[Jesus] Don't let your hearts be troubled. Trust in God, and trust also in me.

JOHN 14:1 NLT

Father God, when I was a child, I heard the congregation sing in my home church, First Baptist of Lancaster, SC, *I'm so glad I learned to trust Him, Precious Jesus, Savior, Friend; and I know that He is with me, Will be with me to the end.* I know, Father, it was your voice all along, singing to me so sweetly through the voices of the saints at First Baptist. And now as an adult, I hear you whispering into my Spiritual ears your Son's message of trust from Holy Scripture. Your Living Word is Jesus my divine Savior in whose name I pray all gratitude for his gifts of grace, forgiveness, trust, and salvation. Thank you, Jesus! Praise your name! Amen.

Every good and perfect gift is from above, coming down from the Father of the heavenly lights, who does not change like shifting shadows.

JAMES 1:17 NIV

NOTES & PRAYERS ....

....

....

....

February

ARE YOU LIVING WITHIN THE MERCY OF GOD THROUGH YOUR SAVIOR? IF SO, YOU ARE IN THE SAFEST PLACE YOU CAN BE.

It wasn't so long ago you were mired in that old stagnant life of sin. You let the world, which doesn't know the first thing about living, tell you how to live. You filled your lungs with polluted unbelief, and then exhaled disobedience. We all did it, all of us, doing what we felt like doing, when we felt like doing it, all of us in the same boat. It's a wonder God didn't lose his temper and do away with the whole lot of us. Instead, immense in mercy and with incredible love, he embraced us. He took our sin-dead lives and made us alive in Christ. He did this all on his own, with no help from us! Then he picked us up and set us down in highest heaven in company with Jesus, our Messiah.

EPHESIANS 2:1-6 MSG

Heavenly Father, though sure of my salvation in Christ, I sometimes find myself tormented by anxiety. Thank you in Jesus' name for helping me realize the root of my unrest is a nagging fear I live at the mercy of a capricious universe, a hateful lie of Satan. For in Truth, I dwell within your safety, sheltered by Jesus' compassionate grace. Let me be merciful to others, as he is merciful to me. Praise the Son. Amen.

[Jesus] Blessed are the merciful, for they shall receive mercy.

MATTHEW 5:7 ESV

NOTES & PRAYERS ....

....

....

....

WHO ARE YOU LIVING FOR, PROFOUND JESUS OR PROSAIC SELF?

The Son is the radiance of God's glory and the exact representation of his being, sustaining all things by his powerful Word.

HEBREWS 1:3A NIV

Lord Jesus, when I consider who you are, I know who self is not. You are extraordinary and worthy. Self is mundane and worthless. You are full of Truth. Self is full of deceit. You are pure. Self is polluted by sin. You are holy. Self is fallen. You are light. Self is dark. You are my Savior, and only by your gifts of love, mercy, forgiveness, grace, and faith, am I redeemed. In your remarkable name – Yeshua, wholly God, loving Savior, Faithful and True, God's Word – thank you for dying on the cross and rising again to save unremarkable me. I pray my gratitude for salvation in you. Amen.

[John the Revelator] I saw heaven standing open and there before me was a white horse, whose rider (Jesus) is called Faithful and True. With justice he judges and wages war. His eyes are like blazing fire, and on his head are many crowns. He has a name written on him that no one knows but he himself. He is dressed in a robe dipped in blood, and his name is the Word of God.

REVELATION 19:11-13 NIV

NOTES & PRAYERS ....

....

....

....

SOME DAYS YOU FEEL TOO DEPLETED TO SERVE YOUR HEAVENLY FATHER OR ANYONE ELSE. ASK GOD TO CURE SELF'S PITY-PARTY BY PROVIDING YOU OPPORTUNITIES TO SERVE MORE AND COMPLAIN LESS.

For I can do everything through Christ, who gives me strength.
PHILIPPIANS 4:13 NLT

Oh, Lord Jesus, sometimes I wake up more tired than when I fell asleep. Remind me to pray for your supernatural strength when I hang my head in exhaustion. Your Word teaches that talking things over with you will restore and re-charge me. In your ministry on earth, you modeled prayer and attentiveness to Scripture as essentials to an effective life in the Spirit, which makes you my perfect example. Thank you, Jesus, for transforming my human depletion into divine vigor. In your formidable name, I pray you will continue to refresh me, so that I, by your miraculous power, may refresh others. Amen.

Be energetic in your life of salvation, reverent and sensitive before God.
That energy is God's energy, an energy deep within you,
God himself willing and working at what will give him the most pleasure.
PHILIPPIANS 2:12A-13 MSG

NOTES & PRAYERS ....

....

....

....

WHEN LIFE IS GOING WELL, DO YOU SOMETIMES FEEL AN ODD SENSE OF ALARM AND DREAD, RATHER THAN JOY AND GLADNESS? JESUS ENCOURAGES YOU TO REJOICE, RESIST WHINING, AND PUT ASIDE FEAR IN ALL SITUATIONS, SOFT AND HARD.

Always be joyful. never stop praying. Be thankful in all circumstances,
for this is God's will for you who belong to Christ Jesus.
1 THESSALONIANS 5:16-18 NLT

Lord Jesus, thank you for waking me up to the sad fact the devil delights in stealing my joy by suggesting doom and gloom, often in the middle of some happy occasion. In your wise name, I beg you to create in me a glad heart in every context, no matter how you choose to fill my days. Thank you, Savior, for the multitude of counterintuitive teachings in your Word that make all the difference in victorious living. Praise your empowering name. Amen.

[Paul] I know what it is to be in need, and I know what it is to
have plenty. I have learned the secret of being content in any and every
situation, whether well fed or hungry, whether living in plenty or in want.
I can do all this through him (Jesus) who gives me strength.
PHILIPPIANS 4:12-13 NIV

NOTES & PRAYERS ....
....
....
....

DO YOU LOVE GOD WITH ALL YOUR HEART THE WAY HE LOVES YOU? REJOICE, O BRIDE OF CHRIST, HIS BELOVED CHURCH. GOD ACCEPTS YOUR LOVE ON THE WORTHINESS OF HIS SON, JESUS, YOUR BRIDEGROOM.

And as the bridegroom rejoices over the bride,
so shall God rejoice over you.

ISAIAH 62:5B ESV

Lord and Savior, I am grateful to be part of your church, the bride of Christ, a beautiful metaphor for your church body. Love is a powerful verb that communicates how a devoted groom behaves toward his treasured bride. He cannot do enough for her, because he loves her. What bride would not respond with love to a husband who cares for her so deeply he would lay down his life to save hers? In your name, thank you, Jesus, for loving your bride both collectively and individually. We return your love with all gratitude. Amen.

Let us rejoice and exult and give him the glory, for the marriage
of the Lamb (Jesus) has come, and his Bride (his church)
has made herself ready.

REVELATION 19:7 ESV

NOTES & PRAYERS ....

....

....

....

JUST BECAUSE SOME PEOPLE LONG AGO BELIEVED THE WORLD WAS FLAT DID NOT MAKE IT ANY LESS SPHERICAL. CONCLUSION: BELIEVE WHAT IS TRUE, NOT WHAT IS FALSE. BELIEVE GOD, JESUS, AND THE HOLY SPIRIT.

God sits high above the round ball of earth. The people look like mere ants. He stretches out the skies like a canvas – yes, like a tent canvas to live under. He ignores what all the princes say and do. The rulers of the earth count for nothing. Princes and rulers don't amount to much. Like seeds barely rooted, just sprouted, they shrivel when God blows on them. Like flecks of chaff, they're gone with the wind.

ISAIAH 40:21B-24 MSG

I praise and worship you, my Heavenly Father, who inspired Isaiah over seven hundred years before the birth of Jesus to write about our physical world as "the round ball of earth." You – Father God, Jesus, and the Holy Spirit – all three, were present in Truth at creation. Thank you, God, in the name of Jesus, for revealing his Good News of salvation to me. Remind me to share his message with others. Amen.

Jesus answered, "I am the way and the truth and the life. No one comes to the Father except through me."

JOHN 14:6 NIV

NOTES & PRAYERS ....

....

....

....

BE ASTOUNDED BY THE DIVINE NATURE OF JESUS – GOD'S SON, THE CHRIST, ANOINTED ONE, LION OF JUDAH, MESSIAH, KING OF KINGS, LORD OF LORDS, FAITHFUL AND TRUE, WHOLLY GOD!

Therefore, Pilate said to him, "So you are a king?"
Jesus answered, "You say correctly that I am a king. For this I have been
born, and for this I have come into the world, to testify to the Truth.
Everyone who is of the Truth hears my voice."

JOHN 18:37 NASB

Thank you, Jesus, for declaring your holy identity. I am in awe of your glory and majesty. Hear my prayer of gratitude in your name for the certainty that in the fullness of time you will return to earth as Lord of lords and King of kings. You will conquer evil forever. Praise you, Jesus, Sovereign Savior. You rule by your mighty power. Amen.

Therefore, God exalted him to the highest place and gave him the name
that is above every name, that at the name of Jesus every knee should
bow, in heaven and on earth and under the earth, and every tongue
acknowledge that Jesus Christ is Lord, to the glory of God the Father.

PHILIPPIANS 2:9-11 NIV

NOTES & PRAYERS ....

....

....

....

GOD WANTS YOU TO KNOW HIM IN HIS HOLY TRINITY. PAY ATTENTION WHEN HE SPEAKS IN SCRIPTURE OF HIS THREE-IN-ONE.

The moment Jesus came up out of the baptismal waters, the skies opened up and he saw God's Spirit – it looked like a dove – descending and landing on him, and along with the Spirit, a voice: "This is my Son, chosen and marked by my love, delight of my life."

MATTHEW 3:16 MSG

Father, I acknowledge you dwell in heaven, but you are also omnipresent in Spirit eternally. You are Mighty God! Savior Jesus, I acknowledge you, too, are wholly God in nature and power of the Father. You came to earth to dwell for a season in the form of a sinless man, but you are now back in heaven until, in your perfect timing, you will return to reign in glory. Though even now, you are omnipresent in Spirit forever, the same as the Father in his Holy Spirit, whom I recognize as the third person of the Trinity, also wholly God, omnipresent and everlasting, even inside my heart. In Jesus' name of Love, Light, and Life, I praise each personality of the Holy Trinity – Father, Son, and Holy Spirit. Amen.

You realize, don't you, that you are the temple of God, and God himself (Holy Spirit in Christ Jesus) is present in you?

1 CORINTHIANS 3:16 MSG

NOTES & PRAYERS

YOU ARE NEVER ALONE IN NAVIGATING LIFE. YOU HAVE THE HOLY SPIRIT OF GOD IN JESUS GUIDING AND HELPING YOU.

For God has said, "I will never fail you. I will never abandon you."
We can say with confidence, "The Lord is my helper. I will have no fear."

HEBREWS 13:5B-6A NLT

Thank you, Jesus, and God my Father, for dwelling with me in the Holy Spirit. I am not solitary in life's joys and sorrows. I have my Savior's peace in the presence of God in the Holy Spirit – Comforter, Counselor, Helper, and Friend – who makes his home with me. Accept my gratitude, Father, for salvation in Jesus. In his name, I glorify your Holy Trinity. Praise you, Mighty God, Three-In-One. Amen.

[Jesus] I will talk to the Father, and he'll provide you another friend (the Holy Spirit) so that you will always have someone with you. This friend is the Spirit of Truth. The godless world can't take him in because it doesn't have eyes to see him, doesn't know what to look for. But you know him already because he has been staying with you, and will even be in you!

JOHN 14:16-17 MSG

So that Christ may dwell in your hearts through faith.

EPHESIANS 3:17A NIV

NOTES & PRAYERS ....

....

....

....

IF YOU ASK WITH A GENUINE HEART, YOUR HEAVENLY FATHER WILL RAIN DOWN BLESSINGS ON YOUR LIFE. PREPARE YOURSELF WHEN YOU MAKE WELL-MEANING REQUESTS WITH PURE MOTIVES WITHIN GOD'S WILL. HAVE YOUR BLESSING BASKET READY TO BE FILLED.

I (God) will bless my people and their homes around my holy hill.
And in the proper season I will send the showers they need.
There will be showers of blessings.

EZEKIEL 34:26 NLT

Thank you, God, for rain as a lovely metaphor for blessings. Showers of rain make it possible for plants to survive in a physically dry landscape, just as showers of blessings make it possible for believers to survive in a Spiritually dry world. But what good is survival without sharing Jesus' Gospel? In his name, I pray for opportunities to glorify you, Father, by proclaiming your Son's message of Good News. Amen.

I give thanks to you, O Lord my God, with my whole heart,
and I will glorify your name forever.

PSALM 86:12 NIV

NOTES & PRAYERS ....

....

....

....

WHAT KINDS OF WORDS DO YOU USE MOST IN YOUR RELATIONSHIPS — HEALTH-GIVING OR HEALTH-STEALING?

Gracious words are like a honeycomb,
sweetness to the soul and health to the body.
PROVERBS 16:24 ESV

Words kill, words give life; they're either poison or fruit – you choose.
PROVERBS 18:21 MSG

Father, you provide an abundance of wise words in Scripture. I am rich in your nourishing discourse. What, then, does it cost me to share? Dear God, in your divine economy, positive words I speak to others lift me up more than they lift the people to whom I am speaking, while negative words sour all our souls. Savior Jesus, I realize health-stealing words come from self, and health-giving words from you. Give me your words to speak to those around me – loving, caring, comforting, nurturing, healing words. And keep me silent when I am tempted to indulge in sarcasm, or even worse. I pray in your name, Jesus, let me imitate your divine utterings only. Amen.

Kind words heal and help; cutting words wound and maim.
PROVERBS 15:4 MSG

NOTES & PRAYERS ....

....

....

....

DOES YOUR TONE OF VOICE BUILD OTHERS UP OR TEAR THEM DOWN? SEASON YOUR SPEECH IN GOD'S CONTEXT: JESUS BUILDS; SELF DESTROYS. WHICH ONE COLORS YOUR TONE, JESUS OR SELF?

A gentle response defuses anger, but a sharp tongue kindles a temper-fire.
PROVERBS 15:1 MSG

Lord Jesus, I am guilty of using a biting tone too often in my relationships. Forgive me! Help me repent with an earnest heart of this unkind habit. Self is the culprit, with its ego-centric expectation that resorting to a hostile tone is acceptable when things do not go self's way. I pray in your name, Savior, remind me to bless others with your kindness, rather than injure anyone, ever, with self's harshness. Amen.

Watch the way you talk. Let nothing foul or dirty come out of your mouth. Say only what helps, each word a gift. Don't grieve God. Don't break his heart. His Holy Spirit, moving and breathing in you, is the most intimate part of your life, making you fit for himself. Don't take such a gift for granted. Make a clean break with all cutting, backbiting, profane talk. Be gentle with one another, sensitive.
EPHESIANS 4:29-32A MSG

NOTES & PRAYERS ....

....

....

....

ARE YOU REGENERATED BY THE HOLY SPIRIT TO BECOME A NEW CREATURE, SAVED TO ETERNAL LIFE IN JESUS' LIGHT? OR ARE YOU DEGENERATED BY SELF TO REMAIN A CONDEMNED CREATURE, UNSAVED TO ETERNAL DEATH IN EVIL'S DARKNESS?

This means that anyone who belongs to Christ has become a new person.
The old life is gone; a new life has begun.

2 CORINTHIANS 5:17 NLT

Holy Spirit, thank you for regrowing me, the dead-and-lost, into the living-and-found (regeneration), despite self's resolve to follow Satan to destruction and death (degeneration). Savior Jesus, I am grateful the Holy Spirit regenerated me and continues to grow and prune me according to God's will. In your name, I ask to flourish, a new creature alive by grace in your righteousness, not dead in impurity. Praise you, Jesus, eternal Light, Life, and Love. Amen.

He (God) saved us, not because of works done by us in righteousness,
but according to his own mercy, by the washing of regeneration
and renewal of the Holy Spirit, whom he poured out on
us richly through Jesus Christ our Savior.

TITUS 3:5-6 ESV

NOTES & PRAYERS ....

....

....

....

JESUS WANTS YOU TO BECOME SELFLESS, AS HE IS SELFLESS. FLESH WANTS YOU TO REMAIN GREEDY, AS FLESH IS GREEDY. WHOM HAVE YOU CHOSEN TO EMULATE – JESUS, YOUR HONORABLE MODEL, OR FLESH, NO ONE'S HONORABLE MODEL?

In your relationships with one another, have the same mindset
as Christ Jesus: who, being in very nature God, did not consider
equality with God something to be used to his own advantage.

PHILIPPIANS 2:5-7 NIV

Thank you, Jesus, for not giving up on me, even as my prideful character works at dragging me down into the dark pit of selfish behavior. I am forever grateful that when I look up, you are there, holding out your hand to lift me out. Teach me to be unselfish, as you are unselfish. In your upright name, I beg you to accept my gratitude you are always willing to be my pristine model. Praise you, Son of God. Amen.

Rather, he (Jesus) made himself nothing by taking the very nature of a
servant, being made in human likeness. And being found in appearance
as a man, he humbled himself by becoming obedient to death –
even death on a cross!

PHILIPPIANS 2:7-8 NIV

NOTES & PRAYERS ....
....
....
....

IF YOU FEEL DISCOURAGED, GIVE THANKS TO GOD. HE WILL BLESS YOU WITH CONFIDENCE IN HIS PLAN FOR YOUR LIFE, ESPECIALLY IF YOU REMAIN FAITHFUL TO PRAISE HIM DURING DIFFICULT TWISTS AND TURNS.

Do not be afraid or discouraged...for the battle is not yours, but God's.
2 CHRONICLES 20:15B NIV

Forgive me, Lord Jesus, for asking so many why-me questions. Remind me to replace my self-centered complaining with God-centered gratitude for whatever is in your plan. Teach me to be grateful for all things, including difficulties. Let me defeat discouragement by giving thanks. Only then will I see your miracle of turning discouragement into encouragement. I am thankful, Savior, for your counterintuitive teaching in Scripture concerning encouragement and discouragement, for I know I can count on your Truth in all situations. I ask in your name, remind me to trust you, no matter what, for I know you will never forsake me. Amen.

I know the plans I have for you, declares the Lord,
plans for your welfare and not for evil, to give you a future and a hope.
JEREMIAH 29:11 ESV

NOTES & PRAYERS ....
....
....
....

IF YOUR HUMAN COMMUNICATION SKILLS LEAD TO MISUNDERSTANDINGS RATHER THAN UNDERSTANDINGS IN YOUR RELATIONSHIPS, ASK JESUS TO TEACH YOU HIS SUPERNATURAL WAYS OF INTERACTING.

Let the words of my mouth and the meditation of my heart be acceptable in your sight, oh Lord, my rock and my redeemer.

PSALM 19:14 ESV

Lord Jesus, during your ministry on earth, you spoke wisely, using phrasing and examples relevant to your listeners' lives. You also understood the healing effect of physical and Spiritual touch. You were not afraid to lay hands on both the sick and healthy to communicate your love, often using touch as a vehicle to perform miracles. It is no wonder you held people's interest so raptly, indeed, kept huge crowds spellbound with stories to which each curious attendee could relate. In your name, I pray to be more like you in connecting with those around me. Help me speak and touch others with empathy and tenderness on your behalf, selflessly. Amen.

The heart of the wise makes his speech judicious and adds persuasiveness to his lips.

PROVERBS 16:23 ESV

NOTES & PRAYERS ....

....

....

....

JESUS IS GOD'S LOVE LETTER TO YOU.

If you ask in prayer, your Heavenly Father will teach you how to become a living love letter from Jesus to others. His instructions are in his Holy Word, God's love letter to you about his Son.

Father, thank you my dad wrote love letters to my mother before they were married. And thank you she never let me read them. His letters belong to her alone, his sweetheart. I am aware the letters in Mother's forbidden letterbox are sweet reflections of Dad in his youth, the reason I would like to see them. But you, God, gave my brother and me much more of him than written reflections. You gave us close association with the actual man. In Jesus' name, I pray to live my life the way Dad did, indeed, the way Jesus did and still does, a living love letter from God to others. Amen.

You yourselves are our letter, written on our hearts, known and read by everyone. You show that you are a letter from Christ, the result of our ministry, written not with ink, but with the Spirit of the living God, not on tablets of stone, but on tablets of human hearts.
2 Corinthians 3:2-3 NIV

And his banner over me is love.
Song of Songs 2:4 NASB

NOTES & PRAYERS ....
....
....
....

YOU HAVE A LIFE-OR-DEATH DECISION TO MAKE – LIFE IN GOD'S SON, OR DEATH IN SELF. CHOOSE LIFE. CHOOSE SALVATION. CHOOSE JESUS!

God gave you free will to decide – life in Jesus, or death in self. But never forget, free will as a gift to you came at great cost to your Savior. He paid for it with his blood, then rose again to guarantee its worth. Use your free will wisely. It is God's grace of undeserved favor given to you through his beloved Son.

Father, you saved me in Jesus, but you did not force me to accept salvation. If you had, what kind of involuntary relationship would that have been? You offered me the choice to accept or reject, just as you offered Adam and Eve the choice to obey or disobey. Yet, even when they chose poorly, you still gave your Son to forgive and pay the sin debt for all believers. I have chosen – decided – to cling to Jesus, in whose name I pray. Amen.

I have set before you life and death, blessing and curse. Therefore, choose life, that you and your offspring may live.
DEUTERONOMY 30:19B ESV

If you declare with your mouth, "Jesus is Lord," and believe in your heart that God raised him from the dead, you will be saved.
ROMANS 10:9 NIV

NOTES & PRAYERS ....

....

....

....

GOD'S GRACE AND GRACE-NOTES ADD BEAUTY TO YOUR LIFE IN THE HERE AND NOW, IN ADDITION TO GUARANTEEING YOUR ETERNAL SALVATION.

We praise God for the glorious grace he has poured out on us who belong to his dear Son. He is so rich in kindness and grace that he purchased our freedom with the blood of his Son and forgave our sins.

EPHESIANS 1:6-7 NLT

Shepherd Jesus, after you saved me by your gifts of grace and faith, you began showering me with more grace. You surprise me daily with grace-notes of joy, humbling me with gratitude as I experience your all-embracing theme of divine grace that floods my life. I am convinced your thoughtful reason for giving me five senses – touch, sight, smell, hearing, and taste – was to enable me to experience the dozens of grace-notes of lovingkindness you pour on me every day. In your name, thank you for blessing me with grace and grace-notes to share with others on your behalf. Amen.

All sin can do is threaten us with death, and that's the end of it. Grace, because God is putting everything together again through the Messiah (Jesus), invites us into life – a life that goes on and on and on, world without end.

ROMANS 5:21 MSG

NOTES & PRAYERS ....

....

....

....

DO YOU SEE THOSE AROUND YOU THROUGH GOD'S DIVINE CLEAR LENS, OR DO YOU PEER AT THEM CRITICALLY THROUGH YOUR OWN FUZZY HUMAN LENS?

God doesn't look at things like humans do. Humans see only what is visible to the eyes, but the Lord sees into the heart.

1 SAMUEL 16:7B CEB

Thank you, Father, for placing more value on a pure heart than an adorned body. Help me keep my heart clean, knowing I cannot achieve something as miraculous as that unless Jesus covers me with his righteousness. I pray in his name to look on others with the same love, grace, patience, and forgiveness with which he looks on me. Amen.

But let your adorning be the hidden person of the heart with the imperishable beauty of a gentle and quiet spirit, which in God's sight is very precious.

1 PETER 3:4 ESV

[Jesus] Woe to you, scribes and Pharisees, hypocrites! For you are like whitewashed tombs, which outwardly appear beautiful, but within are full of dead people's bones and all uncleanness.

MATTHEW 23:27 ESV

NOTES & PRAYERS ....

....

....

....

YOU KNOW THAT YOUR HEAVENLY FATHER IS ALWAYS SOVEREIGN AND GOOD. HE WORKS OUT WITH DIVINE PRECISION EVERY DETAIL OF HIS INTRICATE PLAN FOR ALL CREATION, INCLUDING YOUR INDIVIDUAL LIFE.

Furthermore, because we are united with Christ, we have received an inheritance from God, for he chose us in advance, and he makes everything work out according to his plan.

EPHESIANS 1:11 NLT

Lord Jesus, is it possible to be thankful for trials? My first response is no. But the moment this negative utterance escapes my mouth, I remember you have never asked me to do anything, especially any difficult thing, without your supernatural help. Indeed, you have always turned difficulties into blessings. I pray in your name, Savior, teach me to rejoice in you, no matter my circumstances. Amen.

Dear friends, don't be surprised at the fiery trials you are going through, as if something strange were happening. Instead, be very glad – for these trials make you partners with Christ in his suffering, so that you will have the wonderful joy of seeing his glory when it is revealed to all the world.

1 PETER 4:12-13 NLT

NOTES & PRAYERS ....

....

....

....

COVERT REBELLION AGAINST GOD IS AS DESTRUCTIVE AS OVERT REBELLION. DOES THAT APPLY TO YOUR LIFE?

Honesty lives confident and carefree, but shifty is sure to be exposed.
PROVERBS 10:9 MSG

Lord Jesus, thank you for warning me against pretense in obeying your teachings, while secretly disobeying. Whom do I think I am deceiving when I disobey you covertly? Even if I fool a few people for a little while, I will never be able to fool you, Son of God, wholly God. Better to obey you as conscientiously in secret places as in open places. Otherwise, my life is a sham. Oh, Lord, shine your cleansing Light upon me, rendering my motives transparent and pleasing to you. No pretense. No hypocrisy. No overblown self. In your Light-filled name, Savior Jesus, I ask you to walk with me in your perfection to keep me from stumbling, for alone, I am unsteady, weak, and dark. Purify my heart, Lord and Master. Let my service to you be clean, as you are clean. Praise your spotless name. Amen.

People with integrity walk safely,
but those who follow crooked paths will be exposed.
PROVERBS 10:9 NLT

NOTES & PRAYERS ....

....

....

....

ARE YOU RADIANT WITH YOUR SAVIOR'S CLEAR LIGHT, OR DULL WITH SELF'S SMUDGED FAÇADE? SHINE IN JESUS!

[Jesus] "The religion scholars and Pharisees are competent teachers in God's law. You won't go wrong in following their teachings on Moses. But be careful about following them. They talk a good line, but they don't live it. They don't take it into their hearts and live it out in their behavior. It's all spit-and-polish veneer."

MATTHEW 23:1B-3 MSG

Therefore, do not become partners with them (deceivers); for at one time you (believers) were darkness, but now you are Light in the Lord.

EPHESIANS 5:7-8A ESV

Thank you, Jesus, for making it plain in Scripture that hypocrisy, arrogance, and greed are not of you, but of self. While sincerety, humility, and unselfishness are not of self, but of you. I pray in your name, replace my tarnished façade of self with your authentic Godly Light, for true goodness originates only with you. Wash away my dull veneer, all stained and cracked by sin. Let my life shine from inside out with your divine purity. Praise you, Bright Savior. Amen.

Walk as children of Light!

EPHESIANS 5:8B

NOTES & PRAYERS ....

....

....

....

ARE YOU CLEAR ON GOD'S PURPOSE FOR CREATING YOU?

For we are God's handiwork, created in Christ Jesus to do good works,
which God prepared in advance for us to do.
EPHESIANS 2:10 NIV

For you (God Almighty) created all things, and they exist,
because you created what you pleased.
REVELATION 4:11B NLT

Thank you, Father, for loving me before you created me. Scripture declares it pleased you to love me first, after which you placed a desire in my heart to return your love. You designed me to be in loving relationship with you. I lift up your name in gratitude for creating me to love you. And though you never forced me to accept or return your love, I kneel before you with a grateful heart for the privilege of worshiping you. I am thankful you reconciled yourself to me, a sinner, through Jesus' death and resurrection, and for the Spirit's regeneration of my soul, once dead in sin, but now alive in Christ. In his name, I glorify you, Almighty Creator in your Trinity — Father, Son, and Holy Spirit. Amen.

Bring all who claim me as their God, for I have made them for my glory.
ISAIAH 43:7A NLT

NOTES & PRAYERS ....
....
....
....

LET YOUR SMALLEST ACTIONS AND ATTITUDES BLESS GOD AND OTHERS, FOR LITTLE FOXES OF SIN KILL AND DESTROY. REPENT FROM THEM.

Catch all the foxes, those little foxes, before they ruin the vineyard of love, for the grapevines are blossoming!

SONG OF SOLOMON 2:15 NLT

Savior Jesus, teach me how to tend your divine vineyard in which you invited me to dwell. I want to be a productive branch of your one True vine, a branch that bears good fruit of your Holy Spirit – love, joy, peace, patience, kindness, goodness, faithfulness, gentleness, and self-control. I pray in your name you will show me how to guard against little foxes of sin that destroy good fruit and leave in its place bad fruit – hate, misery, unrest, impatience, cruelty, evil, infidelity, roughness, and lack of self-control. Jesus, banish sins from my heart, especially those that seem small and insignificant, but in reality, are large and destructive. Amen.

If we say we have no sin, we deceive ourselves, and the truth is not in us. If we confess our sins, he [God] is faithful and just to forgive our sins and to cleanse us from all unrighteousness.

1 JOHN 1:8-9 ESV

NOTES & PRAYERS ....

....

....

....

WHICH ARE YOU –
GOD-RELIANT OR SELF-RELIANT?

*Cursed is the strong one who depends on mere humans, who thinks he
can make it on muscle alone and sets God aside as dead weight. He's like
a tumbleweed on the prairie, out of touch with the good earth. He lives
rootless and aimless in a land where nothing grows. But blessed is the
man who trusts me, God, the woman who sticks with God. They're like
trees replanted in Eden, putting down roots near the rivers —
never a worry through the hottest of summers, never dropping a leaf,
serene and calm through droughts, bearing fresh fruit every season.*

JEREMIAH 17:5-8 MSG

My tendency, Lord Jesus, is to give lip service to the idea
of depending on you alone, even as I turn around and take
life's reins back into my own hands. Help me, Savior, to do
what I know is best, to live in reliance on your wisdom, not
human folly. In your steadfast name, accept my gratitude
for your permission and encouragement to lean on you,
my sure guard, along life's pathway. Praise you, dependable
guide. I rest in your power. Amen.

*Listen for God's voice in everything you do, everywhere you go;
he's the one who will keep you on track.*

PROVERBS 3:6 MSG

NOTES & PRAYERS ....
....
....
....

WHAT DO YOU KNOW ABOUT DIVINE CONNECTIONS IN GOD'S ECONOMY AMONG GIVING, TRUSTING, AND BLESSINGS?

You must each decide in your heart how much to give. And don't give reluctantly or in response to pressure. "For God loves a person who gives cheerfully." And God will generously provide all you need. Then you will always have everything you need, and plenty left over to share with others. For God is the one who provides seeds for the farmer and then bread to eat. In the same way, he will provide and increase your resources and then produce a great harvest of generosity in you.

2 CORINTHIANS 9:7-8; 10 NLT

Thank you, Jesus, for reminding me that my level of giving is a measure of my trust in you. Do I believe you will keep your Scriptural promises, astonishing in their generosity, to cheerful givers, especially those who remember the poor? Your teaching is clear: If I believe you keep your promises – and I do! – you will see me rushing to make my giving generous and extravagant, not meager and cheap. In your name, I pray to glorify you through giving, not just for promised blessings, but because giving is your command. Amen.

Honor God with everything you own: Give him the first and the best. Your barns will burst, your wine vats will brim over.

PROVERBS 3:9-10 MSG

NOTES & PRAYERS ....

....

....

....

IS YOUR HEART A SANCTUARY FOR JESUS, OR A MORTUARY FOR SELF?

Jesus replied, "Anyone who loves me will obey my teaching. My Father will love them, and we will come to them and make our home with them."
JOHN 14:23 NIV

Thank you, Jesus, for conquering sin and death on the cross and rising again, both selfless acts that made it possible for the Holy Spirit to regenerate new life in me and abide in my heart. I pray in your name, Savior, for wisdom and knowledge, as I give my present and eternal life over to you. Teach me how to live out your Gospel in my daily interactions with those around me. You, Jesus, are my haven, and yet, until you call me home to you in the eternal, let me live in your will in the temporal. Take my earthly home and regenerated heart and make them yours – body and soul, physical and Spiritual. Abide in me in love as I abide in you in peace. For wherever you are, there is my true home. Amen.

Don't you know that you yourselves are God's temple and that God's Spirit dwells in your midst?
1 CORINTHIANS 3:16 NIV

Christ will make his home in your hearts as you trust in him.
EPHESIANS 3:17 NLT

NOTES & PRAYERS ....
....
....
....

DESIGNED CREATION IS CERTAIN EVIDENCE OF GOD, THE MASTOR CREATOR. PAINTINGS DO NOT PAINT THEMSELVES. MELODIES DO NOT COMPOSE THEMSELVES. STORIES DO NOT WRITE THEMSELVES. AND OUR HIGHLY CALIBRATED AND ELEGANTLY DESIGNED UNIVERSE DID NOT CREATE ITSELF. ALMIGHTY GOD IS THE GREAT DESIGNER, CREATOR, AND CALIBRATOR OF ALL THINGS.

By faith we understand that the universe was created by the word of God,
so that what is seen was not made out of things that are visible.
HEBREWS 11:3 ESV

Mighty God, when you spoke creation into existence, you displayed your divine artistry in form, color, tone, structure, story, beauty, theme, character, dynamics, movement, life, love, light, and sublime thought. Accept my gratitude for everything in the name of Jesus, wholly God himself, just as you are wholly God, loving Father and Holy Spirit. Amen.

Christ is the visible image of the invisible God. He existed before anything
was created and is supreme over creation, for through him God
created everything in the heavenly realms and on earth.
COLOSSIANS 1:15-17 NLT

NOTES & PRAYERS ....

....

....

....

March

YOUR SAVIOR JESUS IS GOD'S BREAD OF LIFE, HIS DIVINE HIDDEN MANNA.

Jesus is your hidden manna. Partake of his divine Spiritual bread
– bread of forgiveness, salvation, and eternal life –
and you will never be Spiritually hungry again.

*[Jesus] To everyone who is victorious, I will give some of
the manna that has been hidden away in heaven.*

REVELATION 2:17B NLT

Heavenly Father, thank you for making me utterly dependent on Jesus' hidden manna. Let my faith, hope, belief, and
trust be strengthened by the Holy Spirit as I read your Word,
the meaning of which is also divine hidden manna. And let
any service I render to others in the name of Jesus become
his own manna in their lives by your grace. In the name of
Jesus, wholly God, as God the Father and the Holy Spirit
are wholly God, I pray my gratitude for salvation, Christ's
heavenly manna of love and rescue for his children. Amen.

---

*[Jesus] I am the living bread that came down from heaven.
Whoever eats this bread will live forever.
This bread is my flesh, which I give for the life of the world.*

JOHN 6:51 NIV

NOTES & PRAYERS ....

....

....

SALVATION IS GOD'S GRACE-GIFT TO YOU, A NEW LIFE AND A NEW NAME IN JESUS.

Everything about you is new in your Savior, even your name. When he returns to earth, he will write your new name on you, leaving no doubt that for all eternity you belong to him – King of kings and Lord of lords, Christ Jesus.

Savior King, Son of God, thank you for sealing me by your Holy Spirit as a child of the Father. I pray in your name with faith, hope, belief, and confidence that on your return, you will write a new name upon me, signifying I belong to you. Lord Jesus, Son of God, fully God, I am grateful you loved me enough to claim me, save me, and name me. In your holy name, I praise, worship, and glorify you. Amen.

[John the Revelator, describing Jesus] His eyes are like blazing fire, and on his head are many crowns. He has a name written on him that no one knows but he himself.

REVELATION 19:12 NIV

[Jesus] I will write on them the name of my God and the name of the city of my God, the new Jerusalem, which is coming down out of heaven from my God; and I will also write on them my new name.

REVELATION 3:12b NIV

NOTES & PRAYERS ....

....

....

....

JESUS' WONDERFUL WAYS ARE SURPRISING, COUNTERINTUITIVE, AND DIVINE.

As Jesus is counterintuitive, so must you be counterintuitive. God's perfect Truth requires you to expect the unexpected and to be the unexpected in God's holy ways.

Lord Jesus, I am grateful your wisdom runs counter to the tendencies of my own vainglorious self. Without your perception, it would never have occurred to me to love an enemy, or do good to someone who hates me, or pray for a person who mistreats me. Without your teaching, I would never have known that focusing on self would cause me to lose my life, and emptying self for your sake would allow me to find my most abundant life in you. Loving Savior, in your name, I ask the Holy Spirit to teach me your counterintuitive wisdom, for without the Spirit's instruction, I cannot think or do anything divinely counterintuitive or productive. Lead me in your ways, Jesus. My faith is in you. Amen.

Then Jesus said to his disciples, "If anyone would come after me, let him deny himself and take up his cross and follow me. For whoever would save his life will lose it, but whoever loses his life for my sake will find it. For what will it profit a man if he gains the whole world and forfeits his soul?"
MATTHEW 16:24-26A ESV

NOTES & PRAYERS ....

....

....

....

AS YOU ANTICIPATE THE SECOND COMING OF JESUS, REMEMEMBER: OBEDIENCE IN SERVICE IS YOUR DIVINE KEY TO PLEASING GOD.

Serving God and others faithfully in the here and now is your best preparation for Jesus' return in the future.

The Son of Man will come at an hour when you do not expect him.
MATTHEW 24:44B NIV

Thank you, Savior, for teaching me in your Word to live in readiness for you to come back by imitating you in service. In your name, I ask you to do good work through me every day, for I can do nothing worthwhile on my own. Amen.

[Jesus about his second coming] "Then the King (Jesus) will say to those on his right, 'Come, you who are blessed by my Father, inherit the kingdom prepared for you from the foundation of the world.' Then the righteous will answer him, saying, 'Lord, when did we see you hungry and feed you, or thirsty and give you drink? And when did we see you a stranger and welcome you, or naked and clothe you? And when did we see you sick or in prison and visit you?' And the King will answer them, 'Truly, I say to you, as you did it to one of the least of these my brothers, you did it to me.'"
MATTHEW 25:34; 37-40 ESV

NOTES & PRAYERS ....
....
....
....

FIRE IS OFTEN A SYMBOL FOR GOD IN SCRIPTURE, THOUGH PHYSICAL FIRE IS NOT GOD, BUT CREATED BY GOD. FIRE OF THE HOLY SPIRIT IS A WHOLE OTHER PHENOMENON, SACRED AND SUPERNATURAL.

John the Baptist answered them, saying, "I baptize you with water, but he (Jesus) who is mightier than I is coming, the strap of whose sandals I am not worthy to untie. He will baptize you with the Holy Spirit and fire."

LUKE 3:16 ESV

Father, thank you for the ever-presence of the Holy Spirit, who blazes with your divine fire of righteousness. For the Spirit is your holy fire of regeneration that refines believers as he shines upon us, indeed, glows from inside our hearts with the Light of Jesus. In your Son's name, thank you for his corporal and Spiritual manifestation of your holy fire – Love, Light, Life, and Salvation. Let me burn brightly in him as I share his Gospel Light with others. Amen.

[John the Revelator] I saw heaven standing open and there before me was a white horse, whose rider (Jesus) is called Faithful and True. With justice he judges and wages war. His eyes are like blazing fire, and on his head are many crowns.

REVELATION 19:11-12A NIV

NOTES & PRAYERS ....

....

....

....

SUBMISSION TO GOD IS HIS EXPECTATION. IT IS ALSO THE BEST POSITION YOU CAN ASSUME TO RECEIVE HIS BLESSINGS.

Humble yourselves, therefore, under God's mighty hand,
that he may lift you up in due time.

1 PETER 5:6 NIV

Father God, teach me to be humble before you. Work in my heart, Lord Jesus, to remind me of your perfect example – complete submission of your sinless corporal body and blood on the cross for my sake. You took the blame and punishment for my sins, died in my place, rose again, and forgave, changed, and saved me, all by grace. I submit to you now and forever out of love, gratitude, and reverence. In your name, thank you for the blessing of surrender. Amen.

Think of yourselves the way Christ Jesus thought of himself. He had equal
status with God but didn't think so much of himself that he had to cling to
the advantages of that status no matter what. Because of that obedience,
God lifted him high and honored him far beyond anyone or anything,
ever, so that all created beings in heaven and on earth, even those long
ago dead and buried, will bow in worship before this Jesus Christ,
and call out in praise that he is the Master of all,
to the glorious honor of God the Father.

PHILIPPIANS 2:5-6; 9-11 MSG

NOTES & PRAYERS ....

....

....

....

GOD SOLVED THE MYSTERY OF HIS GOSPEL BY PROVIDING YOU SALVATION THROUGH JESUS' DEATH AND RESURRECTION.

Your loving Father expressed his enormous regard for you
by opening your Spiritual eyes to Jesus, his Son,
who embodies God's own divine value and eternal love.

Father God, how grateful I am for the Holy Spirit, who quickened my heart with understanding of your sacred mystery in Jesus' Gospel. Through your gifts of grace, mercy, forgiveness, faith, and redemption, you allowed me (a sad sinner) to grasp the Spiritual Truth that Jesus, your Son, is my Savior – mystery solved! In his name, thank you for the privilege of sharing the news of his Power-To-Save. Amen.

[Paul] As you read over what I have written to you, you'll be able to see for yourselves into the mystery of Christ. None of our ancestors understood this. Only in our time has it been made clear by God's Spirit through his holy apostles and prophets of this new order. The mystery is that people who have never heard of God and those who have heard of him all their lives (what I've been calling outsiders and insiders) stand on the same ground before God. They get the same offer, same help, same promises in Christ Jesus. The Message is accessible and welcoming to everyone, across the board.

EPHESIANS 3:4-6 MSG

NOTES & PRAYERS ....

....

....

....

YOUR DEEP AND ABIDING APPRECIATION FOR GOD'S SALVATION MIRRORS YOUR DEEP AND ABIDING LOVE FOR HIS SON.

Your Heavenly Father blessed you with Jesus, who delivered
you from evil, forgave your sins, and saved your soul.
How do you show gratitude to God for those amazing gifts?
Love him. Praise him. Worship him. Thank him.
Surrender to him. Obey him. Honor him.
Glorify his Son!

Give thanks to the Lord, for he is good. His love endures forever.
PSALM 136:1 NIV

Thank you, Father, for showing me strongholds of behavior that diminish my gratitude – pride, striving, overwork, trying to carry on my own shoulders difficulties I should be casting on you. In Jesus' name, I ask you to help me put aside energy-sapping concerns of self and recalibrate my mind to focus on you and the needs of others. Let me follow Jesus as my perfect model for selfless living. Praise the Son. Amen.

For he (God) has rescued us from the dominion of darkness
and brought us into the kingdom of the Son he loves,
in whom we have redemption, the forgiveness of sins.
COLOSSIANS 1:13-14 NIV

NOTES & PRAYERS ....

....

....

....

JESUS KNOWS YOUR NAME, AND YOU KNOW HIS NAME. PRAISE GOD!

The gatekeeper opens the gate for him, and the sheep recognize his voice and come to him. He calls his own sheep by name and leads them out.

JOHN 10:3 NLT

Jesus, my Savior, I love that you called Mary Magdalene by name when you appeared to her near your empty tomb. I love that you called Peter by the name you chose for him when you invited him to follow you and become your disciple. I love that you called Saul by his Hebrew name on the road to Damascus, and you also knew his Roman name, Paul. I love that you called Mary and Martha by name when Martha felt overworked after their brother, Lazarus, had died, and Mary was focusing upon you, while Martha was focusing upon busyness. I love that you called Lazarus by name when you raised him from the dead. And I love that you called me by name when you gave me salvation in your own divine name. For your loving knowledge of all your children's names, I pray my gratitude in your supreme name, Lord of all creation – past, present, and future. Amen.

[God] Fear not, for I have redeemed you;
I have called you by name. You are mine.

ISAIAH 43:1B ESV

NOTES & PRAYERS ....

....

....

....

REST IN THE ASSURANCE NO SHIFTING SHADOW WILL EVER MAR THE BEAUTY OF YOUR HEAVENLY FATHER, OR JESUS, OR THE HOLY SPIRIT.

I am the Lord (Holy God), and I do not change.

MALACHI 3:6 NLT

Jesus Christ is the same yesterday and today and forever.

HEBREWS 13:8 NIV

Father God, you declared to Moses from the unconsumed burning bush in *Exodus* that you are the great *I am*, the one Elohim, who has always been and will always be. Holy Spirit, you, too, are eternal, forever present, even at creation. *The Spirit of God moved upon the face of the waters. Genesis 1:2b KJV.* And, Jesus, you are forever God's Christ, Yeshua, the holy *I am. Jesus answered, "I tell you the truth, before Abraham was even born, I am!" John 8:58 NLT.* In Messiah's name, I pray my gratitude for the three eternal persons of the Holy Trinity – Father, Son, and Holy Spirit. I am in union with them in the Son, along with all other believers. Amen.

For by the power of the eternal Spirit, Christ offered himself to God as a perfect sacrifice for our sins.

HEBREWS 9:14B NLT

NOTES & PRAYERS ....

....

....

....

TIME BELONGS SOLEY TO YOUR HEAVENLY FATHER, JUST AS EVERY OTHER DIMENSION KNOWN (AND UNKNOWN) TO MAN.

In the fullness of time, God will bring to fruition all
his plans for you. Glorify him in his preeminence!

*But when the set time had fully come, God sent his son, born of a woman,
born under the law, to redeem those under the law,
that we might receive adoption to sonship.*

GALATIANS 4:4-5 NIV

Heavenly Father, I stand in awe of your generosity. You healed my self-absorbed past and presented me with a breathtaking future that is God-focused and Spirit-filled. Here I am, least important in all creation, yet you planned my life with as much care as you planned the universe. Your timing is flawless, design unerring, creation magnificent, intention holy, and purpose pure. In Jesus' name, I pray to please you by being on time for every appointment you ever set for me. Thank you, Jesus, for including me in your schedule. Amen.

*You see, at just the right time, when we were still powerless,
Christ died for the ungodly.*

ROMANS 5:6 NIV

NOTES & PRAYERS ....

....

....

....

GOD'S NEW COVENANT IS MADE PERFECT IN HIS SON, JESUS, WHO FULFILLED THE OLD COVENANT AND MADE ALL THINGS NEW.

And he (Jesus) said to them,
"This is my blood of the covenant, which is poured out for many."
MARK 14:24 ESV

Thank you, Father, for loving me enough to save me in Jesus. You made your perfect Son my Mediator, High Priest, and Advocate before you. I am amazed and humbled that when he died for me on the cross, the curtain to the holy of holies ripped from top to bottom, making way for my personal relationship with you. Mighty God, how grateful I am Jesus' resurrection established your New Covenant, which gave me direct access to you through prayer. In your Son's name, accept my gratitude for your every kept promise, especially the abiding presence of the Holy Spirit in my heart. Amen.

With his own blood – not the blood of goats and calves – he (Jesus) entered the Most Holy Place once for all time and secured our redemption forever. That is why he is the one who mediates a new covenant between God and people, so that all who are called can receive the eternal inheritance God has promised them. For Christ died to set them free from the penalty of the sins they had committed under that first covenant.
HEBREWS 9:12; 15 NLT

NOTES & PRAYERS ....

....

....

....

GOD'S INDWELLING HOLY SPIRIT MEANS YOU HAVE A PERMANENT DIVINE FRIEND, COMFORTER, TEACHER, AND GUIDE ALWAYS WITH YOU AND WITHIN YOU.

[Jesus] But the helper, the Holy Spirit, whom the Father will send in my name, he will teach you all things and bring to your remembrance all that I have said to you.

JOHN 14:26 ESV

Father God, what joy knowing your Spirit is ever-present. Jesus assured me when I professed my faith that his Spirit would come to dwell inside me and be my Comforter, Counselor, and Guide, an extraordinary blessing. Thank you in the name of my Savior, for keeping me close in his loving Spirit, whose nearness means I am never alone, never without security, never outside the Kingdom of Heaven. I am grateful for the Holy Spirit's devoted company. Amen.

[Jesus] When the Spirit of truth comes, he will guide you into all the truth, for he will not speak on his own authority, but whatever he hears he will speak, and he will declare to you the things that are to come. He will glorify me, for he will take what is mine and declare it to you. All that the Father has is mine; therefore, I said that he will take what is mine and declare it to you.

JOHN 16:13-15 ESV

NOTES & PRAYERS ....

....

....

....

MALTREATMENT TOWARD YOU IS OFTEN YOUR BEST OPPORTUNITY TO BEHAVE IN A CHRIST-LIKE MANNER.

*[Jesus] But I say to you, love your enemies
and pray for those who persecute you.*
MATTHEW 5:44 ESV

Father God, it hurts me that cruelty and hatred are commonplace toward your children. I would never pretend to suffer equally with those who are tortured and murdered for their faith in you. My mind cannot fathom their pain, though you have taught me in your Word to expect hostility for my belief. Help me – help us all! – as we cling to your assurance in Scripture you have already defeated Satan. In Jesus' name, increase my faith that you, God, are forever sovereign, good, and in control. No matter how fiercely the devil attacks, you always love and protect your children, even me, least of all. Thank you, Father, Son, and Holy Spirit. I glorify you, Holy Trinity, even when I am rejected and injured by others. Praise you, Mighty Godhead. Amen.

---

*Resist him (Satan), firm in your faith, knowing that the same kinds
of sufferings are being experienced by your brotherhood
throughout the world.*
1 PETER 5:9 ESV

NOTES & PRAYERS ....

....

....

....

JESUS PLACES SPECIAL VALUE ON THE GRATEFUL TEARS YOU SHED IN RESPONSE TO HIS FORGIVENESS AND SAVING GRACE.

Your tears of gratitude for salvation are like perfume poured out before God the Father, Son, and Holy Spirit.

Kind Jesus, your Word assures me you value my tears, too many of which are for self alone. And yet, when I shed tears of appreciation for all you have done for me, you always accept my heartfelt love. You treat my thankful tears with as much tenderness as those of the forgiven woman who anointed your feet with perfume. My heart overflows with emotion, just like hers, each time I remember all you sacrificed. In your name, thank you for blessing my tears. I am forgiven and saved in you. Praise you, Deliverer. Amen.

When a certain immoral woman from that city heard he (Jesus) was eating there (at the home of Simon, the Pharisee), she brought a beautiful alabaster jar filled with expensive perfume. Then she knelt behind him at his feet, weeping. Her tears fell on his feet, and she wiped them off with her hair. Then she kept kissing his feet and putting perfume on them.
"I (Jesus) tell you, her sins – and they are many – have been forgiven, so she has shown me much love. But a person who is forgiven little shows only little love." Then Jesus said to the woman, "Your sins are forgiven."
LUKE 7:37-38; 47 NLT

NOTES & PRAYERS ....

....

....

....

SELFLESS SERVICE IS THE HALLMARK OF A GENUINE CHRISTIAN LIFE.

In his ministry on earth, Jesus modeled how a true servant king behaves, demonstrating in his perfection how much he values serving others. Where does service fall on your priority list?

In your relationships with one another, have the same mindset as Jesus: who, being in very nature God, did not consider equality with God something to be used to his own advantage; rather, he made himself nothing by taking the nature of a servant, being made in human likeness.

PHILIPPIANS 2:5-7 NIV

Savior Jesus, I am listening with heightened awareness to your instructions on servanthood. You want me to emulate you – God's One-and-Only Servant King, perfect model of Truth and grace. I pray in your name, make me a vessel filled with the divine virtues of your Holy Spirit. For as I am unable, you are able; as I am weak, you are strong; and as I am impure, you are pure. Thank you for covering me with your righteousness. I pray in your name, make me a loving servant, like you. Amen.

[Jesus] For even the Son of Man (Jesus) did not come to be served, but to serve, and to give His life a ransom for many.

MARK 10:45 NIV

NOTES & PRAYERS ....

....

....

....

HUMBLENESS IS AMONG THE SWEETEST OF YOUR SAVIOR'S TRAITS.

Jesus modeled humility to help you understand who he wants you to become in him. If you want his peace, joy, and actualization in life, be radical as Jesus is radical. Live humbly before God and others.

Therefore, as God's chosen people, holy and dearly loved, clothe yourselves with compassion, kindness, humility, gentleness, and patience.
COLOSSIANS 3:12 NIV

Savior, Son of God, the astounding knowledge of who you are brings me to my knees in humility. Your majesty, power, glory, infinity, holiness, perfection, faithfulness, immutability, generosity, love, omniscience, transcendence, immanence, Truth, and oneness in the Trinity – Father, Son, and Holy Spirit – all make me recognize my insignificance at the foot of your cross. In your loving name, I pray you will erase self's pride from my human heart and replace it with your divine humility. For left to my own designs, I am anything but humble. Forgive me. Change me. Remind me...I am not to chase vanity. I am to be humble in you. Amen.

[Jesus] Take my yoke upon you and learn from me, for I am gentle and humble in heart, and you will find rest for your souls.
MATTHEW 11:29 NIV

NOTES & PRAYERS ....

....

....

....

YOUR HEAVENLY FATHERS'S EXPECTATION OF YOU IN SUFFERING IS TO PUT ASIDE YOUR DESIRE TO UNDERSTAND WHY, AND DERIVE COMFORT BY TRUSTING HIM THROUGH IT.

Suffering refines your trust in God like nothing else. In times of misery and heartbreak, you eventually have to stop praying for an end to your suffering and knowing the why of it, and begin praying for stronger confidence in your Father's perfect will for you.

We can rejoice, too, when we run into problems and trials, for we know that they help us develop endurance. And endurance develops strength of character, and character strengthens our confident hope of salvation.

ROMANS 5:3-4 NLT

Heavenly Father, I pray in Jesus' name, give me comfort and surety your will for me in suffering is for my good. Jesus prayed in sorrow in the Garden of Gethsemane, his face to the ground. *"My Father, if it is possible, may this cup be taken from me. Yet not as I will, but as you will."* Matthew 26:39b NIV. Holy Spirit, mold my clumsy prayers about personal pain into grateful utterings acceptable to God. Let my gratitude shine through in praise and worship. Amen.

Give thanks in all circumstances; for this is God's will for you in Christ.

1 THESSALONIANS 5:18 NIV

NOTES & PRAYERS ....

....

....

....

PERSONAL ACCESS TO YOUR HEAVENLY FATHER IN PRAYER IS A MARVELOUS BLESSING, PAID FOR BY THE BLOOD OF JESUS.

Fellowship with God in personal prayer is a free privilege for you as a believer, but the price Jesus paid for you to have it was enormous. He paid with his death on the cross, then he rose again to assure your salvation.

Jesus, with a loud cry (from the cross), gave his last breath. At that, the temple curtain (to the Holy of Holies) ripped down the middle.
MARK 15:37-38 MSG

Friends, we can now – without hesitation – walk right up to God into "the Holy Place." Jesus cleared the way by the blood of his sacrifice, acting as our priest before God. The "curtain" into God's presence is his body.
HEBREWS 10:19-21 MSG

Father, thank you for allowing me to pray directly to you. Jesus shed his pure blood to open the door for me to talk with you one to one. In his name and with gratitude, I pray without ceasing all day long. Joy! Peace! Love! Amen.

Through him (Jesus) we both share the same Spirit and have equal access to the Father.
EPHESIANS 2:18 MSG

NOTES & PRAYERS ....

....

....

....

SUBMISSION TO GOD IS YOUR FIRST STEP TOWARD FREEDOM OF SALVATION IN JESUS.

You are living proof. Only God can turn total submission into total freedom. For that is what happened when you made your decision to submit your life to Jesus, your Lord and Savior. Through his gifts of grace, forgiveness, faith, and redemption, God freed you from evil when he saved your soul in his pure Son.

Christ has set us free to live a free life. So, take your stand!
Never again let anyone put a harness of slavery (sin) on you.
GALATIANS 5:1 MSG

Son of God, by your grace and mercy, I am free in you. It no longer matters if the devil tries to bind me in chains of sin. You have freed me from his bondage. In your name, Savior Jesus, I pray my gratitude for deliverance in you. Amen.

Jesus said to the people who believed in him, "You are truly
my disciples if you remain faithful to my teachings.
And you will know the truth, and the truth will set you free."
JOHN 8:31-32 NLT

Now the Lord is the Spirit, and where the Spirit of the Lord is,
there is freedom.
2 CORINTHIANS 3:17 NIV

NOTES & PRAYERS ....
....
....
....

JESUS IS GOD'S TRUTH OF FIRST IMPORTANCE.

Reflection on Jesus' Good News of salvation provides
you with quiet moments to thank God for his Son –
his Truth of first importance above all things.

*For what I received I passed on to you as of first importance: that Christ
died for our sins according to the Scriptures, that he was buried,
that he was raised on the third day.*

1 Corinthians 15:3-4a NIV

Lord Jesus, you have written it on my heart, indeed, given
me faith to believe that your work on the cross and your
resurrection established you as worthy to save my soul. You
are God's only begotten Son, cornerstone of all, Spirit along
with God's Spirit in the Holy Spirit, Alpha and Omega, First
Fruit, Messiah, Savior, King of kings, Lord of lords, and Son
in the Holy Trinity. In your name, thank you for being God's
faultless Light and Authority of first importance. Amen.

---

*He (Jesus) is the image of the invisible God, the firstborn of all creation.
For in him all the fullness of God was pleased to dwell, and through him
to reconcile to himself all things, whether on earth or in heaven,
making peace by the blood of his cross.*

Colossians 1:15; 19-20 ESV

NOTES & PRAYERS ....

....

....

....

YOU ARE NOT PARANOID. SATAN AND HIS MINIONS REALLY ARE ATTACKING YOU. BE THANKFUL YOUR HEAVENLY FATHER KEEPS YOU FROM BEING DEVOURED BY THOSE MALEVOLENT ONES. FOR EVIL IS NO MATCH FOR ALMIGHTY GOD, WHO IS FOREVER SOVEREIGN, GOOD, AND VICTORIOUS.

The God of peace will soon crush Satan under your feet.
ROMANS 16:20A NLT

I am grateful, Heavenly Father, you make me victorious in my personal battle against Satan and his evil spirits. I fight their wickedness under the protection of your full armor – Truth, Righteousness, Faith, Salvation, your Holy Word, and Jesus' Gospel of salvation peace – all available to me through obedience, prayer, and alertness to divine instruction by the Spirit from the Word. In Jesus' name, thank you, God. You are my defender. Amen.

And the devil who had deceived them was thrown into the lake of fire and sulfur where the beast and the false prophet were, and they will be tormented day and night forever and ever.
REVELATION 20:10 ESV

NOTES & PRAYERS ....

....

....

....

WALKING IN STEP WITH JESUS MEANS MORE STEPPING LIGHTLY AND LESS STAGGERING.

If you are serious about walking with God, then walk with Jesus.
If you stumble, he will help you up. If you lose your way, he will
help you course-correct. If you get tired, he will give you rest.
You will never find a better traveling companion than your Savior.

Therefore, as you received Christ Jesus the Lord, so walk in him.

COLOSSIANS 2:6 ESV

Lord Jesus, help me with my tendency to lag behind or run
ahead. You are my divine moral compass, my walking companion, my loyal friend who shows me the way. I often think
of Simon of Cyrene, who carried your cross on the road to
Golgotha after you stumbled and fell under its weight. He
did not realize he was walking with the Son of God to his
crucifixion. If he had, he would have begged to walk with
you and help you, instead of having to be forced by Roman
soldiers. In your name, Jesus, thank you for taking my hand
and inviting me to walk with you eternally. I am grateful to
be near you. Keep me forever close. Amen.

---

*Whoever says he abides in him (Jesus) ought to walk
in the same way in which he walked.*

1 JOHN 2:5B-6 ESV

NOTES & PRAYERS ....

....

....

....

ARE YOU JESUS' MESSENGER OF TRUTH, OR SELF'S BABBLER OF LIES?

If you define yourself as a disciple of Jesus, you must define yourself as his messenger. He commands you to share his Good News.

Go ye therefore, and teach all nationss, baptizing them in the name of the Father, and of the Son, and of the Holy Ghost: Teaching them to observe all things whatsoever I have commanded you: and, lo, I am with you always, even unto the end of the world. Amen.
MATTHEW 28:19-20 KJV

Jesus, I pray in your name to become a better helper to the Holy Spirit in witnessing for you. Convict me! Amen.

For "Everyone who calls on the name of the Lord will be saved." But how can they call on him to save them unless they believe in him? And how can they believe in him if they have never heard about him? And how can they hear about him unless someone tells them? And how will anyone go and tell them without being sent? That is why the Scriptures say, "How beautiful are the feet of messengers who bring good news!"
ROMANS 10:13-15 NLT

I said, "Here I am! Send me."
ISAIAH 6:8b NIV

NOTES & PRAYERS ....

....

....

....

CONFIDENCE IN YOUR FAITH IN JESUS IS A BLESSING GOD WILL INCREASE GENEROUSLY. ALL YOU HAVE TO DO IS ASK HIM.

God is good and sovereign. Your certainty of that is a gift from God himself, which means you can pray for more certainty. If you find yourself fretting about some difficult situation, pray for confidence in God's power over all creation, then relax in the increased sureness of his supremacy with which he blesses you.

Let us then with confidence draw near to the throne of grace, that we may receive mercy and find grace to help in time of need.
HEBREWS 4:16 ESV

The Lord will be your confidence and keep your foot from being caught.
PROVERBS 3:26 ESV

Father, in Jesus' name, I pray with certainty your supreme power will never waver. Indeed, I pray for more certainty. Your Son, my Savior, gave me his assurance and peace when he saved me. Praise and glorify him. Amen.

There has never been the slightest doubt in my mind that the God who started this great work in you would keep at it and bring it to a flourishing finish on the very day Christ Jesus appears.
PHILIPPIANS 1:6 MSG

NOTES & PRAYERS ....
....
....
....

IS IT POSSIBLE FOR YOU AS A BELIEVER TO OUTGIVE GOD? NO WAY. CANNOT BE DONE. YET, DO NOT STOP TRYING.

Give thanks to God for the day you surrendered your all to Jesus. You gave him your paltry everything, and he gave you his precious everything – new life with him forever, proof of his promise you cannot outgive your Heavenly Father or his perfect Son.

[Jesus] "Truly, I say to you, there is no one who has left house or wife or brothers or parents or children, for the sake of the Kingdom of God, who will not receive many times more in this time, and in the age to come – eternal life."
LUKE 18:29B-30 ESV

Benevolent Jesus, I surrendered my all, and you made me your child and heir to your Kingdom. I surrendered my all, and you gave me life everlasting. I surrendered my all, and you provided me faith to receive forgiveness and salvation by grace. In your name, Lord, thank you for loving and outgiving me. Let me love and serve you forever. Amen.

[Jesus] "If anyone would come after me, let him deny himself and take up his cross and follow me. For whoever would save his life will lose it, but whoever loses his life for my sake will find it."
MATTHEW 16:24B-25 ESV

NOTES & PRAYERS ....

....

....

....

DEPENDENCE ON GOD NEVER FAILS. DEPENDENCE ON SELF NEVER SUCCEEDS.

Are you counting on God or self as you navigate life?
If self, you are doing it the stressful way,
if God, the peaceful way. Why not shut down stress
by choosing God's peaceful life ordered by his Son –
Jesus Christ, your Lord and Savior.

Don't worry about anything; instead, pray about everything.
Tell God what you need and thank him for all he has done. Then you
will experience God's peace, which exceeds anything we can understand.
His peace will guard your hearts and minds as you live in Christ Jesus.

PHILIPPIANS 4:6-7 NLT

Savior Jesus, where would I be if I did not have your peace? I am grateful my weakness before you is my most valuable strength, which convicts me to reject reliance on self and embrace reliance on you. In your name, I pray my thanks for the privilege of living in your serenity. Thank you, Prince of Peace. Praise your name! Preach your Gospel! Amen.

You (God) will keep in perfect peace all who trust in you,
all whose thoughts are fixed on you!

ISAIAH 26:3 NLT

NOTES & PRAYERS ....

....

....

....

ALWAYS ENCOURAGE OTHERS IN JESUS. NEVER DISCOURAGE ANYONE. NO, NOT EVER.

If you want to be encouraged by God, be an encourager on God's behalf to those around you. He has given you his divine tools – prayer and his Word, plus the Holy Spirit's authentic availability to others through you. Go now and encourage the discouraged.

[God] Be strong and courageous. Do not be afraid; do not be discouraged, for the Lord your God will be with you wherever you go.

Joshua 1:9b NIV

Father, when I consider how faithful you are to encourage me, I am convicted you want me to do the same for others. In Jesus' name, I pray to be a vessel emptied of disheartening self and filled with your heartening Spirit. Amen.

[God] When you go through rivers of difficulty, you will not drown. When you walk through the fire of oppression, you will not be burned up; the flames will not consume you. For I am the Lord your God, the Holy One of Israel, your Savior.

Isaiah 43:2b-3a NLT

Therefore, encourage one another and build each other up.

1 Thessalonians 5:11a NIV

NOTES & PRAYERS ....

....

....

....

YOU ARE ONE OF GOD'S LIVING MIRACLES.

*Then the Lord God formed man of dust from the ground and breathed
into his nostrils the breath of life; and man became a living being.*
GENESIS 2:7 NASB

Have you ever thought of yourself as a miracle? Your Heavenly
Father created you and gave you physical life. Then by grace,
through the blood and resurrection of Jesus, he saved you from
your sins and regenerated you into a new creature in his Son by
the power of the Holy Spirit. Now if all that does not
qualify you as a living miracle, what would?

Savior Jesus, I am grateful you made me newly alive through
regeneration by the Holy Spirit. I belong to you, Lord — your
recreated miracle, forgiven and saved for eternity through
your redemptive grace. In your name, I pray to please you
by loving you with all my heart, mind, and soul and loving
others as I love myself, evidence of my adoration for you.
Thank you for creating and recreating me. Amen.

---

*For God so loved the world, that he gave his only begotten Son,
that whosoever believeth in him should not perish,
but have everlasting life.*
JOHN 3:16 KJV

NOTES & PRAYERS ....

....

....

....

FEAR NOT! YOUR HEAVENLY FATHER IS YOUR DIVINE PROTECTOR. CONQUER YOUR FEAR WITH REJOICING. SUBDUE YOUR ALARM WITH PRAISE. TURN YOUR ANXIETY INTO THANKSGIVING. FEAR NOT!

For God hath not given us a spirit of fear, but of power, and of love, and of a sound mind.

2 TIMOTHY 1:7 KJV

He (God) will cover you with his feathers. He will shelter you with his wings. His faithful promises are your armor and protection. Do not be afraid of the terrors of the night, nor the arrow that flies in the day. Do not dread the disease that stalks in darkness, nor the disaster that strikes at midday. Though a thousand fall at your side, though ten thousand are dying around you, these evils will not touch you.

PSALM 91:4-7 NLT

Father God, in Jesus' name, thank you for delivering me from fear. Your love set me free. Your grace saved me. Your authority empowered me. I am victorious in your Son, brave and unafraid. Glorify you! Amen.

[Jesus] Do not be afraid, little flock, for your Father has been pleased to give you the kingdom.

LUKE 12:32 NIV

NOTES & PRAYERS ....
....
....
....

GOD CREATED YOU AND THE ANGELS TO WORSHIP HIM. HE DID NOT CREATE YOU TO WORSHIP ANGELS. DO NOT EVER LET ANYONE CONFUSE YOU ABOUT THAT.

Angels and their activities are the business of God, not man. Even an angel cautions us in God's Word: *No, don't worship me. I am a servant of God, just like you and your brothers the prophets, as well as all who obey what is written in this book. Worship only God! Revelation 22:9a NLT.*

Heavenly Father, I do not know much about angels, except you created them to worship you and act as aids and *ministering spirits sent to serve those who will inherit salvation. Hebrews 1:14b NIV.* God, I have never seen an angel, certainly no one I recognized as an angel, though I admit to curiosity. One thing I know for certain. When I get to Heaven, I will be thrilled to join your chorus of angels in worshiping you. My day of jubilation in praising you alongside angels is on its way. Thank you, in Jesus' name. Amen.

For he will order his angels to protect you wherever you go.
They will hold you up with their hands,
so you won't even hurt your foot on a stone.
PSALM 91:11-12 NLT

NOTES & PRAYERS ....

....

....

....

April

ON THE DAY JESUS RESCUED YOU FROM SIN, YOU BECAME A LIGHTNING ROD TOWARD OTHERS FOR HIS GRACE.

You saved me, Jesus, then showed me in your Word the Holy Spirit wants to work through me as he draws others to salvation. I am convicted of your inclusive intent, Lord. You took me in as an expression of your love, and not just for me, for everyone. I am humbled by the sentiments in Fanny Crosby's old hymn, "Rescue the Perishing." They are sweet reminders of my responsibility as your disciple. *Rescue the perishing, Care for the dying, Snatch them in pity from sin and the grave;* Thank you, Jesus, in your saving name for including me on your great rescue mission for those who need you so desperately. Amen.

For he (God) has rescued us from the kingdom of darkness
and transferred us into the Kingdom of his dear Son,
who purchased our freedom and forgave our sins.
COLOSSIANS 1:13-14 NLT

The Lord says, "I will rescue those who love me. I will protect those who
trust in my name. When they call on me, I will answer; I will be with
them in trouble. I will rescue and honor them. I will reward them with a
long life and give them my salvation."
PSALM 91:14-16 NLT

NOTES & PRAYERS ....
....
....
....

JESUS' RETURN TO EARTH IS A PROMISE YOU CAN LOOK FORWARD TO GOD KEEPING.

[Jesus] Then, the Arrival of the Son of Man (Jesus himself)! It will fill the skies – no one will miss it. Unready people all over the world, outsiders to the splendor and power, will raise a huge lament as they watch the Son of Man blazing out of heaven.

MATTHEW 24:30 MSG

Lord Jesus, sometimes I just stop for a moment to contemplate how glorious your second coming will be? What a rush! I am overwhelmed with anticipation whenever I consider your promise to return to earth. I wonder if the angels who will accompany you with the loud trumpet blast to gather your elect from the four winds will be the same angels who appeared to shepherds on the night of your birth. I marvel at the details of your thrilling plan, because with you as divine author, every step will play out to perfection. In your name and with great joy and gratitude, I claim and await the fulfillment of your promise in John's *Revelation 22:20 ESV He [Jesus] who testifies to these things says, "Surely I am coming soon."* Amen. Come, Lord Jesus! Again, I say amen.

[Jesus] Keep watch, because you do not know the day or the hour.

MATTHEW 25:13B NIV

NOTES & PRAYERS ....

....

....

....

JESUS, THE WAY, IS YOUR DELIVERANCE FROM WANDERING AROUND IN DARKNESS – LOST.

You have a clear understanding *the way* of Jesus is much more than his one and only path to God. *The way* is Jesus himself. For he is not simply *a way*; he is *the way*, fully God himself, divine Son in the Holy Trinity.

Lord Jesus, I have learned from Scripture your early followers called you and your teachings *the way*, a term drawn directly from your own words as you assured your disciples, along with all other believers – past, present, and future – that you alone are our access to God, because you are God. In your name, I pray you will keep me in the center of *your way, the way*. Thank you for Mary Slade's words in her hymn: *Footprints of Jesus that make the pathway glow; we will follow the steps of Jesus where'er they go. Then, at last, when on high He sees us, our journey done, we will rest where the steps of Jesus end at his throne.* Savior Jesus, you invited me to make *your way* my way, and I accepted your invitation. Remind me to invite others to do the same. Bless them, Lord. Make *your way* their way. Amen.

Jesus said to him [Thomas, the doubter], "I am the way, and the truth, and the life. No one comes to the Father except through me."

JOHN 14:6 ESV

NOTES & PRAYERS ....

....

....

....

YOUR PRAYERS ARE EXCEEDINGLY IMPORTANT TO GOD THE FATHER, JESUS THE SON, AND THE HOLY SPIRIT – MASSIVELY, IMMENSELY, ENORMOUSLY IMPORTANT.

Jesus modeled essential prayer habits during his ministry on earth. Which of his customs in talking to God have you incorporated into your own devotional life?

Your disciples observed you, Jesus, as you retreated to quiet places to pray alone: *Yet, not my will, but yours be done.* And they heard you pray aloud in public as you hung on the cross: *Father, forgive them for they know not what they do.* Your emphasis on daily prayer affirmed its importance – indispensable! I pray now in your name, prayerful Savior, by the leading of the Holy Spirit, who aids me in prayer even as he prays with me, sometimes *in wordless groans* only the Father understands, that my prayers will bring pleasure and glory to Almighty God. Amen.

[Jesus] Our Father which art in heaven, Hallowed be thy name. Thy kingdom come, Thy will be done in earth, as it is in heaven. Give us this day our daily bread. And forgive us our debts, as we forgive our debtors. And lead us not into temptation, but deliver us from evil: For thine is the kingdom, and the power, and the glory, forever. Amen.
MATTHEW 6:9b-13 KJV

NOTES & PRAYERS ....

....

....

....

YOUR HEAVENLY FATHER HAS MADE MANY PROMISES TO YOU IN HIS WORD. FIND OUT WHAT THEY ARE AND CLAIM THEM WITH LOVING THANKFULNESS.

And because of his (God's) glory and excellence, he has given us great and precious promises. These are the promises that enable you to share his divine nature and escape the world's corruption caused by human desires.

2 PETER 1:4 NLT

Jesus, I praise and worship you as I hold fast to the promises you made in Scripture. Kelso Carter's hymn expresses how I feel about your assurances. *Standing on the promises of Christ my King, Thro' eternal ages let His praises ring; Glory in the highest, I will shout and sing, Standing on the promises of God.* In your name, Jesus, thank you for the dozens of kept promises with which you have blessed me, especially the fulfillment of your guarantee of the indwelling Holy Spirit within my heart, beginning on the day you saved me. Praise you, Jesus, for you are God's most important kept promise to the whole world. I stand on you, the Word. My future is in you. Glory to the Son. Amen.

But we are looking forward to the new heavens and new earth he has promised, a world filled with God's righteousness.

2 PETER 3:13 NLT

NOTES & PRAYERS ....

....

....

....

GOD'S FAITHFULNESS TOWARD YOU AFFIRMS HIS LOVE FOR YOU, WHICH MANIFESTS IN HIS SALVATION GRACE MADE POSSIBLE BY JESUS.

Then I saw heaven opened, and behold, a white horse!
The one (Jesus) sitting on it is called Faithful and True.

REVELATION 19:11A ESV

For a better definition of faithfulness and loyalty, think who, instead of what. Jesus himself is God's divine, loving loyalty. As your Savior, he is steadfastly true and faithful to you, which leads to two questions: Are you steadfastly true and faithful to Jesus, and by extension, are you steadfastly true and faithful through him to those around you?

Jesus, you are the foundation of love in God's divine concept of loyalty. *Matthew 22:37b-40 NIV: Love the Lord your God with all your heart and with all your soul and with all your mind. This is the first and greatest commandment. And the second is like it: Love your neighbor as yourself. All the Law and the Prophets hang on these two commandments.* In your name, Savior, make me loyal like you, unwavering. Amen.

Never let loyalty and kindness leave you! Tie them around your neck as a reminder. Write them deep within your heart.

PROVERBS 3:3 NLT

NOTES & PRAYERS ....

....

....

....

WHICH TONES AND OVERTONES
VIBRATE IN YOUR LIFE –
GOD'S HARMONY OR SATAN'S DISSONANCE?

*Good people, cheer God! Right-living people sound best when praising.
Use guitars to reinforce your hallelujahs! Play his praise on a grand
piano! Invent your own new song to him; give him a trumpet fanfare.*
PSALM 33:1-3 MSG

Heavenly Father, it is your divine harmony with Jesus and the Spirit – not my human dissonance in self – that elicits positive responses from people who are searching for you. I beg you, stop me from becoming a part of some dreadful ensemble for Satan, forever clanging out wrong notes. Let me join in the harmony of other believers in praise songs that please you, melodious Father. Help me attract lost ones to your Son. In his name, thank you for drawing me to serve as a faithful member of the divine choir that is his one true church, his precious bride. Amen.

*Let the peace of Christ keep you in tune with each other, in step with each
other. None of this going off and doing your own thing. And cultivate
thankfulness. Let the Word of Christ – the Message – have the run of
the house. Give it plenty of room in your lives. Instruct and direct one
another using good common sense. And sing, sing your hearts out to God!*
COLOSSIANS 3:15-16 MSG

NOTES & PRAYERS ....
....
....
....

PROPHECY IS THE EXCLUSIVE REALM OF GOD REGARDING HIS TRUTHS ABOUT THE FUTURE. ALL DIMENSIONS OF TIME BELONG TO HIM.

Fulfilled prophecies from the Old Testament concerning Jesus' life on earth assure you of God's faithfulness to do what he promises.

Father, thank you for the story of Jesus throughout the Old and New Testaments. I am grateful you quickened my heart to understand your important, essential Truth, that the entire *Bible* is your message of salvation through your Son's sacrifice and resurrection. Your fulfilled prophecies enhance my confidence in the divine hope you have given me that in the fullness of time, Jesus will return to earth on the clouds of heaven. In his name, thank you for kept promises and accomplished prophecies ordered by your Providence. I am confident in my eternal future with you, God. Amen.

[Jesus speaks to the synagogue congregation in Nazareth.] "God's Spirit is on me; he's chosen me to preach the Message of good news to the poor, sent me to announce pardon to prisoners and recovery of sight to the blind, to set the burdened and battered free, to announce, "This is God's year to act!" He rolled up the scroll, handed it back to the assistant, and sat down. Every eye was on him, intent. Then he said, "You've just heard Scripture make history. It came true just now in this place."

LUKE 4:18-21 MSG

NOTES & PRAYERS ....

....

....

....

SERVING OTHERS WITH LOVE IS AN EMPOWERING BEHAVIOR OF JESUS THAT CAN BE YOUR BEHAVIOR. BE POTENT FOR GOD BY SERVING AS JESUS SERVED.

Have you ever wept with gratitude on reading about your Savior's humility as he served his two suppers, the Lord's supper and the marriage supper of the lamb? You wept, because you understood he chose serving others, you included, over being served himself.

In your name, Jesus, I am grateful for the supper you served your disciples before dying and rising again, and for the supper you are preparing to serve believers, your marriage feast to celebrate our union with you. Thank you, Jesus, for inviting me to both meals as your personal guest. Amen.

Jesus took bread, and when he had given thanks, he broke it and gave it to his disciples, saying, "Take and eat; this is my body." Then he took a cup, and when he had given thanks, he gave it to them, saying, "Drink from it, all of you. This is my blood of the covenant, which is poured out for many for the forgiveness of sins."
MATTHEW 26:26B-28 NIV

Then the angel said to me (John), "Write this: Blessed are those who are invited to the marriage supper of the Lamb!"
REVELATION 19:9A NIV

NOTES & PRAYERS ....

....

....

....

GOD CREATED YOU IN THE PHYSICAL. AND THEN, BY THE POWER OF THE HOLY SPIRIT AT THE MOMENT HE SAVED YOU FROM SIN, HE RECREATED YOU IN THE SPIRITUAL IN JESUS, HIS SON AND SALVATION MIRACLE.

When Jesus saved you, the Holy Spirit filled your earthly being with the Spirit of the Father and of Christ, turning your dust body into a regenerated temple of God – born again!

Father, I am astounded when I ponder how you created Adam out of dust and breathed life into him, and then created Eve out of Adam's rib and breathed life into her. And yet, after all you did for them, they still sinned by disobeying you, as have I. Thank you, Father, in the name of Jesus, your love for me and all other believers was/is greater than our disobedience. You proved your love by making a way for us by your gifts of grace, forgiveness, and faith to be reconciled to you through your Son. Praise him. Amen.

Earthly people are like the earthly man (Adam), and heavenly people are like the heavenly man (Jesus). Just as we are now like the earthly man, we will someday be like the heavenly man (our Lord and Savior).

1 CORINTHIANS 15:48-49 NLT

NOTES & PRAYERS ....

....

....

....

PRAY YOUR HEART OUT WITH CONFIDENCE THAT GOD IS LISTENING. HE ALWAYS – YES, ALWAYS! – HEARS AND ANSWERS HIS CHILDREN'S PRAYERS.

[God speaking to Jeremiah] Call to me and I will answer you.
I'll tell you marvelous and wondrous things that
you could never figure out on your own.

JEREMIAH 33:3 MSG

God pays attention when you cry out to him, whether or not you are able to put your needs into words. The Holy Spirit will make your wordless prayers acceptable to your Heavenly Father, who understands the language of your heart.

Father God, I love that music notations as abstract marks on staff paper can be heard in the minds of those who read music. But you, God, hear much more. You hear all things, on all levels, in all dimensions – everything going on in your creation at the same time. Thank you in Jesus' name for hearing my prayers. Help me hear your answers, Lord. I am listening. Amen.

If I had not confessed the sin in my heart, the Lord would not have
listened. But God did listen! He paid attention to my prayer.

PSALM 66:18-19 NLT

NOTES & PRAYERS ....

....

....

....

BE GRATEFUL THAT JESUS, GOD'S SPIRITUAL PROVIDER OF ABUNDANCE, BLESSES AND PRUNES YOU.

Attending to your needs is a loving way your Savior cares for you.

Lord, after dying and rising again, you appeared to your disciples and provided for them when they were having no luck fishing. You told them to cast their net on the right side of the boat, and when they obeyed, they netted too many fish to haul into the vessel. Then you invited them on shore to enjoy a breakfast of bread and broiled fish you had cooked with your own nail-pierced hands. The symbolism is striking. You know our physical, emotional, and Spiritual needs at all times, and you address them in detailed and personal ways. You are our faithful provider, Savior Jesus. In your name, thank you for always including me in your invitation to breakfast. Amen.

[Jesus] "So do not worry, saying, 'What shall we eat?' or 'What shall we drink?' or 'What shall we wear?' For the pagans run after all these things, and your Heavenly Father knows that you need them. But seek first his kingdom and his righteousness, and all these things will be given to you as well."
MATTHEW 6:31-33 NIV

NOTES & PRAYERS ....

....

....

....

MUSIC IS THE UNIVERSAL LANGUAGE GOD CREATED FOR BELIEVERS TO ENJOY IN GLORIFYING HIM, DESPITE THE MULTITUDE OF DIFFERENCES IN OUR NATIVE TONGUES.

Your creator made you, and he made music. Put the two together, and you have a wonderful combination for believers to use in honoring their Heavenly Father in praise and worship.

Sing to the Lord a new song, for he has done marvelous things.
PSALM 98:1A NIV

Father God, how poignant that Jesus sang a praise song with his disciples on the same night he was arrested, tried, convicted, and sentenced to death, all unfairly. He knew everything about to happen to him, including the cross, yet he sang before you in a reverent attitude of prayer and praise. In your Son's name, thank you, God, for music as a loving language to share with other believers in glorifying you. We are new creatures, singing your new songs. Amen.

Let the message of Christ dwell among you richly as you teach and admonish one another with all wisdom through psalms, hymns, and songs from the Spirit, singing to God with gratitude in your hearts.
COLOSSIANS 3:16 NIV

NOTES & PRAYERS ....

....

....

....

PHYSICAL EARS AND SPIRITUAL EARS ARE GIFTS FROM GOD. THANK HIM. PRAISE HIM. WORSHIP HIM!

Just as your physical ears pick up wave-notes of physical sound, your Spiritual ears pick up wave-notes of divine Truth.

Heavenly Father, I am grateful for Clara Scott, who so tenderly described in her hymn lyrics my desire to hear you in Spirit: *"Open my ears, that I may hear voices of truth thou sendest clear; and while the wave-notes fall on my ear, ev'rything false will disappear."* Lord, thank you for helping me understand your important divine teaching, that if I want Truth to vibrate in my Spiritual ears, I must tune in to the supernatural wave-notes you have placed in Scripture. In Jesus' name, open my ears to the Holy Spirit's instruction in your Word and help me obey. Amen.

Ears to hear and eyes to see – both are gifts from the Lord.
PROVERBS 20:12 NLT

Good friend, take to heart what I'm telling you; collect my counsels and guard them with your life. Tune your ears to the world of Wisdom; set your heart on a life of understanding.
PROVERBS 2:1-2 MSG

NOTES & PRAYERS ....

....

....

....

GOD USED YOUR FAITH (GIVEN TO YOU AND EMPOWERED BY DIVINE GRACE AND FORGIVENESS) TO SAVE YOUR SOUL, JUST AS HE USED ABRAHAM'S FAITH (ALSO GIVEN TO HIM AND EMPOWERED BY DIVINE GRACE AND FORGIVENESS) TO SAVE HIS SOUL.

Your New Testament faith is the same type of
God-given faith as Abraham's Old Testament faith.
Be grateful to your Heavenly Father, who is mighty to save.

Faith is confidence in what we hope for and assurance about what we do not see. This is what ancients (like Abraham) were commended for.
HEBREWS 11:1-2 NIV

Heavenly Father, what a blessing to follow your holy concept of faith as it flows gracefully from the Old Testament throughout the New Testament and beyond. I pray in Jesus' name, thank you for faith you gave me out of love. Amen.

[Paul in New Testament] For in the gospel the righteousness of God is revealed – righteousness that is by faith from first to last, just as it is written (and declared by God in Habakkuk in the Old Testament): "The righteous will live by faith."
ROMANS 1:17 NIV

NOTES & PRAYERS ....

....

....

....

JESUS NEVER, EVER MODELED PRIDE.
HE ALWAYS MODELED HUMILITY.

Have this mind among yourselves, which is yours in Christ Jesus,
who, though he was in the form of God, did not count equality with God
a thing to be grasped, but emptied himself, by taking the form of a ser-
vant, being born in the likeness of men. And being found in human form,
he humbled himself by becoming obedient to the point of death,
even death on a cross.

PHILIPPIANS 2:5-8 ESV

Savior Jesus, when I picture you riding into Jerusalem on a donkey, the lowliest beast of burden, I am grateful for your willingness to humble yourself for my sake. You not only became a man, you became a servant of man. In your name, I pray for guidance in imitating your proper conduct for humble service. Remind me to walk as you walked before God and man – in humility. Amen.

[Jesus] You know that the rulers of the Gentiles lord it over them,
and their high officials exercise authority over them. Not so with you.
Instead, whoever wants to become great among you must be your servant,
and whoever wants to be first must be your slave – just as the
Son of Man (Jesus) did not come to be served, but to serve,
and to give his life as a ransom for many.

MATTHEW 20:25B-28 NIV

NOTES & PRAYERS ....
....
....
....

CONTENTMENT IN JESUS IS YOURS FOR THE ASKING. PRAY AND RECEIVE IT.

Contentment in life is a blessing from God.

*[Paul] For I have learned to be content whatever the circumstances.
I know what it is to be in need, and I know what it is to have plenty.
I have learned the secret of being content in any and every situation,
whether well fed or hungry, whether living in plenty or want.
I can do all this through him (Jesus) who gives me strength.*

PHILIPPIANS 4:11B-13 NIV

Heavenly Father, in Jesus' name, help me avoid confusing contentment in self with contentment in Jesus. Your Son is my only Savior and my only contentment. Amen.

*But godliness with contentment is great gain. For we brought
nothing into the world, and we can take nothing out of it.
But if we have food and clothing, we will be content with that.*

1 TIMOTHY 6:6-8 NIV

*Keep your lives free from the love of money and be
content with what you have, because God has said,
"Never will I leave you; never will I forsake you."*

HEBREWS 13:5 NIV

NOTES & PRAYERS ....

....

....

....

WHOSE WILL OPENS WIDE THE DOORWAY TO JOY AND PEACE, GOD'S OR YOURS? YOU KNOW THE ANSWER. TRUE JOY AND PEACE ABIDE IN GOD'S WILL ALONE.

The world and its desires pass away,
but whoever does the will of God lives forever.
1 JOHN 2:17 NIV

Father, I have spent too much time fretting about the question of your will for my life. Thank you for helping me face the Truth that your best plan for me is connected to my dutiful obedience to your commands: 1)Read and study your Word as if my life depends on it, 2)Pray and pray more, and 3)Follow the impeccable example of your Son, Jesus, and his teachings on how to live. Dear God, now that I have admitted I understand the steps required to discern your will, thank you in the name of Jesus for your amazing plans for me. *He (God) leadeth me in the paths of righteousness for his name's sake. Psalm 23:3b KJV.* Abba, crucify my will and replace it with yours Amen.

Do not be conformed to this world, but be transformed by the renewal of
your mind, that by testing you may discern what is the will of God,
what is good and acceptable and perfect.
ROMANS 12:2 ESV

NOTES & PRAYERS ....

....

....

....

COMMITTING TO GOD GAVE YOUR LIFE MEANING, QUALITY, AND PURPOSE. THANK HIM. PRAISE HIM. GLORIFY HIM!

Commit everything you do to the Lord. Trust him, and he will help you.
He will make your innocence radiate like the dawn,
and the justice of your cause will shine like the noonday sun.

PSALM 37:5-6 NLT

Dear God, earthly relationships in my life have become so damaged at times my steadfast commitment to them is the only thing left of value. And then, way too often, my commitment wavers, as well, rendering worthless even that. But you, God, opened my eyes to a new way of experiencing relationships and commitment, according to your promise of reconciliation through your Son, Jesus, my Savior, perfect model for steadfast, supernatural, loving, unfailing, ultimate, eternal commitment. In his holy name, thank you, God, for your loyal commitment to me and all other believers. Teach me to commit faithfully to you and others in imitation of your faithful Son. Amen.

The eyes of the Lord search the whole earth in order to strengthen those whose hearts are fully committed to him.

2 CHRONICLES 16:9A NLT

NOTES & PRAYERS ....

....

....

....

REMEMBRANCE OF JESUS IS A GIFT FROM GOD THAT NEVER STOPS BLESSING.

Remember the Father, Son, and Holy Spirit with delight and rejoicing, as they delight and rejoice in remembering you.

[Jesus] But the helper, the Holy Spirit, whom the Father will send in my name, he will teach you all things and bring to your remembrance all that I have said to you.

JOHN 14:26 ESV

Thank you, Heavenly Father, for giving me remembrance of you through your Word and Spirit. I know you will never forget me, because you loved me before you ever created me. And out of gratefulness and love, I will never forget you. You cared for me enough to give your Son, Jesus, as the perfect model of faithful remembrance for all believers. Accept my gratitude in his name for every nudge of your Spirit and every lesson in your Word, all in remembrance of you, Almighty God – Father, Son, and Holy Spirit. Praise you with sweet remembrance. Amen.

Let all that I am praise the Lord;
may I never forget the good things he does for me.

PSALM 103:2 NLT

NOTES & PRAYERS

GOD'S MIGHTY TRUMPET BLAST WILL BE YOUR CALL TO COME RUNNING ON THE DAY JESUS RETURNS TO COLLECT YOU.

Your ears are tuned perfectly to God's trumpet.
When he blesses you with its blast at Jesus' second coming,
you will hear it clearly with no doubt of authenticity.

Lord Jesus, in your name, thank you for James Black's hymn: *When the trumpet of the Lord shall sound, and time shall be no more, And the morning breaks eternal, bright, and fair; When the saved of earth shall gather over on the other shore, And the roll is called up yonder, I'll be there. Amen!*

[Jesus] Then, the Arrival of the Son of Man (Jesus)! It will fill the skies – no one will miss it. Unready people all over the world, outsiders to the splendor and power, will raise a huge lament as they watch the Son of Man blazing out of heaven. At that same moment, he'll dispatch his angels with a trumpet-blast summons, pulling in God's chosen from the four winds, from pole to pole.
MATTHEW 24:30-31 MSG

We shall not all sleep, but we shall all be changed, in a moment, in the twinkling of an eye, at the last trumpet. For the trumpet will sound, and the dead will be raised imperishable, and we shall be changed.
1 CORINTHIANS 15:51B-52 ESV

NOTES & PRAYERS ....

....

....

....

YOUR HEAVENLY FATHER PREPARED A MINISTRY IN ADVANCE FOR YOUR SERVICE, WHICH, IN FACT, IS HIS OWN MINISTRY. DO NOT MISS OUT ON YOUR MINISTRY BLESSING.

Whoever brings blessing will be enriched,
and one who waters will himself be watered.

PROVERBS 11:25 ESV

Father, you gave Jesus to minister reconciliation with me. Which teaches me that the purpose of any ministry you want me involved in is fundamentally the same for all ministries – communicating to others your message of reconciliation through your Son. In my Savior's name, let me work alongside you, God, for I know whatever I cannot accomplish, you/he can. Praise Jesus for allowing me to help. Amen.

He (God) creates each of us by Christ Jesus to join him in the work
he does, the good work he has gotten ready for us to do,
work we had better be doing.

EPHESIANS 2:10 MSG

Each of you should use whatever gift you have received to serve others,
as faithful stewards of God's grace in its various forms.

1 PETER 4:10 NIV

NOTES & PRAYERS ....

....

....

....

WHEN YOU DO NOT KNOW HOW TO PRAY ABOUT SOMETHING, TELL THE HOLY SPIRIT. HE CAN – AND WILL – INTERPRET YOUR MOST DESPERATE HEARTCRY.

God hears and understands every prayer of your heart on every level, even those you do not understand yourself.

Thank you, Jesus, for hearing my pitiful prayers when life's challenges beat me down. I know you feel my pain, because you suffered the pain of the cross, and even worse, temporary separation from God, our Father. As you took the punishment for my sins, you cried out to him on being forsaken, yet you submitted humbly to his will, knowing it was his perfect will for you. Savior Jesus, help me submit to you in my distress, knowing I am safe and secure in your love. In your name, thank you for the Holy Spirit, who helps me pray when I am too weak to pray on my own. Thank you for prayer and praise, gifts from you to keep me close to you in my need. Amen.

When the righteous cry for help, the Lord hears and delivers them out of all their troubles.
PSALM 34:17 ESV

Weeping may endure for a night, but joy cometh in the morning.
PSALM 30:5B KJV

NOTES & PRAYERS ....

....

....

....

YOU HAVE FACED A CERTAIN TRUTH – GOD DOES NOT TOLERATE AIMLESS DRIFTING.

You are either moving toward God and along with him, or backsliding away from him, out of step.

The backslider in heart will be filled with the fruit of his ways, and a good man will be filled with the fruit of his ways.

PROVERBS 14:14 ESV

Heavenly Father, I am sorry to admit I know too much about the backslidden life. What an arid existence, bereft of good fruit. Thank you, Jesus, for causing me to hunger after your wholesome Spiritual sustenance, the fruit of God's Holy Spirit – love, joy, peace, patience, kindness, goodness, faithfulness, gentleness, and self-control. Help me break self's lazy habit of backsliding and giving in to desires of the flesh, bad fruit. In your name, Savior, I choose divine Truth and reject sinful backsliding. Forward in you, Lord. Amen.

I'm not saying that I have this all together, that I have it made. But I am well on my way, reaching out for Christ, who has so wondrously reached out for me. Friends, don't get me wrong: By no means do I count myself an expert in all of this, but I've got my eye on the goal, where God is beckoning onward – to Jesus. I'm off and running. I'm not turning back.

PHILIPPIANS 3:12-14 MSG

NOTES & PRAYERS ....

....

....

....

IF GOD WERE OBSERVING YOU AS LEAVEN, WHICH KIND WOULD HE SEE, GOOD OR BAD?

For Christ, our Passover lamb, has been sacrificed. Let us therefore celebrate the festival, not with the old leaven, the leaven of malice and evil, but with the unleavened bread of sincerity and truth.

1 CORINTHIANS 5:7B-8 ESV

Father God, you taught me in your Word to think of yeast (leaven) in two ways – either sin or the Kingdom of Heaven. For if yeast as sin is worked through a ball of dough, the whole loaf of bread is affected negatively. But if yeast as the Kingdom of Heaven is worked through, the whole loaf is affected positively. I understand! Your point is a small amount of either kind of yeast, bad or good, goes a long way in effect. For yeast is alive and reproduces according to its nature, which is the reason a small amount makes such a big difference. Heavenly Father, I pray in the name of Jesus, use me as your good and lively yeast within the small circle of influence that is my life. Praise you, God, for the good leaven of your Son, Jesus, my loving Savior. Amen.

[Jesus] What else is the Kingdom of God like? It is like the yeast a woman used in making bread. Even though she put only a little yeast in three measures of flour, it permeated every part of the dough.

LUKE 13:20A-21 NLT

NOTES & PRAYERS ....

....

....

....

JESUS, GOD'S SACRIFICIAL LAMB, DIED AND ROSE AGAIN TO SAVE YOUR SOUL. WORTHY IS THE LAMB!

The next day John the Baptist saw Jesus coming toward him, and said, "Behold, the lamb of God, who takes away the sins of the world!"

JOHN 1:29 ESV

Savior Jesus, you marked me with your shed blood, the same as the Israelites marked their doorposts with the blood of an innocent lamb on the night of the first Passover in Egypt. You, God's lamb, delivered me from sin's bondage of death, just as surely as you delivered the Israelites from Egypt's bondage of slavery. In your name, thank you, Jesus. Amen.

[John the Revelator] They (thousands of angels) encircled the throne and also the living creatures and the elders. In a loud voice they were saying: "Worthy is the Lamb (Jesus), who was slain, to receive power and wealth and wisdom and strength and honor and glory and praise!"

REVELATION 5:11B-12 NIV

For you know that it was not with perishable things such as silver or gold that you were redeemed from the empty way of life handed down to you from your ancestors, but with the precious blood of Christ, a lamb without blemish or defect.

1 PETER 1:18-19 NIV

NOTES & PRAYERS ....

....

....

....

WHEN YOU BELIEVED IN JESUS BY HIS GIFTS OF GRACE AND FAITH, HE DRAPED YOU IN HIS ROBE OF RIGHTEOUSNESS WITH ACCEPTANCE, LOVE, AND JOY

God made him (Jesus) who had no sin to be sin for us,
so that in him we might become the righteousness of God.
2 CORINTHIANS 5:21 NIV

Oh, Lord, if I had to depend on my own righteousness to be saved, I would be lost forever. Thank you for covering me with your white robe of purity by dying for me and rising again. You who were sinless took the blame and punishment for my sins and credited me with your righteousness. In your immaculate name, I pray my love and gratitude for salvation in you. Amen.

[John the Revelator] For the marriage of the Lamb is come, and his
wife (his church) hath made herself ready. And to her was granted
that she should be arrayed in fine linen, clean and white:
for the fine linen is the righteousness of saints.
REVELATION 19:7B-8 KJV

I am overwhelmed with joy in the Lord my God! For he has dressed me
with the clothing of salvation and draped me in a robe of righteousness.
ISAIAH 61:10A NLT

NOTES & PRAYERS ....

....

....

....

OLD CLOTH AND NEW CLOTH, OLD WINE AND NEW WINE, OLD WINESKINS AND NEW WINESKINS – WHAT DO ALL THESE OLD AND NEW THINGS HAVE TO DO WITH YOU AND YOUR SAVIOR JESUS?

[Jesus] Besides, who would patch old clothing with new cloth? For the new patch would shrink and rip away from the old cloth, leaving an even bigger tear than before. And no one puts new wine into old wineskins. For the old skins would burst from the pressure, spilling the wine and ruining the skins. New wine is stored in new wineskins so that both are preserved.
MATTHEW 9:16-17 NLT

Jesus, thank you for replacing my old cloth of sinful self with your white cloth of righteousness. Thank you, also, for replacing my old wineskin of sinful flesh with your pure wineskin that made me a new creature in you, and for filling the new me with the perfect wine of your atoning blood. By your gift of salvation, I am regenerated by the indwelling Holy Spirit. Thank you, Savior, in your name for being sufficient. And not just sufficient, but abundant, and not just abundant, but overflowing. I am new in you. Amen.

Therefore, if anyone is in Christ, he is a new creation. The old has passed away; behold, the new has come.
2 CORINTHIANS 5:17 ESV

NOTES & PRAYERS ....

....

....

....

YOU ARE INVITED TO JESUS' WEDDING SUPPER, WHERE HIS CHURCH WILL BE HIS BRIDE. ATTIRE: HIS ROBE OF RIGHTEOUSNESS WITH WHICH HE COVERED YOU ON THE DAY YOU RECEIVED SALVATION.

Be grateful to Jesus for clothing you in his white wedding robe of righteousness. No other raiment will do for his bride, his church.

Thank you, Jesus, for doing away with my sin-stained rags and dressing me in your shining robe of purity. Only you in your perfection, proven when you died without sin and rose again, could transform me into a new creature. You made me worthy through your own worthiness to be invited to your wedding feast. In your name, Savior, I accept your invitation. Praise you in grateful worship forever. Amen.

[John the Revelator] Let us rejoice and exult and give him (Jesus) the glory, for the marriage of the Lamb has come, and his Bride (his church) has made herself ready; it was granted her to clothe herself with fine linen, bright and pure – for the fine linen is the righteous deeds of the saints. And the angel said to me, "Write this: Blessed are those who are invited to the marriage supper of the Lamb." And he said to me, "These are the true words of God."
REVELATION 19:7-9 ESV

NOTES & PRAYERS ....

....

....

....

ARE YOU READY FOR JESUS' RETURN? IF YOU ARE WORKING ON HIS BEHALF IN THE HERE AND NOW, YOU WILL BE READY WHEN HE COMES BACK TO COLLECT YOU.

Jesus teaches in Scripture the timing of his second coming is not your concern. Your concern is to work, watch, and wait with a confident mind. Your Savior may return at any moment.

Heavenly Father, in Jesus' name, I submit with a grateful heart to your secret timetable for his return. Since I know your will and timing are perfect, let me serve you and others in obedience while I wait. Praise you! Worship you! Amen.

[Jesus] But about that day or hour (of his second coming), no one knows, not even the angels in heaven, nor the Son, but only the Father. As it was in the days of Noah, so it will be at the coming of the Son of Man. For in the days before the flood, people were eating and drinking, marrying and giving in marriage, up to the day Noah entered the ark; and they knew nothing about what would happen until the flood came and took them all away. That is how it will be at the coming of the Son of Man (Jesus). Two men will be in the field; one will be taken and the other left. Two women will be grinding with a hand mill; one will be taken and the other left. Therefore, keep watch, because you do not know on what day your Lord will come.
MATTHEW 24:36-42 NIV

NOTES & PRAYERS ....

....

....

....

May

JESUS CARES ABOUT YOUR SPIRITUAL HUNGER AND YOUR PHYSICAL HUNGER. HE IS YOUR SAVIOR. HE CARES ABOUT ALL YOUR NEEDS.

[Jesus] Blessed are those who hunger and thirst for righteousness,
for they shall be satisfied.

MATTHEW 5:6 ESV

Jesus, you fed five thousand hungry people by a miracle, and four thousand more by a second miracle. It is comforting to read in Scripture about your compassion for the physically hungry, but more comforting to read about your concern for the Spiritually hungry, which includes all of us, especially me. In your name, thank you for feeding and sustaining me physically and Spiritually, for without you, I would starve. You are God's bread of life in every way. Remind me to serve you by feeding others in your name. I am weak alone, but strong in you by your divine power. Savior, help me care for those around me with your selfless love. Amen.

[Jesus] "Then the righteous will answer him, saying, 'Lord, when did we
see you hungry and feed you, or thirsty and give you drink? And when
did we see you a stranger and welcome you, or naked and clothe you?
And when did we see you sick or in prison and visit you?' And the King
(Jesus) will answer them, 'Truly, I say to you, as you did it to one
of the least of these my brothers, you did it to me.'"

MATTHEW 25:37-38 ESV

NOTES & PRAYERS ....

....

....

....

ARE YOU SPIRITUALLY THIRSTY? JESUS WILL GIVE YOU LIVING WATER THAT WILL QUENCH YOUR THIRST FOR ALL ETERNITY.

[Jesus] "If anyone thirsts, let him come to me and drink.
Whoever believes in me, as the Scripture has said,
'Out of his heart will flow rivers of living water.'"
JOHN 7:37B-38 ESV

Wise Jesus, you use my need for physical water to sustain physical life to point me toward a far more important Truth – that only you can satisfy my need for Spiritual water to sustain eternal life. Thank you for pouring living water out on me in abundance through your Holy Spirit, who never runs dry. Now place a dipper in my hand and turn me around to share your living water with others. In your name, Savior, thank you for God's living Spiritual water that heals and rejuvenates believers eternally, even me. Amen.

[Jesus] To the thirsty I will give from the spring of
the water of life without payment.
REVELATION 21:6B ESV

You will be like a well-watered garden, a spring whose waters never fail.
ISAIAH 58:11B NIV

NOTES & PRAYERS ....

....

....

....

ZEAL FOR GOD MEANS ENTHUSIASM AND PASSION FOR GOD, JUST AS ZEAL FOR SELF MEANS ENTHUSIASM AND PASSION FOR SELF.

For whom do you have zeal, God or flesh?

In your name, Jesus, I pray for increasing zeal, enthusiasm, and passion for God in you. Shape my imperfect attitudes and actions into your flawless character. With you as my model, let my life demonstrate zeal for obedience in ways the Holy Spirit instructs me, especially in sharing your righteous zeal with others. I have no righteousness, Lord, only that which you provided when you saved me through your gifts of grace, mercy, and faith, all bound up in you. Praise you, Jesus, in the Holy Trinity – Father, Son, and Holy Spirit. Accept my everlasting zeal for you in your awesome Three-In-One. Glorify you, God. Amen.

For to us a child is born, to us a son is given, and the government will be on his shoulders. And he will be called Wonderful Counselor, Mighty God, Everlasting Father, Prince of Peace. Of the greatness of his government and peace there will be no end. He will reign on David's throne and over his kingdom, establishing and upholding it with justice and righteousness from that time on and forever. The zeal of the Lord Almighty will accomplish this.
ISAIAH 9:6-7 NIV

NOTES & PRAYERS ....

....

....

....

GOD DESIGNED AND CREATED YOU – BODY AND SOUL – BECAUSE HE LOVED YOU. HE LOVES YOU STILL!

For you (God) created my inmost being; you knit me together in my mother's womb. I praise you, because I am fearfully and wonderfully made. Your works are wonderful. I know that full well. My frame was not hidden from you when I was made in the secret place, when I was woven together in the depths of the earth. Your eyes saw my unformed body; all the days ordained for me were written in your book before one of them came to be.

PSALM 139:13-16 NIV

Thank you, God, for being the great designer and creator of DNA (deoxyribonucleic acid). Modern scientists have now proven that nothing about the structure of living cells is random, as if believers in Jesus Christ did not already know this. Although my human brain cannot take in the complexity of it all, I am grateful to you Father God, Son, and Holy Spirit for giving me a living body and a living soul. In Jesus' name, I pray my gratitude to you, Supreme God in your Holy Trinity, for conceptualizing and accomplishing such a creation miracle in me. Praise you, Father! Amen.

When God created mankind, he made them in the likeness of God.

GENESIS 5:1B-2A NIV

NOTES & PRAYERS ....

....

....

....

ARE YOU WILLING TO WAIT FOR THE LORD? OR ARE YOU ALWAYS IN HURRY MODE, TRYING IN VAIN TO SATISFY INSATIABLE SELF?

But they who wait for the Lord shall renew their strength;
they shall mount up with wings like eagles; they shall
run and not be weary; they shall walk and not faint.

ISAIAH 40:31 ESV

Thank you, Heavenly Father, for the lesson of Job. I have situations in my life I would like to see you resolve right now. But if Job persevered in his loyalty as he waited for your deliverance, despite all the calamities Satan rained down on him, then so can I. And if Jesus remained faithful as he waited for you to raise him from the dead, despite being separated from you after he took the blame on the cross for my sins, then so can I. In Jesus' name, I pray for wisdom to persevere in waiting for you, Father God. Though, like Job, I often do not comprehend your reasons or timing. Nevertheless, with your Holy Spirit within and beside me providing comfort and counsel, I wait for you in complete submission. I do not need to understand all your purposes. I just need to wait, knowing your purposes are divinely good from everlasting to everlasting. Amen.

I wait for the Lord, my whole being waits. In his Word, I put my hope.

PSALM 130:5 NIV

NOTES & PRAYERS ....

....

....

....

YOU DO NOT HAVE TO REMAIN A SLAVE TO SATAN'S STRONGHOLDS OF SIN. LOOK TO GOD, YOUR DELIVERER. HE WILL FREE YOU.

No temptation has overtaken you that is not common to man.
God is faithful, and he will not let you be tempted beyond your ability,
but with the temptation, he will also provide the way of escape,
that you may be able to endure it.

1 CORINTHIANS 10:13 ESV

Lord Jesus, I have always thought of besetting sins as strongholds I cannot conquer. Thank you for exposing Satan's lie and giving me faith you are my divine stronghold of goodness. For you are the Father's Righteous One who has the power to vanquish evil. Satan's deceptions and accusations collapse in the face of your advocacy on my behalf before Holy God. I ask for opportunities to tell others about your power over destructive strongholds in their lives. In your name, Savior, I pray for victory in the hearts of believers who trust faithfully you will deliver them from temptation. Praise you, Jesus, for triumph over evil strongholds. Amen.

For though we walk in the flesh, we are not waging war according
to the flesh. For the weapons of our warfare are not of the flesh
but have divine power to destroy (evil) strongholds.

2 CORINTHIANS 10:3-4 ESV

NOTES & PRAYERS ....

....

....

....

WHAT WILL WASH AWAY YOUR SINS?
NOTHING BUT THE BLOOD OF JESUS.

But if we walk in the light, as he (God) is in the light, we have fellowship with one another, and the blood of Jesus his Son cleanses us from all sin.

1 JOHN 1:7 ESV

Jesus, my Savior, thank you for requiring me to confront the stark difference between your purity and my impurity. I am grateful you were willing to shed your precious blood and rise again to redeem me from sin and death. By your love and grace of forgiveness, you cleansed me whiter than wool. Kind Jesus, let me not wander away from you ever again. Guide my steps. Keep me close. Accept my praise. In your holy name, thank you for loving me enough to save me. By your gifts of mercy, forgiveness, grace, and faith, you made me white as snow, as you are white as snow. I beg you, refresh me daily and make me clean again with renewed forgiveness. Praise you, Savior, with all gratitude for covering me with your righteousness. Glorify you, Son in the Trinity – Father, Son, and Holy Spirit. Amen.

"Come now, let us reason together," says the Lord:
"Though your sins are like scarlet, they shall be as white as snow;
though they are red like crimson, they shall become like wool."

ISAIAH 1:18 ESV

NOTES & PRAYERS ....

....

....

....

IN THE BEGINNING, GOD CREATED THE HEAVEN AND THE EARTH. GENESIS 1:1 KJV

All things were made through him (Jesus),
and without him was not anything made that was made.

JOHN 1:3 ESV

Father God, Jesus, and Holy Spirit, thank you for breathing life into my body. I give you all glory in the Holy Trinity for your divine awesomeness. You are God and Creator of everything that is created. Worshiping you comes natural to me. By your wisdom, you formed me to love and praise you. By your power through Jesus, your Son, you brought me from sin into sweet communion and relationship with you. And by your Holy Spirit, you regenerated me into a new creature, born again and saved from sin and death. In Jesus' name, I pour out all praise and gratitude before you, Creator God. Amen.

By faith we understand the universe was created by the Word of God,
so that what is seen was not made out of things that are visible.

HEBREWS 11:3 ESV

By the Word of the Lord the heavens were made,
their starry host by the breath of his mouth.

PSALM 33:6 NIV

NOTES & PRAYERS ....

....

....

....

IF YOU ARE SAVED IN GOD'S SON, HE WILL SERVE AS YOUR MEDIATOR BEFORE HOLY GOD AND DECLARE YOU NOT GUILTY OF SIN. AND WHEN JESUS IN HIS PERFECTION DECLARES YOU NOT GUILTY, YOU ARE NOT GUILTY! YOU ARE FORGIVEN, REGENERATED, JUSTIFIED, AND IN THE PROCESS OF BEING SANCTIFIED BY THE HOLY SPIRIT.

For there is one God and one mediator between God and mankind, the man Christ Jesus, who gave himself as a ransom for all people.

1 TIMOTHY 2:5-6A NIV

Jesus, by your gifts of grace and faith, I am forgiven for my sins, saved, acquitted, set free, and sealed by the Holy Spirit as a new creature in you. In your name, I pray you will continue defending me before God, for I am unworthy to defend myself. You are my divine mediator who loved me enough to save me. Let me show my gratitude to you through service on your behalf. Praise you, worthy Mediator. Amen.

For this reason, Christ is the mediator of a new covenant (Jesus' Good News Gospel), that those who are called may receive the promised eternal inheritance – now that he has died as a ransom to set them free from the sins committed under the first covenant (Mosaic Law).

HEBREWS 9:15 NIV

NOTES & PRAYERS ....

....

....

....

JESUS HAS GIVEN YOU HIS PEACE.
BE GENEROUS IN SHARING IT WITH OTHERS.

[Jesus] Peace I leave with you; my peace I give to you. Not as the world gives do I give. Let not your hearts be troubled, neither let them be afraid.

JOHN 14:27 ESV

[Jesus] I have said that in me you may have peace. In the world you will have tribulation. But take heart; I have overcome the world.

JOHN 16:33 ESV

Savior Jesus, when my heart is impoverished of serenity through neglect of you and your Word, I find myself more likely to jump into worthless chaos. Self instigates inner strife, which leads to outer strife with others, which leads to misery. In your name, Jesus, I ask you to replenish me with your divine calm. Remind me to stay near you in love and gratitude through prayer, your Word, and obedience to wise instruction by your Spirit. I am so grateful for your peace, loving Savior, that I pray you will lead me to share it with others. I am peaceful in you, Lord, Prince of Peace. Amen.

May the God of hope fill you with all joy and peace as you trust in him, so that you may overflow with hope by the power of the Holy Spirit.

ROMANS 15:13 NIV

NOTES & PRAYERS ....

....

....

....

WHAT HAVE YOU CHOSEN FOR YOUR LIFE'S HARVEST? SELF'S SINFUL NATURE THAT IS DEATH, OR THE SPIRIT OF GOD'S PURE NATURE IN JESUS THAT IS LIFE.

Those who are dominated by the sinful nature think about sinful things, but those who are controlled by the Holy Spirit think about things that please the Spirit. So, letting your sinful nature control your mind leads to death. But letting the Spirit control your mind leads to life and peace.

ROMANS 8:5-6 NLT

Savior Jesus, I call my sinful nature self, that same old destructive being I pray for God to empty out and replace with his Spirit. Let me adhere to your wise Truth – sowing to evil desires of sinful flesh reaps death, while sowing to righteous desires of your Holy Spirit reaps life, and not just life, but blessed life, and not just blessed life, but eternal life. In your name and for your sake, Jesus, help me sow, reap, and share your divine love, my harvest in you. Amen.

The person who plants selfishness, ignoring the needs of others – ignoring God! – harvests a crop of weeds. All he'll have to show for his life is weeds! But the one who plants in response to God, letting God's Spirit do the growth work in him, harvests a crop of real life, eternal life.

GALATIANS 6:8 MSG

NOTES & PRAYERS ....

....

....

....

HOW WOULD YOU DESCRIBE YOUR WORKS? DEAD WORKS FOR SELF, OR LIVING WORKS FOR GOD AND OTHERS?

[Jesus] Let your light shine before others, so that they may see your good works and give glory to your Father who is in heaven.

MATTHEW 5:16B ESV

Father, after observing me puzzle too long in my human ignorance over the phrase, dead works, the Spirit took pity on me and led me to a profound Truth in your Word – that even "good works" are dead if done for any other reason than to glorify you. You have convicted me my so-called "good works" have the potential to make me prideful, rather than humble, perhaps even glory-seeking for self, instead of glory-giving to you. In Jesus' name, I pray for help, Father, in putting dead works aside and engaging in living works on your behalf that are good, because you are good. I do not want to die serving self. I want to live serving you, for only you are deserving of honor and glory. Amen.

We continually ask God to fill you with the knowledge of his will through all the wisdom and understanding that the Spirit gives, so you may live a life worthy of the Lord and please him in every way: bearing fruit in every good work, growing in the knowledge of God.

COLOSSIANS 1:9B-10 NIV

NOTES & PRAYERS ....

....

....

....

YOU ARE AN IMPORTANT PART OF GOD'S CREATION MASTERPIECE. HE GAVE YOU LIFE TO PRAISE AND WORSHIP HIM.

*For we are God's masterpiece. He has created us anew in Christ Jesus,
so we can do the good things he planned for us long ago.*

EPHESIANS 2:10 NLT

Father, at first, I thought Scripture meant your masterpiece was the creation of the physical human body, a miracle itself. But now I understand your masterpiece is much more than physical. It is my body saved by your Son and transformed into a new Spiritual creature through your Holy Spirit, and then indwelled by him, a masterpiece of workmanship and miracle beyond compare. Thank you, God, in Jesus' name, who made it possible for a creature of physical skin, muscle, blood, and bone (like me) to be regenerated by the Holy Spirit into a Spiritual masterpiece, all to glorify you and do righteous works in your name. By your divine plan, Father, I beg you to dwell in my heart and use my hands to do your good works. Praise you, Mighty God. Amen.

---

*Do you not know you are God's temple and God's Spirit dwells in you?
If anyone destroys God's temple, God will destroy him.
For God's temple is holy, and you are that temple.*

1 CORINTHIANS 3:16 ESV

NOTES & PRAYERS ....
....
....
....

AS A MEMBER OF GOD'S FAMILY, YOU ARE TRULY AT HOME IN HIS DOMICILE.

So then you are no longer strangers and aliens, but you are fellow citizens with the saints and members of the household of God, built on the foundation of the apostles and prophets, Christ Jesus himself being the cornerstone, in whom the whole structure, being joined together, grows into a holy temple in the Lord. In him you also are being built together into a dwelling place for God by the Spirit.

EPHESIANS 2:19-22 ESV

Father, Will Thompson's hymn lyrics resonate in my heart as he repeats your invitation to all who need you, indeed, who desire peace of salvation in your Son more than anything else: *Earnestly, tenderly, Jesus is calling; Calling, O sinner, come home.* In your name, thank you, Jesus, for planting a desire in my heart to accept your invitation to come home to your Kingdom where I belong, and where I am to invite others to join your family, as well. Praise you, Messiah for welcoming contrite sinners home to you. Amen.

Even before he made the world, God loved us and chose us in Christ to be holy and without fault in his eyes. God decided in advance to adopt us into his own family by bringing us to himself through Jesus Christ. This is what he wanted to do, and it gave him great pleasure.

EPHESIANS 1:4-5 NLT

NOTES & PRAYERS ....

....

....

....

GOD'S GRACE IN JESUS IS THE ONLY PROVISION YOU WILL EVER NEED.

But my God shall supply all your needs
according to his riches in glory by Christ Jesus.
PHILIPPIANS 4:19 KJV

Father, I admit I am still searching for a better understanding of what your provision means. I should be praying for whatever is in your will, yet too often I hear myself praying self-centered prayers. Help me examine my personal motives for wanting things I pretend to need. Give me faith that righteous prayers will flow only from your Son's righteous motives, not self's unrighteous desires. In Jesus' name, remind me to glorify you, God, in your Holy Trinity, by serving others out of love and gratitude for your provision. Help me pray and serve with your right motives, Lord. Amen.

But seek first the kingdom of God and his righteousness,
and all these things will be added to you.
MATTHEW 6:33 ESV

[Jesus] Give, and it will be given to you. Good measure, pressed down,
shaken together, running over, will be put into your lap.
For with the measure you use it will be measured back to you.
LUKE 6:38 ESV

NOTES & PRAYERS ....

....

....

....

WHEN YOU KNOW GOD'S LOVE IN JESUS, YOU KNOW REAL LOVE, TRUE LOVE, PERFECT LOVE, DIVINE LOVE.

And so, we know and rely on the love God has for us. God is love.
Whoever lives in love lives in God, and God in them.

1 JOHN 4:16 NIV

Thank you, Father, for revealing your love for me in the holy perfection of Jesus Christ. In him, you showed the world what divine love looks like in a living person. I am grateful for the faith you gave me to open my heart and accept Jesus as my Lord and Savior and to invite the Holy Spirit to dwell within me. And though self continues the battle to retake my soul, I know you will never let that happen. By the power of your Spirit, you are in me, and I am in you, and together we are in all other believers. In your name, Jesus, I pray my gratitude for your wondrous love and unity. Amen.

Dear friends, let us love one another, for love comes from God.
Everyone who loves has been born of God and knows God. Whoever does
not love does not know God, because God is love. This is how God showed
his love among us: He sent his one and only Son into the world that
we might live through him. This is love: not that we loved God,
but that he loved us and sent his Son as an atoning sacrifice for our sins.

1 JOHN 4:7-10 NIV

NOTES & PRAYERS ....

....

....

....

WHEN YOU MET JESUS, YOU ENCOUNTERED THE RADIANCE AND GLORY OF MIGHTY GOD.

He [Jesus] is the radiance of the glory of God and the exact imprint of his nature, and he upholds the universe by the word of his power.
HEBREWS 1:3A ESV

And the Word became flesh and dwelt among us, and we have seen his glory, glory as of the only Son from the Father, full of grace and truth.
JOHN 1:14 ESV

Thank you, Father, for teaching me in your Word, by the power of the Holy Spirit's instruction, that your bright shining Glory-Light – unbearable for my human eyes to look upon – is not just a metaphor for your righteousness, but exists in shining reality. In Jesus' name, I pray my gratitude you shared your Glory-Light with lowly me in the person of your Son. And then, you blessed my heart with your indwelling Light of the Holy Spirit. Praise you, Jesus, divine radiance of God in all your celestial glory. Amen.

After six days Jesus took with him Peter, James and John the brother of James, and led them up a high mountain by themselves. There he was transfigured before them. His face shone like the sun, and his clothes became as white as the light.
MATTHEW 17:1-2 NIV

NOTES & PRAYERS ....

....

....

....

YOUR HUMAN RELATIONSHIPS REFLECT YOUR SPIRITUAL RELATIONSHIP WITH YOUR HEAVENLY FATHER. IF YOU REMAIN CLOSE TO HIM, HE WILL INSPIRE YOU TO REMAIN CLOSE TO THOSE AROUND YOU.

What a blessing your Heavenly Father has empowered you by the Holy Spirit to improve your human relationships through maintaining your spiritual relationship with God in Jesus.

Be humble and gentle; be patient, bearing with one another in love. Make every effort to keep the unity of the Spirit through the bond of peace.

EPHESIANS 4:2-3 NIV

Father, I try to think of things I can do to make you joyful in your relationship with me. I know glorifying and pleasing you should be among my first priorities, not whining about self's desires. In Jesus' name, I pray to glorify you by nurturing my loving relationship with you in the supernatural, which will help me nurture my loving human relationships in the natural. Be thou glorified, Father, Son, and Holy Spirit. Let my love for you enable me to love others as you love me. Love! Amen.

Love one another with brotherly affection.

ROMANS 12:10A ESV

NOTES & PRAYERS ....

....

....

....

JESUS' FINISHED WORK ON THE CROSS AND HIS RESURRECTION PROVED HIM WORTHY TO ACT AS YOUR ADVOCATE BEFORE GOD.

My dear children, I write this to you so that you will not sin.
But if anybody does sin, we have an advocate with the Father –
Jesus Christ, the righteous one. He is the atoning sacrifice for our sins,
and not only for ours, but also for the sins of the whole world.

1 JOHN 2:1-2 NIV

Savior Jesus, I live on the fact you who are complete in your sinless perfection and fully God in your own right, are willing to stand in the presence of Holy God as my advocate. And you, also, made it possible for me in my sinful imperfection to be in God's presence in personal prayer, a privilege afforded me by your divine worthiness when you saved me. In your name, Jesus, my devoted advocate, thank you for defending me. You are worthy! Amen.

So then, since we have a great High Priest who has entered heaven,
Jesus the Son of God, let us hold firmly to what we believe.
This High Priest of ours understands our weaknesses, for he faced all of
the same testings we do, yet he did not sin. So let us come boldly to
the throne of our gracious God. There we will receive his mercy,
and we will find grace to help us when we need it most.

HEBREWS 4:14-16 NLT

NOTES & PRAYERS ....

....

....

....

JESUS, LAMB OF GOD AND LION OF JUDAH, WILL ADDRESS AND MEET YOUR EVERY NEED.

The next day John the Baptist saw Jesus coming toward him, and said, "Behold, the Lamb of God, who takes away the sin of the world!"

JOHN 1:29 ESV

[John the Revelator] Look, the lion of the tribe of Judah (Jesus), the heir to David's throne, has won the victory. He is worthy to open the scroll and its seven seals.

REVELATION 5:5B NLT

Jesus! You are God's perfect sacrificial Lamb, who died and rose again to pay my sin debt. And you are, also, God's Lion of Judah, who will return to earth in the fullness of time, collect his followers, defeat evil permanently, and reign forever. In your holy name, Son of our Heavenly Father, I pray my gratitude for every bright facet of your divine nature. Thank you for being God's Lamb and Lion all in One. Amen.

[Heavenly Beings] "For you (God's lamb) were slaughtered, and your blood has ransomed people for God from every tribe and language and people and nation. And you have caused them to become a Kingdom of priests for our God. And they will reign on the earth."

REVELATION 5:9B-10 NLT

NOTES & PRAYERS ....

....

....

....

ASK GOD IN THE HOLY SPIRIT
TO GIVE YOU THE MIND OF CHRIST.
HE CAN, AND HE WILL.

Don't copy the behavior and customs of this world, but let God transform you into a new person by changing the way you think. Then you will learn to know God's will for you, which is good and pleasing and perfect.

ROMANS 12:2 NLT

Father, for a long time I tried to equate the learning of facts with the acquisition of Spiritual understanding and wisdom, until I realized I will never be able to grasp Spiritual Truths on my own. Only the mind of Christ can empower me to comprehend the Holy Spirit's teachings. I am grateful, God, for the vital gift of Christ's mind that accompanied my salvation. In his name, teach me to think and behave like him. Father, thank you for your Son's true mind. Amen.

People who aren't spiritual can't receive these truths from God's Spirit. It all sounds foolish to them and they can't understand it, for only those who are spiritual can understand what the Spirit means. Those who are spiritual can evaluate all things, but they themselves cannot be evaluated by others. For, "Who can know the Lord's thoughts? Who knows enough to teach him?" But we understand these things, for we have the mind of Christ.

1 CORINTHIANS 2:14-17 NLT

NOTES & PRAYERS ....

....

....

....

SAY GOODBYE TO ANXIETY BROUGHT ON BY LIVING FOR SELF. ASK JESUS TO LEAD YOUR HEART TOWARD LIVING FOR HIM AND OTHERS. IF YOU ARE SINCERE, HE WILL GIVE YOU HIS DIVINE PEACE OUT OF LOVE.

[Jesus] Peace I leave with you; my peace I give you. I do not give to you as the world gives. Do not let your hearts be troubled and do not be afraid.

JOHN 14:27 NIV

Jesus, Prince of Peace, I believe your tranquility is a function of Spiritual cause/effect; that is, your perfection in character and actions (cause) results in divine peace (effect). In your name, thank you that I can expect the same effect in my regenerated life in you – fulfillment of your promise that Christ-like living for you and others will bring peace provided by you. My Lord and Savior, I pray to grow in your image (by your power, not my own), for I know if I imitate you, Son of God, you will heal my heart with eternal peace. Thank you, Jesus. I am peaceful in you. Amen.

Do not be anxious about anything, but in every situation,
by prayer and petition, with thanksgiving, present your requests to God.
And the peace of God, which transcends all understanding,
will guard your hearts and minds in Christ Jesus.

PHILIPPIANS 4:6-7 NIV

NOTES & PRAYERS ....

....

....

....

JESUS EXPECTS YOU TO BE TENDERHEARTED AND FORGIVING TOWARD OTHERS, AS HE IS TENDERHEARTED AND FORGIVING TOWARD YOU.

If you want to know what it looks like in God's Kingdom to be tenderhearted and forgiving, observe Jesus' life on earth in Scriptural eyewitness accounts.

Be kind to one another, tenderhearted, forgiving one another, as God in Christ forgave you.

EPHESIANS 4:32 ESV

Father God, you have opened my eyes to the divine connections among grace, forgiveness, and tenderheartedness. Is it possible for a saved sinner like me to embody your grace of forgiveness by being merciful toward someone I see as undeserving, someone, perhaps, who has hurt me or someone I love? I could never extend mercy on my own, but with you, God, all things are possible. In Jesus' name, give me your grace to choose mercy and tenderheartedness toward others, when animosity would be self's first choice. Amen.

Finally, all of you, have unity of mind, sympathy, brotherly love, a tender heart, and a humble mind.

1 PETER 3:8 ESV

NOTES & PRAYERS ....
....
....
....

JESUS CHRIST IS LORD OF THE DANCE.

You have turned for me my mourning into dancing;
you have loosed my sackcloth and girded me with gladness.

PSALM 30:11 ESV

In your name, Jesus, Lord of the Dance, be my Lord! Amen.

Dance, then, wherever you may be, I am the Lord of the Dance,
said he. And I'll lead you all, wherever you may be,
and I'll lead you all in the Dance, said he.

I danced on the Sabbath, and I cured the lame. The holy people said it
was a shame. They whipped and they stripped, and they hung me
on high. And they left me there on a cross to die.

I danced on a Friday when the sky turned black. It's hard to dance with
the devil on your back. They buried my body, and they thought I'd gone,
but I am the Dance, and I still go on.

They cut me down, and I leapt up high. I am the life that'll never die.
I'll live in you, if you'll live in me. I am the Lord of the Dance, said he.

("LORD OF THE DANCE" STAINER & BELL LTD.)

Praise him with timbral and dancing; praise him with strings and pipe.

PSALM 150:4 NIV

NOTES & PRAYERS ....

....

....

....

GIVE YOUR TROUBLES TO GOD.
HE WILL FREE YOU OF THEIR DEAD WEIGHT.

Cast your burden on the Lord, and he will sustain you;
he will never permit the righteous to be moved.

PSALM 55:22 ESV

Live carefree before God; for he is most careful with you.

1 PETER 5:7 MSG

Thank you, Jesus, for encouraging me to turn my problems over to you. I am amazed you are interested in every detail of the life of an insignificant believer like me. You are never bored with me, or tired or sick of me. You let me unburden my heart to you without fear of rejection. Joseph Scriven declared in his hymn: *"What a friend we have in Jesus, All our sins and griefs to bear! What a privilege to carry Ev'rything to God in prayer!* In your name, Lord and Savior, I lay my burdens down at the foot of your cross in grateful prayer. Accept my gratitude, Jesus, that you help me so tenderly when I am too weak and worried to help myself. Praise and glory to your holy name, divine Deliverer. Amen.

Be careful for nothing; but in everything by prayer and supplication
with thanksgiving, let your requests be made known unto God.

PHILIPPIANS 4:6 KJV

NOTES & PRAYERS ....

....

....

....

GOD WRAPS HIMSELF IN LIGHT. BOW BEFORE HIS DIVINE RADIANCE. WORSHIP HIM IN HIS GLORY.

[Jesus] I am the light of the world. Whoever follows me will not walk in darkness, but will have the light of life.

JOHN 8:12B ESV

Majestic Father, you blaze brighter than your brightest creations. Your radiance – the divine Light of your Son you are so generous to share with believers – emanates from you in splendor and glory. Out of love and grace, you sent your Light to dwell on earth in the body of Jesus, who to this day fills believers with his Godly Light of the Holy Spirit. You have drawn us to you, Father, and wrapped us in your holy Light along with you. In Jesus' name, I pray you will allow me to shine with your celestial brilliance to the benefit of others until the day you call me home. I pray to dwell in the warmth of your holy Light forever. Amen.

[Jesus] You are the light of the world.

MATTHEW 5:14A NIV

The Lord wraps himself in light as with a garment.

PSALM 104:2A NIV

NOTES & PRAYERS ....

....

....

....

THROUGH THE HOLY SPIRIT'S REGENERATION AT YOUR SALVATION, GOD RESTORED YOU FROM SIN AND DEATH TO NEW LIFE IN JESUS. AND NOW, DAY BY REFINING DAY, HE IS MAKING YOU BEAUTIFUL IN CHRIST BY THE SANCTIFICATION OF HIS SPIRIT. YES, GOD IS PRUNING AND PERFECTING YOU.

*For through the Spirit we eagerly await by faith
the righteousness for which we hope.*

GALATIANS 5:5 NIV

Heavenly Father, I have not measured up to your perfection, yet you love me. You gave your Son to measure up in my place, for he made me righteous in his righteousness. In Jesus' name, thank you, Holy Spirit, for continuing to refine my heart in him as my Savior. For only he can make me worthy of service in his Kingdom. I am grateful. Amen.

---

*Since, then, we do not have the excuse of ignorance, everything – and I do
mean everything – connected with that old way of life has to go. It's rotten
through and through. Get rid of it! And then take on an entirely new way
of life – a God-fashioned life, a life renewed from the inside and working
itself into your conduct as God accurately reproduces his character in you.*

EPHESIANS 4:20-24 MSG

NOTES & PRAYERS ....

....

....

....

JESUS CLOAKED YOU IN HIS WHITE ROBE OF PURITY, WHICH HIS BLAMELESS LIFE, DEATH, AND RESURRECTION MADE HIM WORTHY TO SHARE.

I delight greatly in the Lord; my soul rejoices in my God.
For he has clothed me with garments of salvation and
arrayed me in a robe of his righteousness.

ISAIAH 61:10A NIV

Lord Jesus, help me keep the robe of purity you gave me clean and white. And yet I know, thanks to your salvation mercy that is so abundant, you are willing to cleanse me again and again of current sins. No matter how often I fall short of your glory, you honor your promise that if I humble myself genuinely by asking forgiveness with repentance and a changed life, you will wash away my sins with your perfect blood. In your name, Jesus, I ask to share in your mercy and willingness to forgive others as gracefully and generously as you forgive me. Thank you, Lord, for sharing your righteousness with unrighteous me. Amen.

Your baptism in Christ was not just washing you up for a fresh start.
It also involved dressing you in an adult faith wardrobe –
Christ's life, the fulfillment of God's original promise.

GALATIANS 3:27 MSG

NOTES & PRAYERS ....

....

....

....

DO YOU FIND MOUNTAINTOP EXPERIENCES WITH JESUS WONDERFUL, BUT DAILY LIFE A CONTINUAL CHALLENGE?

Perhaps it is simply the difference between experiencing Jesus for yourself alone and experiencing him to the benefit of others.

Savior Jesus, in your name, thank you for mountaintop experiences with you. By the power of the Holy Spirit and his instruction, those amazing encounters inspire me to love and serve others in the lowlands of daily living, not just hoard the love you shower on me in our special mountaintop moments. Lord, let me glorify you by sharing your love through service in imitation of you. Amen.

Jesus took Peter, James, and John and led them up a high mountain. His appearance changed from the inside out, right before their eyes. His clothes shimmered, glistening white, whiter than any bleach could make them. Elijah, along with Moses, came into view, in deep conversation with Jesus. Peter interrupted, "Rabbi, this is a great moment! Let's build three memorials – one for you, one for Moses, and one for Elijah." He blurted this out without thinking, stunned as they all were by what they were seeing. Just then a light-radiant cloud enveloped them, and from deep in the cloud, a voice: "This is my Son, marked by my love. Listen to him." The next minute the disciples were looking around, rubbing their eyes, seeing nothing but Jesus, only Jesus.

MARK 9:2B-8 MSG

NOTES & PRAYERS ....

....

....

....

YOUR PHYSICAL LIFE IS ONLY A BREATH, THOUGH TO YOUR HEAVENLY FATHER, IT IS AN EXCEEDINGLY IMPORTANT BREATH. HIS PLAN IS TO TAKE YOU BEYOND PHYSICAL LIFE INTO ETERNAL LIFE IN HIS PRESENCE.

Your life is like the morning fog. It's here a little while, then it's gone.
JAMES 4:14B NLT

Dear God, sometimes I find myself believing the devil's lie that the physical life I have now on earth will be my only life. In your Son's perfect name, I pray you will remind me of the glorious eternal life you promised me on the day of my salvation. Father, I am grateful for your Word in Scripture, where the Holy Spirit revealed to me that my present life is but a vapor preceding eternal life. Resting on your promise of everlasting life with you makes way for Jesus' divine peace and puts self's anxiety on the run. Thank you in your Holy Trinity for allowing me to give my life to you. You created me. I am yours. Let me live and serve forever in Jesus, my Lord and Savior. Amen.

Imitate God in everything you do, because you are his dear children. Live a life filled with love, following the example of Christ, who loved us and offered himself as a sacrifice for us, a pleasing aroma to God.
EPHESIANS 5:1-2 NLT

NOTES & PRAYERS ....

....

....

....

YOUR HEAVENLY FATHER AND THE HOLY SPIRIT ARE YOUR PRESENT AND FUTURE HOPE IN JESUS, THE SON.

May the God of hope fill you with all joy and peace as you trust in him, so that you may overflow with hope by the power of the Holy Spirit.

ROMANS 15:13 NIV

Let us hold unswervingly to the hope we profess, for he who promised is faithful.

HEBREWS 10:23 NIV

Father God, my heart rests in the Spiritual hope of Jesus. His loving hope comforts me as I face life's uncertainties. In his name, I cling to his hopefulness and reject self's hopelessness by claiming your promise in 1 Corinthians 13:13 ESV "So now faith, hope, and love abide, these three; but the greatest of these is love." Thank you, God, for faith, hope, and love, all beautiful blessings in your guaranteed promise of eternal life in Christ Jesus. Praise and glorify you for keeping your promises. My hope is in you. Amen.

And hope does not put us to shame, because God's love has been poured out into our hearts through the Holy Spirit, who has been given to us.

ROMANS 5:5 NIV

NOTES & PRAYERS ....

....

....

....

June

GOD AND HIS ANGELS CELEBRATED IN HEAVEN ON THE DAY JESUS SAVED YOU.

For the Son of Man (Jesus) came to seek and to save the lost.
LUKE 19:10 ESV

[Jesus] "Or what woman, having ten silver coins, if she loses one coin, does not light a lamp and sweep the house and seek until she finds it? And when she has found it, she calls her friends and neighbors, saying, 'Rejoice with me, for I have found the coin that I had lost.' Just so, I tell you, there is joy before the angels of God over one sinner who repents."
LUKE 15:8-10 ESV

Compassionate Jesus, thank you for seeking and saving my lost soul. I am grateful my acceptance of your grace-gift of salvation gladdened God's angels to rejoicing. In your name, I pray my gratitude you called me out of darkness into your heavenly Light. Your joy in saving me is my joy in being saved. In your name, lead me to share with others your Good News of salvation. Praise you, Savior. Amen.

[Jesus] "What man of you, having a hundred sheep, if he has lost one of them, does not leave the ninety-nine in the open country, and go after the one that is lost, until he finds it? And when he has found it, he lays it on his shoulders, rejoicing."
LUKE 15:4-5 ESV

NOTES & PRAYERS ....

....

....

....

YOU HAVE NO DEGREE OF SEPARATION FROM YOUR HEAVENLY FATHER AND HIS HOLY SPIRIT. JESUS DIED AND ROSE AGAIN TO BRING YOU CLOSE.

Now you have been united with Christ Jesus.
Once you were far away from God, but now you have
been brought near through the blood of Christ.

EPHESIANS 2:13 NLT

Thank you, Heavenly Father, for drawing me close to you through your Son. Without him, I would be unfit to stand in your presence, indeed, to lie prostrate in submission before you. He is the reason your Holy Spirit dwells inside me – comforting, counseling, and teaching me. In Jesus' name, thank you, God, for nearness to you made possible by the constant presence of the Holy Spirit. Amen.

This is how we know that we live in him (Jesus) and he in us:
He has given us of his Spirit.

1 JOHN 4:13 TLB

The Lord is fair in everything he does and is full of kindness.
He is close to all who call on him sincerely.

PSALM 145:18 TLB

NOTES & PRAYERS ....

....

....

....

UNITING HEARTS IN LOVE REQUIRES INTENTIONAL AND RECIPROCAL DECISIONS TO LOVE. PRAISE GOD YOU HAVE THAT KIND OF RELATIONSHIP WITH JESUS IN THE SPIRIT.

Dear friends, since God so loved us, we also ought to love one another.
No one has ever seen God; but if we love one another,
God lives in us and his love is made complete in us.

1 JOHN 4:11 NIV

Father God, I have learned from the Spirit in your Word the need for decision-making from both parties to love one another is the essence of building a devoted relationship. For if one side chooses to love, and the other does not, how can mutual love flow back and forth? I know you loved me first (by decision) and reconciled yourself to me through Jesus, before I ever returned your love (by decision). I also know you intend for me to love others with the same faithfulness with which you love me, the amazing blessing of which is this: the more I obey your divine commands and precepts on loving others (by decision), the more agape love streams back toward me. In Jesus' name, thank you, God, for you love that never fails. Amen.

Whoever does not love does not know God, because God is love.

1 JOHN 4:8 NIV

NOTES & PRAYERS ....
....
....
....

HOW INSPIRING IT IS TO BE A PART OF GOD'S GREAT CLOUD OF WITNESSES, WHOSE FIRST INTEREST IS LIVING AND LOVING IN JESUS.

Therefore, since we are surrounded by such a huge crowd of witnesses to the life of faith, let us strip off every weight that slows us down, especially the sin that so easily trips us up.
And let us run with endurance the race God has set before us.
HEBREWS 12:1 NLT

Heavenly Father, in Jesus' name, thank you for Christian gatherings, especially warm times of worship in our home churches. We know the comfort of your presence, for you taught us in your Word the Holy Spirit makes his home in the hearts of believers and enters our midst as we join together in praise, prayer, and worship. We are also grateful, Father God, our cloud of witnesses is not small, but a great, growing, dynamic force powered by your supernatural love. Testify, cloud of witnesses! Praise the Holy Trinity – Father, Son, and Holy Spirit – in unity with all believers! Amen.

And let us not neglect our meeting together,
as some people do, but encourage one another,
especially now that the day of his (Jesus') return is drawing near.
HEBREWS 10:25 NLT

NOTES & PRAYERS ....
....
....
....

DO YOU SOMETIMES FEEL YOU ARE LOSING THE BATTLE WITH SIN THAT RAGES WITHIN YOU? GIVE THANKS TO JESUS FOR NOT LEAVING YOU TO FIGHT ALONE.

[Paul] For in my inner being I delight in God's law; but I see another law at work in me, waging war against the law of my mind and making me a prisoner of the law of sin at work within me. What a wretched man I am! Who will rescue me from this body that is subject to death? Thanks be to God, who delivers me through Jesus Christ our Lord.

ROMANS 7:21B-25A NIV

Thank you, God, that your righteousness – a divine blessing with which Jesus covers my impurity – empowers me in my skirmishes with sin. Savior Jesus, I need your perfection to deliver me from evil in your name, for I cannot deliver myself. *He restoreth my soul: he leadeth me in the paths of righteousness for his name's sake. Psalm 23:3 KJV.* Amen.

With the arrival of Jesus, the Messiah, that fateful dilemma is resolved. Those who enter into Christ's being-here-for-us no longer have to live under a continuous, low-lying black cloud. A new power is in operation. The Spirit of life in Christ, like a strong wind, has magnificently cleared the air, freeing you from a fated lifetime of brutal tyranny at the hands of sin and death.

ROMANS 8:1-2 MSG

NOTES & PRAYERS ....

....

....

....

GOD TELLS THE STORY OF JESUS THROUGHOUT SCRIPTURE, FROM THE BEGINNING OF THE OLD TESTAMENT TO THE END OF THE NEW TESTAMENT.

*[Jesus] I am the alpha and the omega, the first and the last,
the beginning and the end.*

REVELATION 22:13 ESV

Thank you, Father, for sharing by divine inspiration to human writers the story of Jesus within the pages of your Word. Indeed, your Word is not just a metaphor for Jesus. It is the Spirit of Jesus himself. In his name, I pray my gratitude for salvation in him. He is my Savior forever. Amen.

[Identity of Jesus prophesied in the Old Testament] For to us a child is born, to us a son is given, and the Government will be on his shoulders. And he will be called Wonderful Counselor, Mighty God, Everlasting Father, Prince of Peace.

ISAIAH 9:6 NIV

[Identity of Jesus fulfilled in the New Testament] In the beginning the Word (Jesus) already existed. The Word was with God, and the Word was God. He existed in the beginning with God.

JOHN 1:1-2 NLT

NOTES & PRAYERS ....

....

....

....

PRAISE GOD FOR HIS PROMISE TO REDEEM YOU – BODY AND SOUL – AND, IN THE FULLNESS OF TIME, TO PROVIDE YOU A GLORIFIED BODY.

But our citizenship is in heaven. And we eagerly await a Savior from there, the Lord Jesus Christ, who, by the power that enables him to bring everything under his control, will transform our lowly bodies so that they will be like his glorious body.

PHILIPPIANS 3:20-21 NIV

Father God, thank you that your future gift to me of a decay-and-death-free body will make it possible for me to worship you in your Holy Trinity throughout eternity – Father, Son, and Holy Spirit. In Jesus' name, I pray my gratitude with confidence that in his perfect timing, he will glorify my body and fulfill his pledge to me of eternity with him. Thank you, Lord, for keeping all your promises. Amen.

We, too, wait with eager hope for the day when God will give us our full rights as his adopted children, including the new bodies he has promised.

ROMANS 8:23 NLT

For this perishable body must put on the imperishable, and this mortal body must put on immortality.

1 CORINTHIANS 15:53 ESV

NOTES & PRAYERS ....
....
....
....

INAPPROPRIATE CURIOSITY ABOUT THINGS BELONGING SOLEY TO GOD WILL LEAD YOU TO APPROPRIATELY CLOSED DOORS. AFTER ALL, GOD IS GOD. AND YOU AND I, WELL...WE ARE NOT GOD.

When they (disciples) had come together, they asked him (Jesus), "Lord, will you at this time restore the Kingdom to Israel?" He said, "It is not for you to know times or seasons the Father has fixed by his own authority."

ACTS 1:6-7 ESV

Father God, in Jesus' name, thank you for sharing with me the mystery of your will concerning Jesus, Savior of all believers, even me. I realize when it comes to your holy secrets, my status is strictly need-to-know, which I accept without question. Your Word teaches me your mysteries and secrets are yours alone, and you share what you will and keep back what you will. I am comforted you are in control of everything known and unknown by your created ones. Praise you, God, in your omniscience. Amen.

God has now revealed to us his mysterious will regarding Christ – which is to fulfill his own good plan. And this is the plan: At the right time he will bring everything together under the authority of Christ, everything in heaven and on earth.

EPHESIANS 1:9-10 NLT

NOTES & PRAYERS ....

....

....

....

YOU ARE YOUR HEAVENLY FATHER'S PURCHASED POSSESSION, BOUGHT BY THE BLOOD OF JESUS.

Blessed be the God and Father of our Lord Jesus Christ, who hath blessed us with all Spiritual blessings in heavenly places in Christ: in whom we have redemption through his blood, the forgiveness of sins, according to the riches of his grace. Ye were sealed with that Holy Spirit of promise, which is the earnest of our inheritance until the redemption of the purchased possession (You!) unto the praise of his glory.

EPHESIANS 1:3; 7; 13B-14 KJV

Father God, I deserved nothing, yet by grace, forgiveness, and your gift of faith, you blessed me with eternal salvation in Jesus in your abiding Spirit presence. Thank you for loving me enough to sacrifice your Son and raise him up again as a ransom for me. I am humbled you placed such great value on my soul. In the name of your Son, I pray my gratitude for your love. Please, God, accept my love in return. How wonderful is the blessing of being your purchased possession, bought by Jesus' blood. Praise him. Thank him. Worship him. Glorify Him! Amen.

But God demonstrates his own love for us in this:
While we were still sinners, Christ died for us.

ROMANS 5:8 NIV

NOTES & PRAYERS ....

....

....

....

IN THE FULLNESS OF TIME, YOU WILL SEE GOD'S HOLY CITY DESCEND FROM HEAVEN TO EARTH, WHICH WILL GIVE NEW MEANING TO THE PHRASE, WELCOME HOME.

[John the Revelator] Then I saw "a new heaven and a new earth," for the first heaven and the first earth had passed away, and there was no longer any sea. I saw the Holy City, the new Jerusalem, coming down out of heaven from God, prepared as a bride beautifully dressed for her husband. And I heard a loud voice from the throne saying, "Look! God's dwelling place is now among the people, and he will dwell with them. They will be his people, and God will be with them and be their God."

REVELATION 21:1-3 NIV

Thank you, Jesus, your New Jerusalem will be a literal dwelling place. How grateful I am for your earnest deposit of promise, the Holy Spirit, who dwells within me now. For the Spirit is my guarantor of future citizenship in your be-jeweled city that will descend in your perfect timing. Praise you, Father, for never failing to keep your promises. Amen.

[Jesus] In my Father's house are many rooms. If it were not so, would I have told you that I go to prepare a place for you? And if I go and prepare a place for you, I will come again and will take you to myself, that where I am you may be also.

JOHN 14:2-3 ESV

NOTES & PRAYERS ....

....

....

....

IF YOU WANT TO ENJOY LIFE TO THE FULLEST, YIELD EVERY DETAIL OVER TO GOD.

Thank you, Father, for closing doors that lead to destruction, especially when I cannot see dangers lurking on the other side.

Lord Jesus, I repent of giving in to irritation over not getting my way at every turn. It often takes time for me to realize a door closed by you is a good thing. In your name, give me wisdom to walk through doors only you open. Amen.

As he (Saul, renamed Paul) neared Damascus on his journey, suddenly a light from heaven flashed around him. He fell to the ground and heard a voice say to him, "Saul, Saul, why do you persecute me?" "Who are you, Lord?" Saul asked. "I am Jesus, whom you are persecuting," he replied. "Now get up and go into the city, and you will be told what you must do."
ACTS 9:3-6 NIV

Then Ananias went to the house (in Damascus, where the Lord had commanded Saul to go), and entered it. Placing his hands on Saul, he said, "Brother Saul, the Lord – Jesus, who appeared to you on the road as you were coming here – has sent me so that you may see again and be filled with the Holy Spirit." Immediately, something like scales fell from Saul's eyes, and he could see again. He got up and was baptized, and after taking some food, he regained his strength.
ACTS 9:17-19 NIV

NOTES & PRAYERS ....

....

....

....

WHOM ARE YOU SERVING, JESUS OR SELF?

*[Jesus] Whoever serves me must follow me; and where I am,
my servant also will be. My Father will honor the one who serves me.*
JOHN 12:26 NIV

Father, it is no fun admitting that on occasion I feel indignant – sometimes to the point of anger – whenever people do not express sufficient gratitude as I serve them, gratitude measured by my own human standard, of course, not your divine standard. Thank you for convicting me of the self-serving nature of my egocentric reactions. In Jesus' name, I ask you to prick me when I need reminders that serving those around me must be to your glory, not mine. Make me grateful for the counterintuitive Truth in your divine economy that serving you and others out of gratitude, obedience, and love brings more blessings to the server than the served. Praise your profound wisdom, God. Amen.

---

*[Jesus] For I was hungry and you gave me something to eat, I was thirsty
and you gave me something to drink, I was a stranger and you invited
me in, I needed clothes and you clothed me, I was sick and you
looked after me, I was in prison and you came to visit me.
The King (Christ) will reply, "Truly, I tell you, whatever you did for one
of the least of these brothers and sisters of mine, you did for me."*
MATTHEW 25:35-36; 40 NIV

NOTES & PRAYERS ....

....

....

....

WHICH WOULD YOU RATHER HAVE – HOLLOW RECOGNITION EARTHLY IN NATURE, OR HOLY REWARDS HEAVENLY IN NATURE?

[Jesus] Beware of practicing your righteousness before other people in order to be seen by them, for then you will have no reward from your Father who is in heaven.

MATTHEW 6:1 ESV

Thank you, Jesus, for instructing me to stop expecting payback for my "good deeds." Compared to your righteousness, my "good deeds" done by flesh for self's glory are pitiful and puny, like filthy rags in the sight of Holy God. In your name, let my human deeds be your divine deeds with your own pure motives, not self's impure gesturing. Amen.

[Jesus] Thus, when you give to the needy, sound no trumpet before you, as the hypocrites do in the synagogues and in the streets, that they may be praised by others. Truly, I say to you, they have received their reward. But when you give to the needy, do not let your left hand know what your right hand is doing, so that your giving may be in secret. And your Father who sees in secret will reward you. And when you pray, you must not be like the hypocrites. For they love to stand and pray in the synagogues and at the street corners, that they may be seen by others. Truly, I say to you, they have received their reward.

MATTHEW 6:2-5 ESV

NOTES & PRAYERS ....

....

....

....

DO YOU EVER GET A PROMPTING FROM GOD TO SAY AND DO NOTHING FOR A TIME?

The Lord is in his holy temple; let all the earth be silent before him.
HABAKKUK 2:20 NIV

Lord, I see myself as a can-do individual, which makes it hard for me to acknowledge that sometimes my best help to you and others is to practice can-do-not. You are God. You can get along just fine without my jumping in and trying to take control of situations belonging to you alone. Indeed, there are times my chattering prayers go down roads to nowhere, even to my own ears. Why am I not composed in your presence? Why do I not let you handle things? Help me, Lord, with my tendency to keep doing, doing, doing and talking, talking, talking at times you want me to be still. Thank you, Jesus, for your restorative blessings of silence and tranquility. In your name, I pray you will remind me to wait quietly before you in love and reverence. Let me be near you in silent adoration, Lord and Savior. Amen.

He (God) says, "Be still and know that I am God."
PSALM 46:10A NIV

Be silent before the Sovereign Lord, for the day of the Lord is near.
ZEPHANIAH 1:7A NIV

NOTES & PRAYERS ....
....
....
....

YOUR HEAVENLY FATHER'S COMMAND TO FORGIVE IS MORE THAN ENOUGH REASON TO PRACTICE FORGIVENESS. OBEY HIM! FORGIVE!

Be kind and compassionate to one another, forgiving each other, just as in Christ God forgave you.

EPHESIANS 4:32 NIV

Father God, I need your help to stop asking the same old question: If I forgive someone, what is in it for me? It is a self-centered question I ask in secret and silence, not openly and aloud, yet I ask it all the same. Guide me toward a better question, Lord: How can I learn to forgive others, as you have forgiven me? Scientists have proven if I choose to forgive, I will reap much good emotionally and psychologically, even physically. It is not surprising you would shower down such wonderful blessings in response to obedience. But in Jesus' name, do not let me forgive just to garner blessings. I pray for grace to forgive out of obedience to you and a genuine desire to grow more Christ-like. Amen.

Put on as God's chosen ones, holy and beloved, compassionate hearts, kindness, humility, meekness, and patience, bearing with one another and, if one has a complaint against another, forgiving each other; as the Lord has forgiven you, so you also must forgive.

COLOSSIANS 3:12-13 ESV

NOTES & PRAYERS ....

....

....

....

REST IN THE KNOWLEDGE YOU ARE ONE OF YOUR HEAVENLY FATHER'S INTENTIONAL AND FINELY WROUGHT CREATIONS OF PARTICULAR IMPORTANCE TO HIS KINGDOM.

Now ye are the body of Christ, and members in particular.

1 CORINTHIANS 12:27 KJV

Father God, I rejoice as I consider how you view me *in particular.* You created me as an individual *in particular* with a myriad of specially selected characteristics all melded together in a way unique unto me *in particular.* And you did the same for each of your children *in particular.* Then you prepared places for us, singularly and collectively, within your body of believers. Each of us is a distinctive member *in particular* of the church of Jesus Christ – your Son and our Savior – full of grace and Truth. Thank you, God, in Jesus' name for loving us enough to make each one a member of your Kingdom *in particular.* Praise you! Glorify you! Amen.

For as the body is one, and hath many members, and all the members of that one body, being many, are one body: so also is Christ. For by one Spirit are we all baptized into one body.

1 CORINTHIANS 12:12-13a KJV

NOTES & PRAYERS ....

....

....

....

GOD'S LIVELY HOPE IN JESUS IS ENERGETIC, SPARKLING, GENEROUS, ACTIVE, HEALTHY, LOVING, ANIMATED, DYNAMIC, SPRIGHTLY, BUOYANT, VIGOROUS, VIVACIOUS, ETERNAL!

Your Heavenly Father has given you his loving, lively hope
that his beloved and worthy Son, who laid down his life
for you and rose again, will rescue you from sin and death.

Father God, your divine hope would have been sufficient
grace for my lifetime into eternity. But since you are the
provider of abundance, not just bare necessities, you gave
me lavish, lively hope. I love the robust, astounding, siz-
zling, exciting, amazing, thrilling hope you provided me in
your Son in his thousands of surprising layers and moving
parts. Jesus' hope is multi-dimensional – spinning, revolv-
ing, shining, glowing, burning with Holy Light. Thank you,
God, in the Savior's name for his lively hope. Amen.

---

*Blessed be the God and Father of our Lord Jesus Christ, which according
to his abundant mercy hath begotten us again unto a lively hope
by the resurrection of Jesus Christ from the dead, to an inheritance
incorruptible, and undefiled, and that fadeth not away,
reserved in heaven for you, who are kept by the power of God through
faith unto salvation ready to be revealed in the last time.*

1 PETER 1:3-5 KJV

NOTES & PRAYERS ....

....

....

....

NO MATTER THE CHALLENGES YOU FACE AS A BELIEVER, GOD WILL KEEP YOU SAFE ALONG LIFE'S HIGHWAYS AND BYWAYS. SAFE PASSAGE IS YOUR HEAVENLY FATHER'S BIBLICAL PROMISE TO YOU.

For the Scriptures say, "He will order his angels to protect and guard you."
LUKE 4:10 NLT

The Lord keeps you from all harm and watches over your life.
The Lord keeps watch over you as you come and go, now and forever.
PSALM 121:7-8 NLT

Father God, how comforting it is to know that your Holy Spirit is with me. His companionship is a treasure, but you do not stop at providing his mere company. You make – and keep – all your calming promises of safety and security in his presence. I walk with confidence along the paths upon which the Holy Spirit shines his Light, knowing he will take me to, through, or above whatever trials I encounter. Savior Jesus, I claim your assurance that if I seek diligently what is right, you will show me the right way to go. In your name, I pray in humility and faith for safe travels in you. Amen.

He (God) guards the paths of the just and protects those faithful to him.
PROVERBS 2:8 NLT

NOTES & PRAYERS

ASK GOD TO MAKE YOUR LIFE A WELL-WATERED GARDEN, IRRIGATED BY HIS EVER-FLOWING SPRING OF DIVINE LOVE.

Behold, I am doing a new thing; now it springs forth, do you not perceive it? I will make a way in the wilderness and rivers in the desert.

ISAIAH 43:19 ESV

Dear God, by your loving power, you planted a garden in Eden and placed Adam and Eve there to live near you in sinless harmony and obedience. How sad they chose dissonance and disobedience. And how sad I have made so many of the same poor choices. I repent of my parched, lifeless disobedience. In its place, I choose thriving, Spiritual obedience, knowing I need the Holy Spirit's strength to accomplish it, since I have no strength of my own. Make my life a Spirit-watered garden that glorifies you, God, not a wilderness committed to self. And let my harvest be your fruit of the Spirit – love, joy, peace, patience, kindness, goodness, faithfulness, gentleness, and self-control. I am thirsty for you, Father, and in need of your watering. Amen.

The Lord will guide you continually, giving you water when you are dry and restoring your strength. You will be like a well-watered garden, like an ever-flowing spring.

ISAIAH 58:11 NLT

NOTES & PRAYERS ....

....

....

....

ON MAUNDY THURSDAY, JESUS' LAST PASSOVER MEAL WITH HIS DESCIPLES, HE LED THEM IN A SPECIAL WORSHIP SERVICE TO HELP THEM REMEMBER HIM AND HIS SAVING LOVE – THE FIRST HOLY COMMUNION.

[Jesus] Do this in remembrance of me.

1 CORINTHIANS 11:24B ESV

Lord Jesus, Maundy Thursday was not just a regular Thursday evening for you and your disciples, considering the monumental events of the next day, Good Friday, the day you were led to Golgotha and crucified in payment for the sins of the world. You spent the night before (Maundy Thursday) communing with your disciples. Maundy derives from the Latin word, mandatum, meaning commandment. And what was your commandment? *Love each other!* Then you washed the feet of your disciples in service and love and told them they were to imitate you and wash each other's feet. And, lastly, to seal their memories, you celebrated with them the first Holy Communion. Thank you, Jesus! Amen.

[Jesus] So now I am giving you a new commandment:
Love each other. Just as I have loved you, you should love each other.

JOHN 13:34 NLT

NOTES & PRAYERS ....

....

....

....

GOD'S GOOD PLEASURE IS IN JESUS, HIS SON, WHOM HE SACRIFICED AND RESURRECTED TO COVER YOUR UNRIGHTEOUSNESS, ALL TO FULFILL HIS LOVING DESIRE TO FIND GOOD PLEASURE IN YOU.

Your Heavenly Father of reconciliation delights in you with good pleasure and wants you to delight in him. Thank him! Love him!

Father God, your good pleasure is perfect. The question is: How could you find good pleasure in a fallen creature like me? I am so grateful you made a way through Jesus. You are pleased by his purity. And because he covered me (a lowly sinner) with his own virtue, you are pleased by me. Your salvation by grace is grand like that! In my Savior's name, thank you, God, for finding good pleasure in me through your perfect Son. Amen.

And Jesus, when he was baptized, went up straightway out of the water: and, lo, the heavens were opened unto him, and he saw the Spirit of God descending like a dove, and lighting upon him: And lo a voice from heaven, saying, This is my beloved Son, in whom I am well pleased.

MATTHEW 3:16-17 KJV

Work out your own salvation with fear and trembling, for it is God who works in you, both to will and to work for his good pleasure.

PHILIPPIANS 2:12B-13 ESV

NOTES & PRAYERS ....

....

....

....

GOD WATERS YOUR LIFE WITH HIS HOLY RAIN OF RIGHTEOUSNESS AND SALVATION. REJOICE AT BEING REJUVINATED BY THE HOLY SPIRIT'S LIVING WATER.

[God]: You heavens above, rain down my righteousness; let the clouds shower it down. Let the earth open wide. Let salvation spring up. Let righteousness flourish with it; I, the Lord, have created it.

ISAIAH 45:8 NIV

Heavenly Father, I love that you use rain in Scripture as a metaphor for Jesus' righteousness. As rain cleanses the earth naturally, Jesus cleanses our souls supernaturally. As rain provides the proper environment for healthy physical life, Jesus creates the proper environment for healthy Spiritual life. And as rain is an earthly blessing, Jesus is God's most important heavenly blessing. Rain washes with water. Jesus washes with his blood. Thank you, God, in your Son's name for rain and righteousness – amazing blessings both. Amen.

[God's prophecy of Messiah Jesus] May he be like rain falling on a mown field, like showers watering the earth. In his days may the righteous flourish and prosperity abound till the moon is no more. He will take pity on the weak and the needy and save the needy from death. He will rescue them from oppression and violence, for precious is their blood in his sight.

PSALM 72:6-7; 13-14 NIV

NOTES & PRAYERS ....

....

....

....

YOUR GREATEST PLEASURE IS TO PRAISE GOD AND REJOICE THAT HE SAVED YOU IN JESUS. HALLELUJAH! THE NEW HAS COME!

[John the Revelator, speaking about Jesus] And he that sat upon the throne (in heaven) said, Behold, I make all things new.

REVELATION 21:5B KJV

Thank you, Heavenly Father. Your beloved Son is the new that has come. Savior Jesus, I feel as joyful about your arrival on earth as the angels who announced your birth to shepherds watching over their flocks outside Bethlehem. How loving of you to proclaim your Good News first to lowly shepherds out-of-doors, awake and guarding their sheep, instead of to earthly kings and princes inside their palaces, asleep and guarded by servants. Any announcement made in a manner as unique as that would be considered a new thing even in today's society, the lowly being selected over the prominent to hear angels sing. Thank you, God, for sending Jesus, your holy and new thing – new, yet he always was and will always be. In his name, thank you for making me new in him through your salvation grace. Amen.

Therefore, if anyone is in Christ, he is a new creation. The old has passed away; behold, the new has come.

2 CORINTHIANS 5:17 ESV

NOTES & PRAYERS ....

....

....

....

MEET MELCHIZEDEK, KING PRIEST OF THE OLD TESTAMENT. LOOK CLOSELY, AND HE WILL REMIND YOU OF YOUR KING, LORD, MASTER, SAVIOR, AND HIGH PRIEST – JESUS!

God prophesied concerning Jesus with perfect accuracy in the Old Testament, using lives of real people like Melchizedek to foreshadow his Son, our perfect new-covenant High Priest.

Father, when I met Melchizedek, Old Testament King Priest in *Genesis,* I wondered what his purpose was in your Word. Then I met him again in *Psalms* and *Hebrews* and asked a better question: Toward whom was Melchizedek pointing prophetically? The answer – Jesus, our High Priest and Mediator before you, Holy God. In his name, praise! Amen.

The Lord (God) says to my Lord (Jesus): "Sit at my right hand, until I make your enemies your footstool." The Lord has sworn and will not change his mind, "You are a priest forever after the order of Melchizedek."
PSALM 110:1; 4 ESV

Jesus has become the guarantor of a better covenant. Unlike the other high priests, he does not need to offer sacrifices day after day, first for his own sins, and then for the sins of the people. He sacrificed for their sins once and for all when he offered himself.
HEBREWS 7:22B; 27 NIV

NOTES & PRAYERS ....

....

....

....

YOUR SAVIOR, JESUS, IS GOD'S ONE AND ONLY SON, WHILE AT THE SAME TIME, FULLY GOD IN HIS OWN RIGHT, AS IS THE HOLY SPIRIT.

He (Jesus) is the radiance of the glory of God and the exact imprint of his nature, and he upholds the universe by the word of his power. After making purification for sins, he sat down at the right hand of the Majesty on high, having become as much superior to angels as the name he has inherited is more excellent than theirs.

HEBREWS 1:3-4 ESV

Jesus! You are as much God as our Heavenly Father is God, and as much God as the Holy Spirit is God. Thank you for coming to earth as God in corporal form, full of grace and truth, to dwell among us. In your name, my Lord and Savior, I shout Alleluia in gratitude for your gift of salvation! Praise you Father, Son, and Holy Spirit. Praise you, Mighty God, in your Holy Trinity. Amen.

[Jesus] These things I have spoken to you while abiding with you. But the Helper, the Holy Spirit, whom the Father will send in My name, He will teach you all things, and bring to your remembrance all that I said to you.

JOHN 14:25-26 NASB

NOTES & PRAYERS ....

....

....

....

IF YOU ARE DROWNING, YOUR REDEEMER WILL SAVE YOU. JUST CALL OUT TO HIM, "HELP ME, JESUS!" THEN YIELD YOUR FEAR OVER TO GOD'S SON, WHO TRANSFORMS HUMAN FEAR INTO DIVINE FAITH, HOPE, BELIEF, TRUST, ASSURANCE, AND CONFIDENCE IN HIS SALVATION FOR BELIEVERS.

Jesus saved Peter (and you!) from drowning in stormy seas.

Lord Jesus, Peter walked on water through your power, not his, for you gave him so great a faith. But more astonishing and humbling is you continue to hold out your hand to me in present day. In your name, Master and Savior, thank you for safety in your arms. Amen.

"Lord, if it is you (walking on water), command me to come to you."
He (Jesus) said, "Come." So Peter got out of the boat and walked on the
water and came to Jesus. But when he saw the wind, he was afraid,
and beginning to sink he cried out, "Lord, save me."
Jesus immediately reached out his hand and took hold of him, saying to
him, "O you of little faith, why did you doubt?" And when they got into
the boat, the wind ceased. And those in the boat worshiped him, saying,
"Truly you are the Son of God."
MATTHEW 14:26-33 ESV

NOTES & PRAYERS ....

....

....

....

GOD ADDRESSES ALL YOUR QUESTIONS IN SCRIPTURE. STUDY HIS WORD TO FIND SOLUTIONS TO YOUR PROBLEMS.

Lord Jesus, I have faith to ask you anything,
knowing you will answer much more than I ask.

Concerned Savior, I love the questions Paul called out to you when you appeared before him on the road to Damascus: *Who are you, Lord? What shall I do, Lord?* And I also love that you answered him in Hebrew, a language Paul understood. Thank you for addressing me in a tongue I understand, as well. I hear your voice clearly in prayer and Scripture. In your name, I offer my gratitude, another language I learned from you. Thank you, Jesus, for being available whenever I need you. I am blessed by your nearness. Amen.

[Jesus] "Saul, Saul, why are you persecuting me? It is hard for you to kick against the goads (thorns)." And I (Paul) said, "Who are you, Lord?" And the Lord said, "I am Jesus whom you are persecuting."
ACTS 26:14-15 ESV

[Paul] "And I said, 'What shall I do, Lord?' And the Lord said to me, 'Rise, and go into Damascus, and there you will be told all that is appointed for you to do.'"
ACTS 22:10 ESV

NOTES & PRAYERS ....
....
....
....

HOPE IN JESUS CHRIST IS THE ANCHOR FOR YOUR SOUL THAT WILL SUSTAIN YOU.

We have this hope as an anchor for the soul, firm and secure. It enters the inner sanctuary behind the curtain (Holy of Holies), where our forerunner, Jesus, entered on our behalf. He is High Priest forever.

HEBREWS 6:19-20A NIV

My Lord and Savior, Jesus, how I love to send up praise and gratitude to you as I sing Edward Mote's hymn: "The Solid Rock." *My hope is built on nothing less than Jesus' blood and righteousness.* And not just hope, but surety of hope. Father God, you made it possible by the power of your Spirit for my heart to abound in hope. In Jesus' name, thank you. Amen.

May the God of hope fill you with all joy and peace in believing, so that by the power of the Holy Spirit you may abound in hope.

ROMANS 15:13 ESV

Praise be to the God and Father of our Lord Jesus Christ! In his great mercy he has given us new birth into a living hope through the resurrection of Jesus Christ from the dead, and into an inheritance that can never perish, spoil, or fade. This inheritance is kept in heaven for you, who through faith are shielded by God's power until the coming of the salvation that is ready to be revealed in the last time.

1 PETER 1:3-6 NIV

NOTES & PRAYERS ....

....

....

....

IF YOU MAKE AN EFFORT BY THE POWER OF JESUS, YOUR WORDS WILL BECOME LIKE GOLDEN APPLES THAT NOURISH OTHERS.

A word fitly spoken is like apples of gold in a setting of silver.
PROVERBS 25:11 ESV

Lord Jesus, convict me to mourn all the compassionate words I have left unsaid. It has been too easy for me to use the minimalist rule when I come in contact with others, allowing a certain self-centered phrase run through my mind as I interact, particularly with strangers: Don't engage! Don't engage! Don't engage! Why do I deem it acceptable to retreat into my own selfishness when I look into someone else's tired, overworked, stressed, unloved eyes? The answer is self does not want to reach out. But you, Jesus, always want to connect, because, unlike flesh, you are unselfish. Change my heart, Lord. Replace self's petty purposes with your holy intentions and high purposes. In your name, I beseech you, turn my speech toward others into divine golden apples that could only ever be of you. Amen.

A good man brings good things out of the good stored up in his heart,
and an evil man brings evil things out of the evil stored up in his heart.
For the mouth speaks what the heart is full of.
LUKE 6:45 NIV

NOTES & PRAYERS ....

....

....

....

ELIJAH'S OLD TESTAMENT ASCENSION TO HEAVEN IN A WHIRLWIND POINTS TO JESUS' NEW TESTAMENT ASCENSION TO HEAVEN THROUGH A CLOUD, PROOF THE STORY OF JESUS THREADS THROUGHOUT SCRIPTURE.

[An angel] This very Jesus who was taken up from among you (disciples) to heaven will come as certainly, and mysteriously, as he left.

ACTS 1:11B MSG

Mighty God, thank you for the astonishing eyewitness accounts in your Word describing Elijah (Old Testament) and Jesus (New Testament) being taken up from earth and transported to heaven by your power in the Spirit. In both cases, those left behind on earth were expected to continue serving you in the same manner as their teachers – Elisha according to Elijah, and the twelve disciples (plus all other believers, including me) according to Jesus. Thank you, God, for convicting me that I, too, am expected to live my life in service to others, just as your Son did. I pray for faithfulness to abide always in my Savior's name and for his sake. Keep me close, Father. Amen.

As they (Elisha and Elijah) were walking along, suddenly a chariot of fire appeared, drawn by horses of fire. It drove between the two men, separating them, and Elijah was carried by a whirlwind into heaven.

2 KINGS 2:11-13 NLT

NOTES & PRAYERS ....

....

....

July

GOD WILL AMAZE YOU WITH HIS WONDERS. INQUIRE OF EZEKIEL WHO PROVIDES EYEWITNESS DESCRIPTIONS OF GOD'S POWER.

[Ezekiel] I looked, and I saw a windstorm coming out of the north – an immense cloud with flashing lightning and surrounded by brilliant light. The center of the fire looked like glowing metal, and in the fire was what looked like four living creatures (cherubim). The appearance of the living creatures was like burning coals of fire or like torches. Fire moved back and forth among the creatures; it was bright, and lightning flashed out of it. The creatures sped back and forth like flashes of lightning.

EZEKIEL 1:4-5A; 13-14 NIV

Father, when I am feeling down, I consider how you blessed Ezekiel by giving him extraordinary visions to remind him and your people of your sovereignty, goodness, and omnipresence, even as they were being held captive in Babylon. In Jesus' name, thank you, God, for reassuring Ezekiel – and me! – of your supremacy. You have transformed my heart from hopeless to hopeful. You are my God. Amen.

[Ezekiel] As I looked at the living creatures, I saw a wheel on the ground beside each creature with its four faces. Wherever the spirit would go, they would go, and the wheels would rise along with them, because the spirit of the living creatures was in the wheels.

EZEKIEL 1:15; 20 NIV

NOTES & PRAYERS ....

....

....

....

ENJOY YOUR GLORIOUS FREEDOM IN GOD'S SON. BE NOT IN BONDAGE TO ANYONE OTHER THAN YOUR SAVIOR – JESUS!

So if the Son (Jesus) sets you free, you will be free, indeed.
JOHN 8:36 ESV

Lord Jesus, thank you for the treasure of freedom with which you blessed me at salvation. By your grace, I am no longer a prisoner of sin, no longer judged, convicted, nor condemned to death. I am forgiven and set free to live forever in your presence. I offer you all my gratitude for the priceless liberty only you could provide – incalculable, undeserved, eternal liberty, yet temporal, as well. I am free into eternity, yes, but also in the here and now, guarded from darkness by the Light of the Holy Spirit. Thank you, Jesus, for joy in knowing that evil no longer controls me. In your name, I pray my gratitude for the blessing of freedom in you made possible by your grace of forgiveness. You are my Savior. Amen.

So now there is no condemnation for those who belong to Christ Jesus. And because you belong to him, the power of the life-giving Spirit has freed you from the power of sin that leads to death.
ROMANS 8:1-2 NLT

NOTES & PRAYERS ....
....
....
....

WHAT KIND OF LIFE-HARVEST DO YOU PRODUCE, GOOD FRUIT OF JESUS, OR THORNS AND THISTLES OF SELF?

When the ground soaks up the falling rain and bears a good crop for the farmer, it has God's blessing. But if a field bears thorns and thistles, it is useless. The farmer will soon condemn that field and burn it.

HEBREWS 6:7-8 NLT

Father, your good fruit is polar opposite to thorns and thistles: love/hate, joy/gloom, peace/conflict, patience/impatience, kindness/cruelty, goodness/evil, faithfulness/disloyalty, gentleness/harshness, self-control/weakness. Thank you, God, for helping me see that bearing good fruit for your Kingdom is a conscious choice I must make each day with your loving help. For only by your wisdom and power can I be the ground that soaks up your rain of righteousness and produces a crop of good fruit. Apart from you, I can do nothing. But with you, I can do the work you prepared for me. In Jesus' name, guide and prune me to your service. Make me a producer of your Son's good fruit. Amen.

[Jesus] I am the vine; you are the branches. If you remain in me and I in you, you will bear much fruit; apart from me you can do nothing.

JOHN 15:5 NIV

NOTES & PRAYERS ....

....

....

....

FROM ONE DEGREE TO ANOTHER TOWARD HIS GLORY...THAT IS HOW JESUS IN THE SPIRIT CONTINUES TO TRANSFORM YOU.

And we all, who with unveiled faces contemplate the Lord's glory, are being transformed into his image with ever-increasing glory, which comes from the Lord, who is the Spirit.

2 CORINTHIANS 3:18 NIV

And so we are transfigured much like the Messiah (Jesus), our lives gradually becoming brighter and more beautiful as God enters our lives and we become like him.

2 CORINTHIANS 3:18 MSG

Father, thank you for saving me and taking me on as your project to the purpose of transforming me into the image of Christ, sanctifed. I could never achieve such a miracle. But when Jesus returns and completes the work he began in me when he saved my soul, he will bring me into his glory. In the Son's perfect name, thank you, God in your Holy Trininty, for the wonderful and eternal future you have assured me in your glorious presence. Amen.

I am certain that God, who began the good work within you, will continue his work until it is finished when Christ Jesus returns.

PHILIPPIANS 1:6 NLT

NOTES & PRAYERS ....

....

....

....

ARE YOU SPENDING YOUR LIFE GLORIFYING GOD OR SELF?

Not to us, O Lord, not to us, but to your name give glory,
for the sake of your steadfast love and your faithfulness!

PSALM 115:1 ESV

Heavenly Father, why am I obsessed with my own needs? Why do I nurture the upside-down idea I deserve this or that? Too often my prayers turn into a boring list of my shallow wishes that I think if you would grant, I would finally be happy. Why can't I see focusing on this kind of prayer is glorifying self? And more importantly, why can't I see glorifying self will never make me happy, not even in the short run. It is only when I set about doing the work you planned for me that I will find joy and peace. You created me, Father God, to spend my life glorifying you, so let me glorify you every day in every way. In Jesus' name, accept my gratitude for your gifts of grace, forgiveness, faith, and salvation. Be thou glorified, Almighty God. All praise and honor to you in your Holy Trinity. Praise and worship you, Father, Son, and Holy Spirit. Glory, glory, glory! Amen.

Then everything you do will bring glory to God through Jesus Christ.
All glory and power to him forever and ever! Amen.

1 PETER 4:11B NLT

NOTES & PRAYERS ....

....

....

....

ARE YOU MEASURING YOURSELF AGAINST THE PROPER STANDARD? NEVER FORGET, GOD'S HOLINESS IS THE ONE AND ONLY PROPER STANDARD.

If you are kind only to your friends, how are you different from anyone else? Even pagans do that. But you are to be perfect, even as your Father in heaven is perfect.

Matthew 5:47-48 NLT

Father God, I understand, at last. The Old Testament law you gave Moses was a mirror to show your faithful ones how far off their own lives were from your Godly standard. They were never the good people they may have thought, for they could never keep your law to perfection. Does that mean I cannot keep your law, either? Of course, I cannot, certainly not in my own strength. You are my standard, Jesus, that I can meet only through the grace of your purity, not my impurity. In your name, thank you for giving your righteousness to me through salvation by your shed blood and resurrection. Guide me toward sharing your generosity with others through the power of the Holy Spirit. Amen.

He (Christ) is your example, and you must follow in his steps. He never sinned, nor ever deceived anyone.

1 Peter 2:21b-22 NLT

NOTES & PRAYERS ....
....
....
....

IS IT IMPORTANT TO YOU TO BE KNOWN AS A CHILD OF YOUR HEAVENLY FATHER?

See what great love the Father has lavished on us,
that we should be called children of God! And that is what we are!
1 JOHN 3:1A NIV

Savior, thank you for my friend who calls me her BFFF – Best Friend Forever Fanatic. She says I am a little too much into you. In our conversations, she focuses on fanatic, while I focus on forever. She does not seem to realize we are going to be friends eternally, for that is how long your gift of salvation will last for both of us. In your name, Lord, I give you all gratitude for allowing me to be my pal's Best Friend Forever Fanatic (BFFF), but thank you more for allowing me to be your friend forever, and not just your friend, but a cherished member of your everlasting family. Amen.

[Jesus] Greater love has no one than this: to lay down one's life for
one's friends. You are my friends if you do what I command.
JOHN 15:13-14 NIV

Jesus and the ones he makes holy (believers) have the same Father.
That is why Jesus is not ashamed to call them his brothers and sisters.
HEBREWS 2:11 NLT

NOTES & PRAYERS ....
....
....
....

SHOUT AMEN IF YOU KNOW JESUS IS WHOLLY GOD. AMEN! AMEN! AMEN!

In him (Jesus) lives the fullness of the Godhead bodily. And you (believers) are complete in him, who is the head of all authority and power.
COLOSSIANS 2:9-10 MEV

Jesus, I rejoice with my Christian family and friends in acknowledging your divinity. You are God manifested in corporal form, Creator and Upholder of all things, Righteous Judge and Savior – God's Messiah! You are the King of Righteousness and our Heavenly Father's Bright Morning Star. You are worthy of worship and praise lifted up to you by all creation. Thank you for being Lord of lords, King of kings, and Prince of Peace. You are the Mighty One, yet you love me on a personal level. You are the King of Glory, yet you nurture a relationship with lowly me. In your name, I praise you, Jesus – Deliverer, Healer, Counselor, Comforter, and Friend. You are the Son in God's Holy Trinity. Amen.

"Very truly I tell you," Jesus answered, "before Abraham was born, I am!"
JOHN 8:58 NIV

[Jesus] "I am the First and the Last. I am He who lives, though I was dead. Look! I am alive forevermore."
REVELATION 1:17B-18A MEV

NOTES & PRAYERS ....

....

....

....

BE GRATEFUL YOUR HEAVENLY FATHER LOVED YOU ENOUGH TO GIVE YOU SPIRITUAL EARS. USE THEM TO HEAR JESUS' VOICE IN PRAYER AND SCRIPTURE.

[Jesus] My sheep hear my voice, and I know them, and they follow me. I give them eternal life, and they will never perish.

JOHN 10:27-28A ESV

Thank you, God, for designing my Spiritual ears in a way that leaves me no excuse for not listening. Lord Jesus, I hear your wisdom so clearly in your Word that not listening would be more difficult than listening. I hear you plainly. Forgive me when I pretend I do not. Speak to my heart, Savior, as I pray in your name for wisdom to hearken to your Spirit voice in prayer and Scripture. I am listening with my Spritual ears. Speak, Lord! Amen.

[Jesus] Anyone who listens to my teaching and follows it is wise, like a person who builds a house on solid rock. Though the rain comes in torrents and the floodwaters rise and the winds beat against that house, it won't collapse because it is built on bedrock. But anyone who hears my teaching and doesn't obey it is foolish, like a person who builds a house on sand. When the rains and floods come and the winds beat against that house, it will collapse with a mighty crash.

MATTHEW 7:24-27 NLT

NOTES & PRAYERS ....

....

....

....

JESUS IS YOUR LOYAL, LOVING – AND LEGAL – ADVOCATE BEFORE HOLY GOD.

My dear children, I (Paul) am writing this to you so that you will not sin. But if anyone does sin, we have an advocate who pleads our case before the Father. He is Jesus Christ, the one who is truly righteous.

1 JOHN 2:1 NLT

Jesus, only you have the right to plead my case moment by moment before Holy God, because only you paid the price for my sins by dying for me in perfection and rising again. Wholly God yourself, only you have the right to advocate for me formally, legally, lovingly, and loyally. Only you are worthy to speak with authority on my behalf, having covered me with your own righteousness the day I accepted you as my personal Savior, which rendered me innocent of my sins and saved me from prosecution, conviction, and punishment. Only you, Jesus, can defend me before God, at the same time Satan stands accusing me. In your worthy, legal, and loving name, Savior Jesus, I am grateful. Amen.

So now there is no condemnation for those who belong to Christ Jesus. And because you belong to him, the power of the life-giving Spirit has freed you from the power of sin that leads to death.

ROMANS 8:1 NLT

NOTES & PRAYERS ....
....
....
....

YOU ARE A CITIZEN OF YOUR HEAVENLY FATHER'S KINGDOM, SEALED AS HIS SAVED CHILD.

Be grateful for God's seal of approval to dwell eternally in his presence. Welcome to the family! You are home!

Heavenly Father, thank you the Holy Spirit sealed me as your child when I accepted Jesus as my Lord and Savior. I am secure in my citizenship in your Kingdom. And though I understand you desire me to be Christ-like in the here and now, as well as in New Jerusalem when you establish your eternal Kingdom, I am grateful you are aware I can do neither on my own. In Jesus' name, I beseech you, God, help me defeat weakness, sloth, and lack of faith. Make me your Son's selfless servant in your Kingdom. Amen.

[Jesus] Now I confer on you the royal authority my Father conferred on me so you can eat and drink at my table in my Kingdom.
LUKE 22:29-30A MSG

In him (Jesus) you also, when you heard the word of truth, the gospel of your salvation, and believed in him, were sealed with the promised Holy Spirit, who is the guarantee of our inheritance until we acquire possession of it, to the praise of his glory.
EPHESIANS 1:13-14 ESV

NOTES & PRAYERS ....

....

....

....

GOD IS PLEASED WHEN YOU DANCE WITH JOY AS YOU WORSHIP HIM. AND IF YOU CANNOT DANCE, RELAX AND ENJOY THE DANCING OF OTHERS, FOR LITURGICAL PRAISE DANCE IS THE ULTIMATE HAPPY DANCE.

Let them praise his name with dancing,
making melody to him with tambourine and lyre!
PSALM 149:3 ESV

Father, thank you for encouraging your children to worship you through rhythm and dance. Although I cannot dance well myself, I love that others can. You have taught us you expect worship, Father, even require it. *Isaiah 66:23 ESV From new moon to new moon, and from Sabbath to Sabbath, all flesh shall come to worship before me, declares the Lord.* Let us now come into your presence, God, with joyful hearts in happy praise. Let us sing, shout, play instruments, clap, and dance. In Jesus' name, we praise you for all eternity with music and dancing. Amen.

You [God] have turned my mourning into joyful dancing. You have taken away my clothes of mourning and clothed me with joy, that I might sing praises to you and not be silent. Lord, my God, I give you thanks forever!
PSALM 30:11-12 NLT

NOTES & PRAYERS ....

....

....

....

DO YOU NOT KNOW? HAVE YOU NOT HEARD? THE LORD IS THE EVERLASTING GOD, THE CREATOR OF THE ENDS OF THE EARTH. HE WILL NOT GROW TIRED OR WEARY, AND HIS UNDERSTANDING NO ONE CAN FATHOM. HE GIVES STRENGTH TO THE WEARY AND INCREASES THE POWER OF THE WEAK. ISAIAH 40:28-29 NIV

Even youths will become weak and tired, and young men will fall in exhaustion. But those who trust in the Lord will find new strength. They will soar high on wings like eagles. They will run and not grow weary. They will walk and not faint.

ISAIAH 40:30-31 NLT

Father, I am grateful for your loving support when I am too weak to stand. You give me divine strength that transcends human frailty. You make me all right with the world, when the world is not all right with me. And you make your Son my rock of salvation. In his name, thank you, God. Amen.

I pray that out of his glorious riches he (God) may strengthen you with power through his Spirit in your inner being, so that Christ may dwell in your hearts through faith.

EPHESIANS 3:16-17A NIV

NOTES & PRAYERS ....

....

....

....

GOD WILL ALLOW YOUR SPIRITUAL EYES TO SEE FAR MORE THAN YOUR PHYSICAL EYES WILL EVER SEE. PRAISE YOUR HEAVENLY FATHER WHO GAVE YOU SPIRITUAL VISION.

Rather, we fix our gaze on things that cannot be seen. For the things we see now will soon be gone, but the things we cannot see will last forever.

2 CORINTHIANS 4:18B NLT

Thank you, Jesus, for directing my gaze toward unseen wonders promised by you – your second coming, eternal life, heaven, your physical presence in addition to your Spiritual presence, and more! And though I cannot see the eternal future you are preparing for me, I know it is real. I am even conscious of much failed effort and useless activity in the air around me as evil ones try to take control of your creation. Those cosmic battles are invisible to my physical eyes, yet I know they have already been won by you, conquering Savior. In your name, accept my gratitude for your eternal victory over evil, the reality of which I train my Spiritual eyes upon with joy and relief. Praise you, Son of God, Lion of Judah, Lord of lords, King of kings – Christ Jesus! Amen.

Look not to the things that are seen but to the things that are unseen. For the things that are seen are transient, but the things unseen eternal.

2 CORINTHIANS 4:17-18 ESV

NOTES & PRAYERS ....

....

....

....

YOU HAVE THE PRIVILEGE OF GLORIFYING GOD WITH ONE MIND AND ONE VOICE WITH ALL OTHER BELIEVERS IN CHRIST JESUS AND THE HOLY SPIRIT.

May the God who gives endurance and encouragement give you the same attitude of mind toward each other that Jesus had, so that with one mind and voice you may glorify the God and Father of our Lord Jesus Christ.

ROMANS 15:5-6 NIV

King Jesus, not only did you give me personal access to God through your cross and resurrection, you gave me very your mind. And not only did you give me your mind, you gave me your definitive instruction book in your Word to show me how to think and behave like you. And not only did you give me your Word, you infused it with the Holy Spirit. In your name, Jesus, thank you for making me one with you and other believers. Praise you, Father, Son, and Spirit for unity in you that you have given your church, not just collectively, but individually. We are one together with you. Glory to God in the Son and Spirit for divine unity. Amen.

[Jesus praying to Father God for believers] I have given them the glory you gave me, that they may be one as we are one – I in them and you in me – so that they may be brought to complete unity.

JOHN 17:22-23 NIV

NOTES & PRAYERS ....

....

....

....

YOU ARE MORE THAN THE SINGULAR YOU. YOU ARE ALSO THE COLLECTIVE YOU, UNIFIED INTO ONE MINDSET WITH FATHER GOD, JESUS THE SON, AND THE HOLY SPIRIT, ALONG WITH ALL OTHER FELLOW BELIEVERS.

[Jesus] Abide in me, and I in you. As the branch cannot bear fruit by itself, unless it abides in the vine, neither can you, unless you abide in me.

JOHN 15:4 ESV

Heavenly Father, with mystery and generosity, you allowed me to remain uniquely me at my salvation, at the same time becoming one with you in Jesus and the Spirit. If you were willing to bless me – lowliest of all sinners – with such a miracle, I know you will bless any other sinner with the same. In Jesus' name and by the power of the Spirit, out of love and gratitude, lead me, God, to share your Oneness with those around me. Blest be the tie that binds us all together, which is your sacred love manifested in Jesus, your Son. Amen.

Make every effort to keep yourselves united in the Spirit, binding yourselves together with peace. For there is one body and one Spirit, just as you have been called to one glorious hope for the future. There is one Lord, one faith, one baptism, one God and Father, who is over all, in all, and living through all.

EPHESIANS 4:3-6 NLT

NOTES & PRAYERS ....

....

....

....

JESUS IS YOUR KINSMAN REDEEMER. HE GUARANTEED YOU HIS BLESSING OF SALVATION ON THE DAY YOU ACCEPTED IT.

Jesus gave himself for us to redeem us from all wickedness.

TITUS 2:14A NIV

Lord Jesus, I am grateful the Old Testament account of Boaz and Ruth's love relationship points to your relationship with your saved ones. You are like Boaz, who rescued Ruth in her time of need, because he loved her, just as you rescued me in my time of need, because you loved me. You made me part of your family, your kin, by redeeming me from my lost condition. You are my kinsman redeemer and Savior! And I noticed, also, that Boaz saved Ruth's beloved mother-in-law, Naomi, as well, just as you saved so many loved ones in my own family. In your redeeming name, thank you for making your mission-to-save inclusive, not exclusive. I know how Ruth felt when Boaz loved and saved her, for I know how I felt when you loved and saved me. Lead me to tell others who are in need of your restorative grace you are their kinsman redeemer, too, just as you are mine. Thank you, God. Amen.

And she answered (Boaz), "I am Ruth, your servant.
Spread your wings over your servant, for you are my redeemer."

RUTH 3:9B ESV

NOTES & PRAYERS ....

....

....

....

YOUR TEARS ARE UNIQUE UNTO YOU ALONE, PHYSICALLY AND SPIRITUALLY.

You (God) keep track of my sorrows. You have collected all my tears
in your bottle. You have recorded each one in your book.

PSALM 56:8 NLT

Jesus, thank you for weeping with me no matter the reason for my sadness, as you wept with Martha and Mary, mourning their dead brother, Lazarus. It is a comfort to call out your name – Oh, Jesus! I say it over and over in silence and aloud whenever I cry. Just the sound of it brings me peace, as does remembering that you, too, wept when you dwelt among us in corporal body. Your sorrow in tears shows me you understand how it feels to be brokenhearted. I love you, Jesus, for crying with me, loving me, and assuring me that one day, you will return to earth and collect me with all other believers. We will live in gladness forever in your presence. In your name, I praise you, Savior Jesus in the Spirit Comforter, for drying my tears. Amen.

All night I flood my bed with weeping, drenching it with my tears.

PSALM 6:6B NLT

He [Jesus] will wipe every tear from their eyes.

REVELATION 21:4A NIV

NOTES & PRAYERS ....

....

....

....

IF YOU LOVE AND CARE FOR OTHERS IN VIEW OF ETERNITY AND NOT JUST THE PRESENT, YOU ARE TREATING THEM THE WAY JESUS TREATS YOU.

[Jesus] As I have loved you, so you must love one another.

JOHN 13:34B NIV

Love never ends.

1 CORINTHIANS 13:8A ESV

Jesus, thank you for caring for me as personally and individually as you care for all believers, as if each one were the most important child in your creation. You, Savior, are my model for how to treat those around me. You are loving and compassionate, and you want me to be the same. Yet, I am weak, Lord. I beg you to place your love and compassion inside my heart, and then turn me around to share with others, for I cannot accomplish that good thing on my own. In your name, teach me to love as you love, for your healing love never wavers. Thank you, Jesus, for embodying love and compassion. Fill my heart with you. Amen.

The Lord appeared to us in the past, saying: "I have loved you with an everlasting love; I have drawn you with unfailing kindness."

JEREMIAH 31:3 NIV

NOTES & PRAYERS ....
....
....
....

JESUS' RESURRECTION IS ALL THE EVIDENCE YOU WILL EVER NEED TO PROVE HIS CONQUEST OVER SIN AND DEATH.

Jesus paved the way with his victorious resurrection,
so that you could have your own resurrection to life in him.
What a glorious resurrection promise.

*Jesus said to her [Samaritan woman at the well], I am the resurrection
and the life. Whoever believes in me, though he die, yet shall he live,
and everyone who lives and believes in me shall never die.*

JOHN 11:25-26A ESV

Savior Jesus, I give you all my gratitude for sharing your resurrection blessing with me. You rose from the dead in triumph over sin and death. You redeemed me. You gave me living hope for eternal life with you. And, in the fullness of time, you will make my body fit for your Kingdom by transforming it from perishable to imperishable. In your name and with love, thank you for the empty tomb that proves you rose again. I worship you, risen Jesus. Amen.

---

*[Jesus] And this is the will of him who sent me, that I shall lose none
of all those he has given me, but raise them up at the last day.*

JOHN 6:39 NIV

NOTES & PRAYERS ....
....
....
....

ASK GOD TO FILL YOUR CUP WITH BLESSINGS, SO THAT YOU CAN FILL SOMEONE ELSE'S CUP.

Lord, you alone are my inheritance, my cup of blessing.

PSALM 16:5A NLT

Heavenly Father, you have taught me in your Word to keep the inside of my cup as clean as its outside. I understand you mean the cup of my life, the vessel I should be down on my knees beseeching you daily to cleanse and fill with your Holy Spirit. Consider me not just beseeching, but begging, imploring, and entreating you to fill my cup to the brim and overflowing with the blessing of your loving Spirit. For only then can I share in the blood and body of Christ, and only then can I share his blood and body with others. My cup is your cup, Jesus, the cup of salvation. In your name, I ask you to keep it filled with your essence – your shed blood, righteousness, and living water – given to me by your grace, forgiveness, and gift of faith, the Good News of which you want me to share. Praise you, Savior, for being God's One-And-Only pure cup of refreshing living water given to me in divine abundance meant to pour out on others. Amen.

Thou preparest a table before me in the presence of mine enemies: thou anointest my head with oil; my cup runneth over.

PSALM 23:5 KJV

NOTES & PRAYERS ....

....

....

....

YOU MADE A LIFE-SAVING DECISION THE DAY YOU PUT YOUR HEART AND SOUL INTO SEEKING CHRIST FIRST AND SELF LAST.

You've been raised with Christ and have set your hearts on things above, where Christ is seated at the right hand of God.

COLOSSIANS 3:1B NIV

Lord Jesus, you existed before time was ever a concept in the human mind. You are eternal – as far into the past as the future. Thank you for giving me an everlasting future as a new creature in you. I am grateful that when I lose my way along the path you planned for me (by following my own will instead of yours), I can always look to you for divine resets. In your name, Master and Savior, thank you for being infinitely you in whom I am infinitely hidden. I belong to you forever. Praise your name in gratitude. Amen.

[Jesus] Father, the hour has come. Glorify your Son, that your Son may glorify you. For you granted him authority over all people that he might give eternal life to all those you have given him. Now this is eternal life: that they know you, the only true God, and Jesus Christ, whom you have sent. I have brought you glory on earth by finishing the work you gave me to do. And now, Father, glorify me in your presence with the glory I had with you before the world began.

JOHN 17:1B-5 NIV

NOTES & PRAYERS ....

....

....

....

WHEN GOD CALLED YOU TO SALVATION, JESUS BECAME YOUR FIRST RESORT, NOT YOUR LAST RESORT. PRAISE THE FATHER FOR THE PRIVILEGE OF MAKING HIS SON YOU FIRST PRIORITY.

Trust God from the bottom of your heart; don't try to figure out everything on your own. Listen for God's voice in everything you do, everywhere you go; he's the one who will keep you on track.

PROVERBS 3:5-6 MSG

Lord Jesus, I do not know why I sometimes forget the power of trusting in you. I start thinking I am doing well enough on my own without your strength and guidance. Forgive me for turning to self, Lord, when I need to be turning to you. Without you, I would be in a constant fret. But with you, I am calm in the divine trust with which you blessed me at salvation. In your name, thank you, Jesus, for peace of mind. You are my first priority. I trust in you. Amen.

[Jesus] So don't worry about these things, saying, What will we eat? What will we drink? What will we wear? These things dominate the thoughts of unbelievers, but your heavenly Father already knows all your needs. Seek the Kingdom of God above all else, and live righteously, and he will give you everything you need.

MATTHEW 6:31-33 NLT

NOTES & PRAYERS ....

....

....

....

YOU FOUND ABUNDANT LIFE WHEN YOU GAVE EVERYTHING YOU ARE AND EVERYTHING YOU HAVE OVER TO JESUS. HE PROMISED TO GIVE BACK YOUR BEST LIFE, AND HE DID!

[Jesus] If you try to hang on to your life, you will lose it.
But if you give up your life for my sake, you will save it.

MATTHEW 16:25 NLT

Heavenly Father, you created me to have free will. Then you stood back and waited for me to acknowledge the obvious – that I would not exist at all were it not for you, the one Creator. What arrogance on my part to think self of any consequence with the certainty of death staring me in the face? When I realized your Son knows me better than I could ever know myself and still wants the best for me, despite my shortcomings, I knew I had just one sound decision to make, from which all other sound decisions would flow, that is, giving my life to your Son, in whom all life originated. In your name, Savior Jesus, I cherish your Light and Life. Thank you for reconciliation and salvation. Amen.

[Jesus] If you grasp and cling to life on your terms, you'll lose it,
but if you let that life go, you'll get life on God's terms.

LUKE 17:33 MSG

NOTES & PRAYERS ....

....

....

....

JESUS CALLED; YOU ANSWERED; AND YOU HAVE NOT STOPPED PRAISING, WORSHIPING, AND GLORIFYING HIM EVER SINCE.

God lifted him (Jesus) high and honored him far beyond anyone or anything, so that all created beings in heaven and on earth – even those long ago dead and buried – will bow in worship before this Jesus Christ, and call out in praise that he is the master of all to the glorious honor of God the Father.

PHILIPPIANS 2:9B-11 MSG

Father God, help me recognize my prayers for what they are. Am I chattering in your presence about things of concern only to me, without addressing anything of concern to you? What would a prayer to you alone, about you alone, dedicated to you alone, sound like? In Jesus' name, remind me to think with more gratitude about what kinds of prayers would please you most. Father, guide me by the Holy Spirit as I approach you in your throne room. Teach me to pray fervently, submissively, respectfully, and reverently. Make my praise and prayers perfume rising up to you. Amen.

So we praise God for the glorious grace he poured out on us who belong to his dear Son (Jesus).

EPHESIANS 1:6 NLT

NOTES & PRAYERS ....

....

....

....

YOU ARE NO CUT FLOWER THAT WILL WILT AND WITHER IN THE DRY AND ROOTLESS SEASONS OF LIFE. YOU ARE A BRANCH OF THE TRUE VINE OF JESUS, CREATED TO BLOOM AND BEAR HIS GOOD FRUIT INFINITELY.

[Jesus] I am the vine; you are the branches.
Whoever abides in me and I in him, he it is that bears much fruit,
for apart from me you can do nothing.

JOHN 15:5 ESV

Lord Jesus, you are the eternal author of all life. Thank you for grafting my human life, created by you, into your own divine being that was never created, but always was, is, and ever shall be. I know, Savior, any good fruit I bear is your fruit, for apart from you, I am nothing and can do nothing. In your name, thank you for allowing me to be a living part of the everlasting vine of Truth that you are. I want to live in you and for you forever. Praise you, Jesus. Amen.

[Jesus] Anyone who does not remain in me is thrown away like a useless
branch and withers. Such branches are gathered into a pile to be burned.
But if you remain in me and my words remain in you, you may ask for
anything you want, and it will be granted! When you produce much fruit,
you are my true disciples. This brings great glory to my Father.

JOHN 15:6-8 NLT

NOTES & PRAYERS ....
....
....
....

YOUR LIFE IS A CLASSIC RAGS-TO-RICHES STORY, FOR WHEN KING JESUS SAVED YOU, HE REPLACED YOUR FILTHY SIN RAGS WITH HIS OWN ROYAL RAIMENT OF PURITY.

For he has clothed me with garments of salvation and arrayed me in a robe of righteousness, as a bridegroom adorns his head like a priest, and as a bride adorns herself with her jewels.

ISAIAH 61:10B NIV

Thank you, Jesus, for having mercy on me, a soiled sinner washed clean by your divine compassion of grace! If not for my salvation made possible by the perfection of your shed blood, resurrection, forgiveness, grace, and gift of faith, I would have dried up like a dead stick and been cast on a brush pile to be burned, not clothed by you in your bright white shining robe of virtue. I deserved to be tried, convicted, and sentenced to death for my sins, yet you saved me. In your name, thank you for clothing me in your white robe of purity, knowing I have no purity of my own. Praise you, Jesus. Amen.

For the time has come for the wedding feast of the Lamb (Jesus), and his bride (his church) has prepared herself. She has been given the finest of pure white linen to wear. For the fine linen represents the good deeds of God's holy people.

REVELATION 19:7B-8 NLT

NOTES & PRAYERS ....

....

....

....

BE PROXIMATE, NOT APPROXIMATE, IN YOUR RELATIONSHIPS. MODEL YOUR STYLE OF RELATING TO OTHERS AFTER THE NEARBY STYLE OF JESUS, FOR HE IS THE ULTIMATE BUILDER OF HEALTHY RELATIONSHIPS.

I know the Lord is always with me. I will not be shaken,
for he is right beside me.

PSALM 16:8 NLT

Thank you, Jesus, for allowing me to count on your constant proximity. Your Holy Spirit is always with me – not distant, but attentive; not neglectful, but conscientious; not indifferent, but interested; not false, but genuine. Help me to infuse those same loving blessings of grace into my relationships with others, knowing any comfort I provide will be of you, Lord, not of me. Jesus, you have shown me by your divine presence how meaningful my own presence can be in the lives of those around me. If you are near me, and I am near them, then you are near them, also. In your name, Savior, lead me to grow closer to you as I seek to grow closer to other believers and lost ones for your sake. Amen.

Let your gentleness be evident to all. The Lord is near.
PHILIPPIANS 4:5 NIV

NOTES & PRAYERS ....

....

....

....

YOU HAVE DISCOVERED SOMETHING WONDERFUL ABOUT JESUS. ON THE DAY YOU DECIDED TO BECOME HIS AMBASSADOR, HIS TOUCH BECAME YOUR TOUCH.

And he (Jesus) took them (little children) in his arms
and blessed them, laying hands on them.

MARK 10:16 ESV

Lord Jesus, I pray often for your healing mercy on myself and others, knowing I cannot heal anyone on my own. I am aware, however, that at times you have used my personal touch as your touch to bring relief to the sad, lonely, sick, or lost. My hugs, handshakes, shoulder pats, fist bumps, high fives, and cheek kisses have, on occasion, become your own soothing touches, made possible by your selection and power. Thank you for being generous with your touches, Lord, and for the miracle of touching others through believers. Your power flows through us, Jesus, whenever and to whomever you choose. I pray in your name, choose me often to be your divine channel of touch. Live in me, and I in you, to your service. Amen.

[Jesus] Anyone who believes in me will do the same works I have done,
and even greater works, because I am going to be with the Father.

JOHN 14:12B NLT

NOTES & PRAYERS ....

....

....

....

JESUS IS THE KINGDOM OF GOD.

[Jesus] The Kingdom of God doesn't come by counting the days on the calendar. Nor when someone says, Look, here! or, There it is! And why? Because God's Kingdom is already among you (meaning himself).

LUKE 17:20B-21 MSG

Lord Jesus, you ushered in God's redemptive Kingdom with your birth, sealing your office as King of kings and Lord of lords, for the Kingdom of God is wherever you are. Thank you, Son of God, for teaching by personal example and by Spirit instruction in your Holy Scripture what it means to be a citizen of your Kingdom, which is to live as you live now and for eternity. In your name, King Jesus, I praise you. I am grateful to be a part of your Kingdom. Amen.

[Foretelling Jesus] For a child has been born – for us! The gift of a Son – for us! He'll take over the running of the world. His names will be: Amazing Counselor, Strong God, Eternal Father, Prince of Wholeness. His ruling authority will grow, and there'll be no limits to the wholeness he brings. He'll rule from the historic David throne over that promised Kingdom. He'll put that Kingdom on a firm footing and keep it going with fair dealing and right living, beginning now and lasting always. The zeal of God-of-the-Angel-Armies will do all this.

ISAIAH 9:6-7 MSG

NOTES & PRAYERS ....

....

....

....

YOUR HEAVENLY FATHER REGENERATED YOU BY THE HOLY SPIRIT'S POWER WHEN HE SAVED YOU IN JESUS. THEN HE CONTINUED TRANSFORMING YOU – ONGOING – TO BE LIKE YOUR SAVIOR, A PROCESS HE WILL COMPLETE WHEN HE CALLS YOU HOME TO ETERNITY. YOUR PART IS TO CONFORM AS GOD TRANSFORMS.

God accomplished your salvation through the blood of Jesus once and for all by his grace, forgiveness, and gift of faith. He then began perfecting you in the character of Christ through the continuing process of sanctification, also powered by grace.

Father, through your mercy and provision, you called me to rebirth and reconciliation in Jesus. What blessings! In his name, thank you that when you bring me home to eternity in your presence, you will complete my makeover in your Son. Give glory and honor to the Holy Trinity – Father, Son, and Holy Spirit. I am reborn in my Savior Jesus. Amen.

But when the kindness and love of God our Savior appeared, he (Jesus) saved us, not because of righteous things we had done, but because of his mercy. He saved us through the washing of rebirth and renewal by the Holy Spirit.

TITUS 3:4-5 NIV

NOTES & PRAYERS ....

....

....

....

August

WHAT BETTER WAY TO SHOW GRATITUDE TO GOD FOR ENCOURAGING YOU THAN TO ENCOURAGE SOMEONE ELSE IN HIS NAME.

[God to Joshua] This is my command – be strong and courageous!
Do not be afraid or discouraged. For the Lord your
God is with you wherever you go.
JOSHUA 1:9 NLT

Lord Jesus, why do I find it easier to encourage others than myself? Maybe it has to do with knowing I do not deserve it. Thank you, Savior, for giving me your special brand of encouragement only your agape love can provide. I deserve nothing, yet you never stop lifting me up with care and assurance from your Word and Spirit. Through grace, mercy, forgiveness, and generosity, you give me value that is your value, strength that is your strength, and work that is your work, none of which originates with me. In your name, I ask you to use me to fill someone else's cup with the same divine love and encouragement with which you fill mine. Praise you, encouraging Savior. Amen.

Christ died for us so that, whether we are dead or alive when he returns,
we can live with him forever. So encourage each other and
build each other up, just as you are already doing.
1 THESSALONIANS 5:10-11 NLT

NOTES & PRAYERS ....

....

....

....

WHAT BREAD DO YOU SERVE OTHERS FROM THE TABLE OF YOUR LIFE – NATURAL BREAD OF SELF THAT WILL GROW MOLDY IN TIME, OR SUPERNATURAL BREAD OF JESUS THAT WILL REMAIN FRESH FOREVER?

[Jesus] The true bread of God is the one who comes down from heaven and gives life to the world. Sir, they said, Give us that bread every day. Jesus replied, I am the bread of life. Whoever comes to me will never be hungry again. Whoever believes in me will never be thirsty.

JOHN 6:33-35 NLT

Lord Jesus, I remind myself of the grasping contingent of the five thousand-plus throng you fed by miracle with the little boy's two fish and five loaves. Greedy ones in the crowd continued following you in hopes of receiving more free physical bread, instead of falling down on their knees and begging for your Spiritual bread, the holy bread of you, Son of God. In your name, Jesus – God's bread of life – thank you for encouraging me to share your bounty with others who are starving Spirituallt in their need of you. Amen.

And when He (Jesus) had taken some of the bread and given thanks, He broke it and gave it to them, saying, This is My body which is given for you; do this in remembrance of Me.

LUKE 22:19 NASB

NOTES & PRAYERS ....

....

....

....

COMMON CONFLICT BECOMES UNCOMMON WHEN HEALED BY THE GRACE OF JESUS.

Summing up: be agreeable, be sympathetic, be loving, be compassionate, be humble. That goes for all of you, no exceptions. No retaliation. No sharp-tongued sarcasm. Instead, bless – that's your job, to bless. You'll be a blessing and also get a blessing. Whoever wants to embrace life and see the day fill up with good, here's what you do: say nothing evil or hurtful; snub evil and cultivate good; run after peace for all you're worth.

1 Peter 3:8-11 MSG

Blessed are the peacemakers, for they will be called children of God.

Matthew 5:9 NIV

Savior Jesus, I love your descriptive title, Prince of Peace. And since I also love being your loyal subject, I understand I, too, must be peaceful. So why is it self so often claims justification in being contentious? In your name, Lord, I pray to put self's ill temper aside and embrace your wisdom concerning peacefulness. Let your Spirit in the Word be my instruction guide for healing conflict, indeed, for avoiding conflict altogether. In your name, Peaceful Savior, I pray to share your divine serenity with others. Amen.

Work at living in peace with everyone, and work at living a holy life.

Hebrews 12:14a NLT

NOTES & PRAYERS ....

....

....

....

IN YOUR SEARCH FOR AUTHENTIC LIFE PRESENTLY, YOU DISCOVERED JESUS WANTS TO PROVIDE YOU AUTHENTIC LIFE ETERNALLY. PRAISE HIM. WORSHIP HIM. REVERE HIM. LOVE HIM. HE IS YOUR AUTHENTIC SAVIOR.

Your old life is dead. Your new life, which is your real life – even though invisible to spectators – is with Christ in God. He is your life.

COLOSSIANS 3:3 MSG

Lord Jesus, thank you for making your authenticity my authenticity. I am acceptable to God for the sole reason you are acceptable. You – begotten Son of God, worthy One, sinless One, perfect One, authentic One – bought me with your spilled blood and resurrection. In your authentic name, I pray to live in a way so genuine it makes you glad you saved me. Praise you, Savior. Amen.

Chosen by God for this new life of love, dress in the wardrobe God picked for you: compassion, kindness, humility, quiet strength, discipline. Be even-tempered, content with second place, quick to forgive an offense. Forgive as quickly and completely as the Master (Jesus) forgives you. And regardless of what else you put on, wear love. It's your basic, all-purpose garment. Never be without it.

COLOSSIANS 3:12-14 MSG

NOTES & PRAYERS ....

....

....

....

MEEK DOES NOT MEAN WEAK IN YOUR WALK WITH JESUS. MEEK MEANS QUIETLY STRONG IN YOUR SAVIOR.

God blesses those who are humble, for they will inherit the whole earth.

MATTHEW 5:5 NLT

Lord Jesus, though fully God, you humbled yourself in meekness by becoming mortal, sacrificing yourself on the cross, and rising again for the sake of others. You did not have to do anything, being God, yet you chose to do everything, being God, paragon of power in your meekness. Which makes you the perfect model for me. In your name, Savior, show me how to be meek in ways you are meek and strong in ways you are strong. Teach me to love others with your selfless love – meek and strong simultaneously for all eternity. Amen.

Be humble, thinking of others as better than yourselves. Don't look out only for your own interests, but take an interest in others, too. You must have the same attitude Christ Jesus had.

PHILIPPIANS 2:3B-5 NLT

For the Lord taketh pleasure in his people;
he will beautify the meek with salvation.

PSALM 149:4 KJV

NOTES & PRAYERS ....

....

....

....

WHEN LIFE BRINGS MOURNING, JESUS BRINGS COMFORT AND RELIEF.

He (Jesus) will wipe every tear from their eyes, and there will be no more death or sorrow or crying or pain.
REVELATION 21:4A NLT

Lord Jesus, my experience with mourning has become more about how to help others than myself. Which does not mean I have not gone through periods of mourning. I certainly have, and they wounded me deeply and still do. Thank you for your presence, Lord, during my mourning, for soothing and supporting me, for holding me up when I felt like falling down. I pray you will comfort others through me as they face their own trials. Remind me not to resort to shallow human sentiments in my clumsy efforts to ease their pain. Make me graceful in you, Jesus, by reminding me to rely on your consoling Spirit in your Word. And if you decide to use me to comfort someone else, I will be honored and humbled before you. In your reassuring, cheering, up-lifting, encouraging name, my Savior, thank you for loving me tenderly in my times of mourning and for prompting me to love others in theirs. Amen.

Weeping may stay for the night, but rejoicing comes in the morning.
PSALM 30:5B NIV

NOTES & PRAYERS ....

....

....

....

CHOOSE JESUS AS SUPREME TRUTH FOR YOUR LIFE, FOR HE IS GOD'S ONE-AND-ONLY PERFECT TRUTH.

Then Pilate said, "So, are you a king or not?" Jesus answered, "You tell me. Because I am King, I was born and entered the world so that I could witness to the truth. Everyone who cares for truth, who has any feeling for the truth, recognizes my voice."
JOHN 18:37 MSG

Thank you, Jesus, for living and speaking God's Truth, indeed, for being God's Living Truth. You are Truth, my Lord and Savior, which makes every Spirit instruction in your Word worthy of obedience. You have authority, because you are authority. In your name, Faithful and True, I pray my gratitude for the privilege of worshiping you in Spirit and Truth and for obeying you with the aid of the Spirit. Amen.

Jesus said, "I am the Road, also the Truth, also the Life. No one gets to the Father apart from me. If you really knew me, you would know my Father, as well. From now on, you do know him. You've even seen him!" Philip said, "Master, show us the Father; then we'll be content." "You've been with me all this time, Philip, and you still don't understand? To see me is to see the Father."
JOHN 14:6-9A MSG

NOTES & PRAYERS

EVEN AS SATAN TRIED TO KEEP YOU IN CHAINS WITH EVIL LIES, YOUR HEAVENLY FATHER SET YOU FREE WITH DIVINE TRUTH. PRAISE JESUS, YOU BELONG TO HIM, GOD'S ULTIMATE TRUTH AND FREEDOM.

[Jesus] You are truly my disciples if you remain faithful to my teachings. And you will know the truth, and the truth will set you free.

JOHN 8:31B-32 NLT

Jesus, you are plainspoken concerning realities of Truth and deceit. You are Truth; whereas, Satan is "a liar and the father of lies." And not only a liar, "a murderer from the beginning," who has always "hated the truth." Lying is not simply disobeying you, Lord. Lying is obeying Satan. In your name, Savior, thank you for rescuing me from Satan's deception. I am free from sin and death by the power of your authentic Truth, which is You! Praise you, Deliverer. Amen.

Guide me in your truth and teach me, for you are God my Savior.

PSALM 25:5A NIV

[Jesus] He (Satan) was a murderer from the beginning. He has always hated the truth, because there is no truth in him. When he lies, it is consistent with his character; for he is a liar and the father of lies.

JOHN 8:44B NLT

NOTES & PRAYERS ....
....
....
....

GIVE YOUR ANGER OVER TO JESUS.
HE WILL TURN YOUR TOXIC FEELINGS
INTO HIS OWN DIVINE PEACE.

Post this at all the intersections, dear friends: lead with your ears, follow up with your tongue, and let anger straggle along in the rear. God's righteousness doesn't grow from human anger.

JAMES 1:19-20 MSG

Lord Jesus, where did I get the idea it was all right to thrash about in sinful anger and excuse it by claiming righteous indignation? Only you are righteous, Savior, never me. Thank you for revealing in your Word my anger is just one more worthless human habit. In your peaceful, yet all powerful and holy name, I pray for redirection when I feel angry and frustrated. I need you in my weakness, for I have proven my inability to redirect myself. I would never be able to put wrath into submission without your power and gift of faith. Please, Jesus, give me your peace. I need help in keeping anger from blocking me. Let me be peaceful in you, Prince of Peace. Amen.

Let all bitterness and wrath and anger and clamor and slander be put away from you, along with all malice.

EPHESIANS 4:31 ESV

NOTES & PRAYERS ....

....

....

....

WHICH IS THE CONSTANT YOU IN RELATIONSHIPS – THE YOU WHO SEEKS UNDERSTANDING, OR THE YOU WHO OFFERS UNDERSTANDING?

Look not only to your own interests, but also to the interests of others.
PHILIPPIANS 2:4B ESV

Savior Jesus, why do I clamor to be understood in part by other human beings, when your Word assures me I am already understood in full by you. You, Savior, wholly God in your own right, have convicted me that my attitude toward understanding has been backward far too long. Instead of working so hard to get others to meet my needs, I should have been working harder to meet theirs. In your name, replace my unwillingness with your willingness to understand those around me. Remind me to share your divine sympathy and compassion as I relate, for without your prompting and guidance, I will just keep on seeking understanding instead of offering it, which is self's way, not your way. Let me emulate you, Lord. Grow me to be more Christ-like in understanding others with your agape love. Amen.

[Jesus] Do to others whatever you would like them to do to you.
This is the essence of all that is taught in the law and the prophets.
MATTHEW 7:12 NLT

NOTES & PRAYERS ....

....

....

....

SPEECH CAN BE WISE OR FOOLISH. WHICH ONE CHARACTERIZES YOUR SPEECH?

Watch the way you talk. Let nothing foul or dirty come out of your mouth. Say only what helps, each word a gift. Don't grieve God. Don't break his heart. Make a clean break with all profane talk.
EPHESIANS 4:29-30A; 31 MSG

Heavenly Father, over my lifetime, as I have tried to communicate positively with others, I have discovered (without ever once consulting you, which I should have done at the start), that talking much and listening little is less helpful than talking little and listening much. In fact, my chatty habit has often been downright unhelpful along life's journey, to the point of wreaking havoc at times in my relationships. I am asking you now to tap me – no, thump me! – on the shoulder every time I give in to my habit of talk, talk, talking, all the while ignoring the needs of others to express themselves. Father God, as I pray to you for wisdom, stop my rush of self-serving words and replace them with your profound and giving Word. In the name of Jesus, I ask for insight into my own speech. Thank you for hearing my plea. I will hush now and listen for your instruction. Amen.

Set a guard, O Lord, over my mouth; keep watch over the door of my lips!
PSALM 141:3 ESV

NOTES & PRAYERS ....

....

....

....

WHICH IS YOUR DEFAULT RESPONSE TO LIFE'S DIFFICULT CHALLENGES, NATURAL PANIC OR SUPERNATURAL PEACE?

[Jesus] I'm leaving you well and whole, my parting gift to you. Peace.
I don't leave you the way you're used to being left –
feeling abandoned, bereft. So don't be upset. Don't be distraught.

JOHN 14:27 MSG

Lord Jesus, thank you for your comforting Spirit, who abides in me and shares his peace with me every moment of every day. I am grateful the peace you promised in your Word is literal peace embodied in your Spirit, not just a state of mind subject to the ebb and flow of human emotion. Self chases that brand of counterfeit peace in vain. Savior Jesus, I cannot generate or search out true peace on my own. The only true peace in my heart is the Holy Spirit, who is the very presence of your serene nature and my heavenly blessing. I have no peace in flesh, Lord, just in you. Accept my gratitude in your sacred name for your gift of divine peace. I am calm in you. Amen.

I (Jesus) have told you these things that in me you may have peace.
In this world you will have trouble. But take heart!
I have overcome the world.

JOHN 16:33 NIV

NOTES & PRAYERS ....

....

....

....

AS A BELIEVER, YOU RADIATE THE BRIGHT LIGHT OF JESUS, BLAZING FORTH WITH DIVINE RADIANCE FROM INSIDE YOUR HEART, WHEREIN DWELLS GOD'S SPIRIT OF HIS BELOVED SON.

It started when God said, "Light up the darkness!"
And our lives filled up with light as we saw and understood
God in the face of Christ, all bright and beautiful.

2 Corinthians 4:6 MSG

Savior Jesus, it has taken me too long to understand that your Holy Spirit, who entered my heart to dwell the moment God saved me, is Your Life and the Light of the Father. When I confessed my sin, repented, received forgiveness, turned from sin, and professed my faith in you, your Spirit and Light filled my heart, banishing evil's darkness. In your name, thank you, bright Savior. You are God's Son and Light of Life. Amen.

[Jesus] You're here to be light, bringing out the God-colors in the world.
God is not a secret to be kept. We're going public with this, as public as a
city on a hill. If I make you light bearers, you don't think I'm going to
hide you under a bucket, do you? I'm putting you on a light stand.
Now that I've put you there on a hilltop, on a light stand – shine!

Matthew 5:14b-15 MSG

NOTES & PRAYERS ....

....

....

....

JESUS – YOUR SAVIOR AND FULLY GOD – PRAYED FOR YOU TO THE FATHER. THANK HIM WITH PRAISE AND WORSHIP FOR LOVING YOU ENOUGH TO PRAY FOR YOU.

[Jesus' prayer for believers] I am praying now not only for these disciples, but also for all who will ever believe in me through their message. I pray that they will all be one, just as you and I are one – as you are in me, Father, and I am in you. And may they be in us so that the world will believe you sent me.

JOHN 17:20-21 NLT

Jesus, thank you for your prayer recorded in John's Gospel that you offered up for all believers under God's New Covenant. I am grateful your message of unity for your followers shines with the Light of God's love as brightly today as it did in New Testament times. You declare in your Word you want all who profess belief in you to stand in unity, not just to bless themselves, but to bless the lost by sharing your Gospel Truth. In your name, Jesus, use me to deliver your Good News of salvation to those around me. Draw them, Lord, to be in unity with you and all other believers. Amen.

[Excerpt from Jesus' prayer for believers] I am in them (believers) and you (God) are in me.

JOHN 17:23A NLT

NOTES & PRAYERS ....

....

....

....

WHEN YOU STOPPED LOOKING FOR EARTHLY MEANING IN SELF-REFLECTION, YOU FOUND HEAVENLY MEANING IN CHRIST-REFLECTION. DWELL ON THINGS OF JESUS, NOT SELF.

Summing it all up, friends, I'd say you'll do best by filling your minds and meditating on things true, noble, reputable, authentic, compelling, gracious – the best, not the worst; the beautiful, not the ugly; things to praise, not things to curse.

PHILIPPIANS 4:8 MSG

Thank you for reminding me, Lord Jesus, my all-about-me reflections have never come to anything but miseries. Not until I redirected my thinking toward you, rather than self, did I get my first glimpse of true joy – sparkling, shimmering, glimmering, gleaming, glowing, dazzling, radiating God-joy, Christ-joy, Spirit-joy! In your name, I lift up all devotion and gratitude as I focus my heart and mind on your goodness. Hallowed be your Godhead – Father, Son, and Holy Spirit. Amen.

[Paul] By no means do I count myself an expert in all of this, but I've got my eye on the goal, where God is beckoning us onward – to Jesus.

PHILIPPIANS 3:13B MSG

NOTES & PRAYERS ....

....

....

....

DO YOU BELIEVE JESUS WANTS TO BEAR YOUR CARES AND WOES? IF YOU DO, LAY THEM DOWN AT THE FOOT OF THE CROSS, ONCE AND FOR ALL.

[Jesus] Are you tired? Worn out? Burned out on religion? Come to me. Get away with me and you'll recover your life. I'll show you how to take a real rest. Walk with me and work with me – watch how I do it. Learn the unforced rhythms of grace. I won't lay anything heavy or ill-fitting on you. Keep company with me and you'll learn to live freely and lightly.

MATTHEW 11:28-30 MSG

You are my model, selfless Jesus. Your blood and resurrection delivered me from sin in two ways: You saved me from the awful fate of being separated from you eternally, and you relieve me every day of my burden of current sin and guilt by allowing me to confess new offenses, repent, change, and accept your grace of forgiveness. Generous Jesus, your ongoing mercy clarifies the meaning in *Matthew 11:30 ESV For my yoke is easy and my burden is light.* In your name, Savior, thank you for helping me with my cares and woes. Give me a tender heart on your behalf to help others with theirs. Amen.

Share each other's burdens, and in this way obey the law of Christ.

GALATIANS 6:2 NLT

NOTES & PRAYERS ....

....

....

....

WHICH DO YOU ENGAGE IN MORE, GRIEVING OR PLEASING THE HOLY SPIRIT? YOUR ANSWER LIES IN WHETHER YOUR PRIORITY IS GOD OR SELF.

And do not bring sorrow to God's Holy Spirit by the way you live.
Remember, he has identified you as his own,
guaranteeing that you will be saved on the day of redemption.
EPHESIANS 4:30 NLT

Father God, help me remember the Spirit is a distinct personality of your Holy Trinity who wants to manifest the character of Jesus through me. I am grateful to be regenerated by the Spirit – transformed into a new creature, saved, born again! Which means he now dwells in my heart as a permanent resident. What a marvel, the actual Spirit of the living God caring enough about my personal welfare to indwell me. In your name, Lord, and out of gratitude for all you have done for me, I pray for help in pleasing your Holy Spirit and never grieving him. Amen.

Focusing on the self is the opposite of focusing on God. Anyone completely
absorbed in self ignores God, ends up thinking more about self than God.
That person ignores who God is and what he is doing.
And God isn't pleased at being ignored.
ROMANS 8:7-8 MSG

NOTES & PRAYERS ....

....

....

....

GOD, THE GREAT CREATOR, MADE YOU IN HIS IMAGE. CLAIM YOUR BIRTHRIGHT BY LIVING CREATIVELY NOW AND FOR ETERNITY IN YOUR HEAVENLY FATHER. YOU BELONG TO HIM IN JESUS AND THE HOLY SPIRIT.

He (God) chose to give birth to us by giving us his true Word (Jesus).
And we, out of all creation, became his prized possession.

JAMES 1:18 NLT

Father, make me a good steward of your gift of life, both physical and Spiritual. As I read in Scripture about your creative process, I see and feel how much you enjoyed creating all things. And I cannot help but think you created men and women in your image with the intention of allowing us to enjoy creating, as well, albeit in our limited human capacity. For though you created everything out of nothing, we can create only by putting together in different ways the things you have already created. I know your Spirit and Jesus were also present at creation, and the three of you were not created, but always existed – Father, Son, and Holy Spirit. In Jesus name, thank you, Great Creator. Amen.

So God created human beings in his own image. In the image of God,
he created them; male and female he created them.

GENESIS 1:27 NLT

NOTES & PRAYERS ....

....

....

....

IS THE CHARACTER OF YOUR HEART THE AWESOMENESS OF JESUS OR THE AWFULNESS OF SELF?

Celebrate God all day, every day. I mean, revel in him! Make it as clear as you can to all you meet that you're on their side, working with them and not against them. Help them see that the Master (Jesus) is about to arrive. He could show up any minute!

PHILIPPIANS 4:4-5 MSG

Heavenly Father, it is shocking how brazen Satan and his evil minions are in today's world. Shocking, but not terrorizing. For I remain secure in your Word you are always sovereign, good, and in control. Whenever I feel unnerved by some event that makes evil appear to have the upper hand, I turn my attention back to your all-powerful name. Praise you, God, in your supremacy. You rule! You reign! Amen.

Stay away from every kind of evil.

1 THESSALONIANS 5:22 NLT

Do that, and God, who makes everything work together, will work you into his most excellent harmonies.

PHILIPPIANS 4:9 MSG

NOTES & PRAYERS ....
....
....
....

DO YOU BELIEVE YOU CAN ASK GOD TO PURIFY THE MOTIVES OF YOUR HEART? YES, YOU CAN. AND, YES, HE WILL. PRAY TO YOUR HEAVENLY FATHER IN YOUR NEED. HE WANTS YOUR HEART TO BE IMMACULATE IN JESUS.

The heart is hopelessly dark and deceitful, a puzzle no one can figure out. But I, God, search the heart and examine the mind. I get to the heart of the human. I get to the root of things.
JEREMIAH 17:9-10a MSG

Father, you know the selfish nature of my motives better than I do. Self's motives in my heart are like stinking weeds that choke off fragrant fruit. It is ridiculous how offended I become when I observe evidence of the same self-oriented motives in the hearts of others. I am aware of my dual thinking, yet I cannot curb it on my own. Help me turn my judgmental attitudes and questionable motives (so much heavy baggage) over to the Spirit. Forgive my selfishness as I pray in Jesus' name, your perfect example of a heart overflowing with pure motives. Cure me, Lord, of the sinful habit of judging others. Cleanse my heart, Father. Amen.

Create in me a clean heart, O God, and renew a right spirit within me.
PSALM 51:10 ESV

NOTES & PRAYERS ....

....

....

....

YOU CAN BE FEARLESS IN THE FACE OF DEATH, FOR YOUR SAVIOR, JESUS, CONQUERED SIN AND DEATH BY RISING AGAIN AFTER DYING ON THE CROSS.

For the Lord himself will descend from heaven with a cry of command, with the voice of an archangel, and with the sound of the trumpet of God. And the dead in Christ will rise first. Then we who are alive, who are left, will be caught up together with them in the clouds to meet the Lord in the air, and so we will always be with the Lord.

1 THESSALONIANS 4:16-17A ESV

Lord Jesus, thank you that on dying, I will enter your presence in spirit in paradise, and that later, when you return to earth, you will resurrect my physical body from the grave, glorify it, and bring me up to meet you in the air. But if I am still alive in my physical body when you come back, I know you will glorify my body then, in the twinkling of an eye, and fly me up to meet you in the clouds. I pray in your name with confidence, my Savior, as I watch and wait for your victorious return. Praise you, Jesus. Amen.

Then he (criminal on the cross beside Jesus) said, "Jesus, remember me when you come into your kingdom." Jesus answered him, "Truly I tell you, today you will be with me in paradise."

LUKE 23:42-43 NIV

NOTES & PRAYERS ....

....

....

....

BE THANKFUL AND HUMBLED THE HOLY SPIRIT DWELLS WITHIN YOU, FOR THE SPIRIT IS A DISTINCT INDIVIDUAL WHO IS FULLY GOD, JUST AS THE FATHER AND SON ARE FULLY GOD.

[Paul] In him (Jesus) you also, when you heard the word of truth, the gospel of your salvation, and believed in him, were sealed with the promised Holy Spirit, who is the guarantee of our inheritance until we acquire possession of it, to the praise of his glory.

EPHESIANS 1:13-14 ESV

Father God, thank you for your Holy Spirit who abides within me. In Jesus' divine name, I pray my gratitude. Amen.

After his baptism, as Jesus came up out of the water, the heavens were opened, and he saw the Spirit of God descending like a dove and settling on him. And a voice from heaven said, "This is my beloved Son, who brings me great joy."

MATTHEW 3:16-17 NLT

[Jesus] And I will ask the Father, and he will give you another Helper, to be with you forever, even the Spirit of truth, whom the world cannot receive, because it neither sees him nor knows him. You know him, for he dwells with you and will be in you.

JOHN 14:16-17 ESV

NOTES & PRAYERS ....

....

....

....

JESUS IS YOUR SOURCE OF DIVINE CERTITUDE, THE REASON YOU DO NOT SETTLE FOR HUMAN PLATITUDES.

Jesus said, "I am the road, also the truth, also the life. No one gets to the father apart from me. If you really knew me, you would know my father, as well. From now on, you do know him. You've even seen him (in me)!"

JOHN 14:6-7 MSG

Savior Jesus, you have shared – and continue to share – your Truth in Scripture. You taught me that God saved me by grace through your death on the cross and subsuquent resurrection. Though innocent of sin, you bore the punishment for my sins and clothed me in your purity. And then, as God's blameless Son and wholly God in your own right, you gave me the faith I needed to accept your Word as Truth, after which the Holy Spirit regenerated me into a new creature in you and began refining me toward your image. Now, in your holy name, I ask for opportunities to share your Truth with others. Thank you, Jesus, God's Son, for setting me free. Your Truth saved me. Amen.

Guide me in your truth and teach me, for you are God my Savior, and my hope is in you all day long.

PSALM 25:5 NIV

NOTES & PRAYERS ....

....

....

....

JESUS PLACED A PROFOUND REALIZATION IN YOUR HEART – CONFESSION, EVEN WHEN ACCOMPANIED BY A REQUEST FOR FORGIVENESS, IS EMPTY WITHOUT REPENTANCE AND CHANGED BEHAVIOR.

You will never succeed in life if you try to hide your sins.
Confess them and give them up; then God will show mercy to you.
PROVERBS 28:13 GNT

Father, help me break the habit of confessing the same sins over and over (besetting sins), then launching right back into them the moment Satan dangles temptation before me. In Jesus' name, thank you for your presence as you grow me in the recreated life of peace and joy you gave me at my salvation. I pray, Holy Spirit, convict me to repent of my evil ways. Jesus, change me, even as you forgive me. I submit to your divine authority. Amen.

There at the Jordan River those who came to confess their sins were
baptized (by John the Baptizer) into a changed life. When John realized
that a lot of Pharisees and Sadducees were showing up for a baptismal
experience because it was becoming the popular thing to do, he exploded:
"Brood of snakes! What do you think you're doing slithering down
here to the river? Do you think a little water on your snakeskins is going
to make any difference? It's your life that must change, not your skin!"
MATTHEW 3:6-10 MSG

NOTES & PRAYERS ....

....

....

....

YOU ARE SUSPICIOUS WHEN SOMEONE DECLARES, "I HAVE A CLEAR CONSCIENCE!" FOR YOU HAVE LEARNED IN GOD'S WORD NO ONE'S CONSCIENCE CAN EVER BE CLEAR, UNLESS JESUS WASHES IT WITH HIS RIGHTEOUS BLOOD AND RESURRECTION.

And since we have a great High Priest who rules over God's house, let us go right into the presence of God with sincere hearts fully trusting him. For our guilty consciences have been sprinkled with Christ's blood to make us clean, and our bodies have been washed with pure water.

HEBREWS 10:21-22 NLT

Father, I am grateful you revealed to me that aspiring to obey my conscience – no matter how hard I try – will never be enough to save my soul. Only your gifts of grace, forgiveness, and faith are enough to ransom me through the atoning sacrifice of your Son's death and resurrection. In his name, thank you, God, for redeeming me in your Son's divine superiority to my failed conscience. Praise Jesus, who cleansed me of sin with his pure blood. Amen.

Cling to your faith in Christ, and keep your conscience clear. For some people have deliberately violated their consciences; as a result, their faith has been shipwrecked.

1 TIMOTHY 1:19 NLT

NOTES & PRAYERS

FINISHING WELL IS IMPORTANT TO YOUR HEAVENLY FATHER. HIS DIVINE EXPECTATION IS FOR YOU TO FINISH YOUR ENTIRE LIFE WELL FOR JESUS' SAKE.

[Paul] I have fought the good fight. I have finished the race.
I have kept the faith.

2 TIMOTHY 4:7 ESV

[Jesus] His master said to him, "Well done, good and faithful servant."

MATTHEW 25:21A ESV

Jesus, you are the finest example of finishing well who has ever been and will ever be. When you said from the cross, "It is finished," and then gave up your Spirit to the Father, you finished your earthly ministry in the best way possible. God deemed you alone worthy to pay for the iniquity of us all. I pray in your name for forgiveness of my sins and the chance to start over each day with a clean heart. Thank you, Jesus, for stressing in Holy Scripture how important finishing well is to you. And thank you, also, for being the perfect model of quality in excellent completion. Help me finish well for you, Savior, as you finished well for me. Amen.

I press on toward the goal for the prize of the
upward call of God in Christ Jesus.

PHILIPPIANS 3:14 ESV

NOTES & PRAYERS ....

....

....

....

ARE YOU LIVING YOUR LIFE BASED ON GOD'S RELIABLE TRUTH, OR SELF'S UNRELIABLE FICTION?

[About God] The sum of your word is truth,
and every one of your righteous rules endures forever.
PSALM 119:160 ESV

Savior Jesus, I have come to a sobering conclusion about my diligent gauging of things I think will make me "feel good." It is hard to admit these things are usually rooted in serving self. And since self is deceitful about what will and will not bring joy, I often find myself deceived and joyless. Where, then, can I find the sum Truth about lasting joy in you? You do not have to tell me, Lord. I already know. Your sum Truth is available at all times in your Scriptural Word. Remind me to order my life around your Truth, Lord, instead of self's cruel deceptions. In your name, I pray to share your Truth with others. Amen.

What you say goes, God, and stays, as permanent as the heavens.
Your truth never goes out of fashion; it's as up-to-date as the earth when
the sun comes up. Your Word and truth are as dependable as ever.
PSALM 119:89-91 MSG

NOTES & PRAYERS ....

....

....

....

IS YOUR FAITH A SUCCESSFUL VOYAGE OR A DISASTROUS SHIPWRECK?

Cling to your faith in Christ, and keep your conscience clear.
For some people have deliberately violated their consciences;
as a result, their faith has been shipwrecked.

1 TIMOTHY 1:19 NLT

Oh, Lord Jesus, you are patient and merciful, even when my faith encounters storms. Convict my conscience to help me stop my sins from shipwrecking my faith. Direct me toward calm seas and the peace that follows righteousness. As life rages around me, guide me to still waters and safe havens belonging only to you. I have learned from your Word that following you leads to life and blessing, and following self leads to death and destruction. In the refuge of your divine name, Savior Jesus, I pray for grace of safe travel in your company eternally. Keep me from being shipwrecked by weak faith. Yes, hold me close in the power of strong faith, which I have learned is a gift from you just for the asking. I beg you now for invincible faith that only you can provide. Thank you, Jesus, for unshakable faith. Amen.

[Jesus] He replied, "You of little faith, why are you so afraid?" Then he got
up and rebuked the winds and the waves, and it was completely calm.

MATTHEW 8:26 NIV

NOTES & PRAYERS ....

....

....

....

YOU ARE BECOMING AN EXPERT ON GOD'S ECONOMY. CASE IN POINT: IF YOU DO NOT WANT GOD TO JUDGE YOU, THEN DO NOT JUDGE OTHERS.

[Jesus] "It's easy to see a smudge on your neighbor's face and be oblivious to the ugly sneer on your own. Do you have the nerve to say, 'Let me wash your face for you,' when your own face is distorted by contempt? It's this I-know-better-then-you mentality again, playing a holier-than-thou part instead of just living your own part. Wipe that ugly sneer off your face, and you might be fit to offer a washcloth to your neighbor."

LUKE 6:41-42 MSG

Jesus, who but you would have been wise enough to turn my bad habit of judging those around me into a mirror image of how I will be judged by you? In your Word, you made a hard teaching simple enough for even me to understand: I will be judged by the same measure that I judge. I do not know why it took me so long to accept the fact that judging others is more injurious to myself than those I judge. In your name, teach me to show mercy to others, just as you show mercy to me. Praise you, compassionate Jesus. Amen.

[Jesus] Do not judge, and you will not be judged. Do not condemn, and you will not be condemned. Forgive, and you will be forgiven.

LUKE 6:37 NIV

NOTES & PRAYERS ....

....

....

....

JESUS DIED ON THE CROSS AND ROSE AGAIN FOR SOMETHING, NOT NOTHING. AND THAT SOMETHING WAS YOUR UNDESERVED SALVATION.

I do not treat the grace of God as meaningless. For if keeping the law could make us right with God, then there was no need for Christ to die.

GALATIANS 2:21 NLT

Savior Jesus, why do I go back to the past and condemn myself for sins you have already forgiven? Satan gets into my ear, accusing and shaming me, reminding me of old guilt. Oh, God, help me stop cheapening your gifts of forgiveness, grace, and faith. You saved me, once and for all, at great cost to yourself. Never again do I have to be imprisoned for my transgressions, even as Satan tries to convince me otherwise. He is my enemy and a liar, the father of lies. He wants me to forget I am free in you. In your name, Jesus, I pray my guilt-free gratitude for your gift of salvation, blood-bought by you. Praise you, worthy Son of God. Amen.

[John the Revelator] And I heard a loud voice in heaven, saying, "Now the salvation and the power and the kingdom of our God and the authority of his Christ have come, for the accuser (Satan) of our brothers has been thrown down, who accuses them day and night before our God."

REVELATION 12:10 ESV

NOTES & PRAYERS ....

....

....

....

FEAR-OF-MISSING-OUT (FOMO) IS ONE MORE REASON TO ACCEPT GOD'S SON AS YOUR PERSONAL SAVIOR, FOR IF YOU REJECT JESUS, YOU WILL MISS OUT ON THE MOST VALUABLE GIFT YOU WILL EVER RECEIVE – SALVATION!

[Jesus] If you cling to your life, you will lose it;
but if you give up your life for my sake, you will find it.
MATTHEW 10:39 NLT

Savior Jesus, I sometimes catch myself wondering if giving my life to you might result in your requiring me to give up things I enjoy. I am embarrassed to admit these senseless episodes of Fear-Of-Missing-Out (FOMO) with which Satan afflicts me. Thank you, Lord, for showing me in Scripture that not giving my life to you would be the cause of my missing out on the most important good thing ever – You, Jesus! In your name, I am grateful for the abundant life you have given me in eternal salvation by your grace. Let me share your Good News with others, not waste time on self's greedy worries about missing out on things of the temporal world. I am not missing out, Lord. I have you! Amen.

And God is able to bless you abundantly, so that in all things at all times,
having all that you need, you will abound in every good work.
2 CORINTHIANS 9:8 NIV

NOTES & PRAYERS ....

....

....

....

September

SILENCE IS ONE OF GOD'S LOVELIEST LANGUAGES.

Silent prayer with your Heavenly Father often enhances communication. It is true God knows what you need even when you are silent, which is a given, though not the main point. The main point of being silent before God is to hear what your Heavenly Father wants from you, not what you want from him.

For God alone, O my soul, wait in silence, for my hope is from him.
PSALM 62:5 ESV

It is good that one should wait quietly for the salvation of the Lord.
LAMENTATIONS 3:26 ESV

Father, remind me to be silent before you. Stop my mindless chatter. Prompt me to listen to your voice, not my own. Bless me with your nearness as you move my heart toward quiet study and reverent worship. In Jesus' name, thank you, for revealing to me that unless I draw near to you and be silent, I will not be able to detect your soft whisper. I wait now in humble silence for you to speak. Amen.

The Lord is in his holy temple; let all the earth be silent before him.
HABAKKUK 2:20 NIV

NOTES & PRAYERS

GOOD WORK BELONGS TO GOD, NOT YOU. GIVE YOUR HANDS AND HEART OVER TO YOUR FATHER IN ALL YOU DO. THAT IS THE ONLY WAY WORK CAN BE GOOD. ASK YOURSELF – FOR WHOM AM I WORKING?

Be energetic in your life of salvation, reverent and sensitive before God. That energy is God's energy, an energy deep within you, God himself willing and working at what will give him the most pleasure.

PHILIPPIANS 2:12b-13 MSG

Father, you know me through and through. You know I work too much, too hard, and too long at the expense of rest and everything else. My constant search is for reasonable balance between work and repose. In Jesus' name, thank you for revealing to me work done for any other reason than your glory belongs to self and the devil. Help me course-correct my path. In Jesus' name, direct me to worthwhile work that glorifies you, not counterfeit busywork that glorifies self (also counterfeit). Give me rest in you, Lord. Heal me from self's trumped-up exhaustion from misdirected labor. I need your wisdom concerning work. Amen.

And whatever you do, whether in word or deed, do it all in the name of the Lord Jesus, giving thanks to God the Father through him.

COLOSSIANS 3:17 NIV

NOTES & PRAYERS ....

....

....

....

WHEN YOU HAVE BEEN FORGIVEN BY GOD, GUILT IS A THIEF OF TIME AND EMOTION.

You can let guilt ravage your energy by making you too miserable
to embrace abundant life in Jesus, or you can enjoy abundant
life in him by rejoicing in his deliverance from guilt.
Time wasted on guilt after your sins have been dealt with
by God in his Son through loving forgiveness and
salvation is time stolen from you by the devil.

Father, close my ears to Satan, who clamors to stand before
you, accusing me of sin. He tries to convince me I am still
guilty even after I have confessed, repented, changed my behavior, and been forgiven by you. Open my ears to Jesus,
my forgiver and Savior, who shed his blood and rose again
to cleanse me from sin and guilt. Now I just need a daily
foot washing as I confess to you and ask forgiveness for new
sins, if I repent and change my ways. In Jesus' name, I pray
all gratitude, for he is my Savior. By his love and mercy, he
delivered me from old and new sins, plus old and new guilt
and debilitating shame. Thank you, God, for freedom in
Jesus. He is my salvation. No more guilt! Amen.

[God] And I will forgive their wickedness,
and I will never again remember their sins.

HEBREWS 8:12 NLT

NOTES & PRAYERS ....

....

....

....

GIVE THANKS TO YOUR HEAVENLY FATHER FOR TURNING FORGIVENESS INTO HEALING BALM FOR THE FORGIVEN AND FORGIVER. IMITATE YOUR SAVIOR JESUS. FORGIVE!

It is easy to focus on the fact that people do not deserve your forgiveness, especially after they have done or said something hurtful to you or someone you love. It is harder to admit you yourself never deserved God's forgiveness. By grace, your Heavenly Father forgave you through Jesus, whose shed blood and resurrection on your behalf made him the model of a forgiving heart.

Be kind to one another, tenderhearted, forgiving one another,
as God in Christ forgave you.
EPHESIANS 4:32 ESV

Savior Jesus, each time I pray the Lord's Prayer, I am reminded of your expectation of me to forgive. *And forgive us our sins, as we forgive those who sin against us. Matthew 6:12 NLT.* Thank you for forgiving me through your loving grace to set a standard for how I am to forgive others. In your name, Jesus, help me forgive as you forgive – with God's grace of love and mercy, no matter how undeserved. Amen.

[Jesus] Forgive others, and you will be forgiven.
LUKE 6:37B NLT

NOTES & PRAYERS ....

....

....

....

LIVING HOPE IS A GIFT FROM YOUR HEAVENLY FATHER. WHAT A BLESSING GOD'S LIVING HOPE IN JESUS ASSURES YOU OF SALVATION IN HIM.

Praise be to the God and Father of our Lord Jesus Christ! In his great mercy he has given us new birth into a living hope through the resurrection of Jesus Christ from the dead, and into an inheritance that can never perish, spoil, or fade.

1 PETER 1:3 NIV

If you feel a need for hope, ask God in prayer. He will send you certain hope that everything he has ever told you is his Truth.

Father God, I pray all gratitude for your gift of living hope in your Son. And thank you for encouraging me to pray for more hope. Edward Mote wrote in his inspiring hymn: *My hope is built on nothing less than Jesus' blood and righteousness.* My hope is Jesus! Jesus is my hope! Almighty God, in the name of Messiah, thank you for salvation in him, who blesses my heart with his certain hope. Amen.

May the God of hope fill you with all joy and peace as you trust in him, so that you may overflow with hope by the power of the Holy Spirit.

ROMANS 15:13 NIV

NOTES & PRAYERS ....

....

....

....

LET DOWN YOUR FULL WEIGHT ON THE SECURITY YOU HAVE IN JESUS. HE IS THERE FOR YOU IN GOOD TIMES AND BAD. PRAY WITH PERSEVERANCE FOR HIS HELP. THEN ACCEPT IT IN JOY AND PEACE.

Rejoice in the Lord always; again, I will say, rejoice!
PHILIPPIANS 4:4 NASB

No matter what is happening in your life, rejoice, pray, and thank God, who gave you his beloved Son to assure your unfailing joy and peace in the Holy Spirit in all circumstances.

I am grateful, Father, for divine connections and counter-intuitive teachings in your Word; for example, rejoicing in Jesus increases his gift of peace whenever I face trials. It is such a blessing that no matter my difficulties, I can count on your promise: *Weeping may tarry for the night, but joy comes with the morning. Psalm 30:5b ESV.* In Jesus' name, thank you, God, for adversities. I rejoice in you with praise and worship. Amen.

Consider it all joy, my brethren, when you encounter various trials, knowing that the testing of your faith produces endurance. And let endurance have its perfect result.
JAMES 1:2-4A NASB

NOTES & PRAYERS ....

....

....

....

YOUR ABUNDANT NEW LIFE IN JESUS WILL ENDURE FOREVER, WHICH IS NOT JUST A HOPE, BUT A CERTAINTY.

*I (Jesus) am come that they might have life,
and that they might have it more abundantly.*
JOHN 10:10B KJV

Thank you, Father God, for giving me abundant, eternal life through Jesus' salvation. Remind me to share your Son's Good News Gospel with others. Spreading the Word of his Spirit-gift of regeneration to recreated life causes the blessing of new life to increase, person to person. Its healing multiplies Jesus' vibrant fresh life expansively and extravagantly, believer to believer. Let my grace-gift of new life in you, Jesus, overflow with your goodness to aid the Spirit in drawing others to God's salvation. In your name, Lord and Savior, thank you for everlasting life. Amen.

---

*He (God) brought us to life using the true Word (Jesus),
showing us off as the crown of all his creatures.*
JAMES 1:18 MSG

*For this is how God loved the world: He gave his one and only Son,
so that everyone who believes in him will not perish but have eternal life.*
JOHN 3:16 NLT

NOTES & PRAYERS

GLORY IS THE EXCLUSIVE REALM OF YOUR HEAVENLY FATHER, HIS BELOVED SON, AND THE HOLY SPIRIT.

Hallelujah! Salvation and glory and power belong to our God.

REVELATION 19:1B NIV

Mighty Jehovah, thank you for the privilege of glorifying you in the mysterious Three-In-One of your divine Trinity – Father, Son, and Spirit. In Jesus' name, I worship you in Spirit and Truth. Honor and glory are yours forever. Amen.

Who is this King of glory? The Lord strong and mighty, the Lord mighty in battle. Who is he, this King of glory? The Lord Almighty – he is the King of glory.

PSALM 24:8; 10 NIV

The Word [Jesus] became flesh and made his dwelling among us. We have seen his glory, the glory of the one and only Son, who came from the Father, full of grace and truth.

JOHN 1:14 NIV

There is one body (the church) and one Spirit, just as also you were called in one hope of your calling; one Lord (Jesus), one faith, one baptism, one God and Father of all, who is over all and through all and in all.

EPHESIANS 4:4-6 NASB

NOTES & PRAYERS ....

....

....

....

IF YOU TREAT OBEDIENCE TO GOD AS A PRIVILEGE, YOU WILL OPEN HIS FLOODGATE TO FAVOR AND BLESSINGS.

Only Jesus in the Spirit can empower you to obey God. He will help you heed the promptings of the Spirit to obey the Father.

We know we have come to know him (Jesus) if we obey his commands.
1 JOHN 2:3 NIV

Thank you, Jesus, for helping me understand Spiritual obedience and disobedience in terms of cause/effect. I have seen a pattern in my life: If I am obedient to your commands and precepts, things go smoothly, meaning I am able to cope, no matter my circumstances, easy or difficult. Conversely, if I am disobedient, things go poorly, meaning I lose my ability to cope at all. I do not like admitting how much trouble the disobedient nature of self has caused me in disastrous effects. Even Paul, the Apostle, shared in Scripture his personal experience with the tyranny of self's disobedience. In your name, Savior, I pray my gratitude Paul recognized you as his rescuer from disobedience. Please, Lord, rescue me. I need you in my weakness. Amen.

[Jesus] If you love me, you will keep my commandments.
JOHN 14:15 ESV

NOTES & PRAYERS ....

....

....

....

SALVATION IS GOD'S GRACE-GIFT TO YOU.

When you put your earthly problems into perspective,
they become small alongside God's great gift of eternal salvation.
Let today be the day you ask Jesus to carry the load of your earthly concerns, all the while expressing gratitude for his blessings
of forgiveness for your sins and deliverance from guilt,
plus the miraculous gift of eternal life in his presence.

Heavenly Father, I am grateful you drew me close and loved
me before I ever loved you. You planned for my salvation by
your grace, not my works, because you knew I would never have the strength of character to measure up, not without you covering me with your perfection. You gave me the
gift of redemption from my sins when I confessed, asked
forgiveness, repented, and changed my life through your
strength, not mine. I believed by your gift of faith that Jesus,
your Son, came to earth to save my soul and indwell my
heart by his Holy Spirit. In his generous name, I pray my
unending gratitude for salvation in him. Thank you. Amen.

Christ Jesus came into the world to save sinners – of whom I (Paul) am
the worst. But for that very reason I was shown mercy so that in me,
the worst of sinners, Christ Jesus might display his immense patience as
an example for those who would believe on him and receive eternal life.

1 TIMOTHY 1:15B-16 NIV

NOTES & PRAYERS ....

....

....

....

HOLY SCRIPTURE IS GOD'S COMPREHENSIVE NARRATIVE EXPLAINING JESUS, HIS BELOVED SON AND YOUR WORTHY SAVIOR.

From *Genesis* through *Revelation*, God's Word is Jesus,
and Jesus is God's Word – his saving Messiah.

[Jesus] You search the Scriptures, because you think they
give you eternal life. But the Scriptures point to me!

JOHN 5:39 NLT

Thank you, Heavenly Father, for imparting the Good News of Jesus from the beginning to the end of your *Bible*. In his name, I pray my gratitude that when I read your Word, I hear and see your Son – Jesus, my Savior! – on every Spirit-alive page. Thank you, Father, for Messiah Jesus and his message of salvation. Jesus is your Word. Glorify, praise, honor, and worship him. Amen.

Then Jesus said to them, "You foolish people! You find it so hard to believe
all that the prophets wrote in the Scriptures. Wasn't it clearly predicted
that the Messiah would have to suffer all these things before entering his
glory?" Then Jesus took them through the writings of Moses and all the
prophets, explaining from all the Scriptures the things concerning himself.

LUKE 24:25-27 NLT

NOTES & PRAYERS ....

....

....

....

CAN YOU ARTICULATE WHAT IT MEANS TO BE BORN AGAIN? IT IS IMPORTANT TO BE ABLE TO EXPLAIN IN PLAIN LANGUAGE GOD'S MIRACLE OF SPIRITUAL REBIRTH TO MAKE THE BLESSING OF IT CLEAR TO OTHERS,

Jesus replied, "I tell you the truth, unless you are born again, you cannot see the Kingdom of God." "What do you mean?" exclaimed Nicodemus. "How can an old man go back into his mother's womb and be born again?" Jesus replied, "I assure you, no one can enter the Kingdom of God without being born of water and the Spirit. Humans can reproduce only human life, but the Holy Spirit gives birth to Spiritual life. So don't be surprised when I say, 'You must be born again.'"

JOHN 3:3-6 NLT

Lord Jesus, I became alive in the flesh at physical conception and was born of my mother, yet I remained dead in sin. But when I came to the age of accountability, I accepted your Good News of salvation and became a new creature in you, regenerated and indwelt by the Spirit – born again! In your name, thank you, Savior, for Spiritual rebirth. Amen.

You, however, are not in the flesh but in the Spirit, if in fact the Spirit of God dwells in you. Anyone who does not have the Spirit of Christ does not belong to him.

ROMANS 8:9 ESV

NOTES & PRAYERS ....

....

....

....

BAPTISM IS THE OUTWARD AFFIRMATION OF YOUR INNER COMMITMENT TO JESUS.

Thank God for giving you baptism as a way of confirming your love and commitment to his Son. You belong to him.

Savior Jesus, ever my model for goodness, I am grateful you insisted on being baptized by John the Baptist, a special occasion at which all three personalities of God's Holy Trinity manifested – Father, Son and Spirit – making clear how much value my Heavenly Father places on baptism as a sign of love for him. I pray in your name, Savior, and with the Spirit's aid you will accept my baptism as a public demonstration of my commitment to you and the Father and Holy Spirit. Lord Jesus, let me imitate you with gratitude in every way you enable me, especially in baptism. Amen.

Then Jesus came from Galilee to the Jordan to John, to be baptized by him. John would have prevented him, saying, "I need to be baptized by you, and do you come to me?" But Jesus answered him, "Let it be so now, for thus it is fitting for us to fulfill all righteousness." Then he (John) consented. And when Jesus was baptized, immediately he went up from the water, and behold, the heavens were opened to him, and he saw the Spirit of God descending like a dove and coming to rest on him; and behold, a voice from heaven said, "This is my beloved son, with whom I am well pleased."
MATTHEW 3:13-17 ESV

NOTES & PRAYERS ....

....

....

....

AGAPE LOVE IS GOD'S DIVINE LOVE FOR YOU.

God's love is charitable. He loved you deeply enough to give his beloved Son to redeem you from sin, though you had nothing with which to pay him back. Agape love – God's brand of love – is the sacrificial, all-embracing love with which he cares for his children, including you. And he expects you, with his divine help, to care for him and others with that same extravagant love.

Dear friends, let us continue to love one another, for love comes from God. Anyone who loves is a child of God and knows God. But anyone who does not love does not know God, for God is love.

1 JOHN 4:7-8 NLT

Father God, thank you for agape love that you constantly rain down upon those whom the world would describe as unlovable – sinners, prisoners, the poor, disenfranchised, weak, mournful, sick, and dying, all of whom have nothing to give back except their own agape love for you. In my Savior Jesus' name, teach me to love others the way he loves me – unselfishly and faithfully. Amen.

God remembered us when we were down, His love never quits. Rescued us from the trampling boot, His love never quits. Takes care of everyone in time of need. His love never quits. Thank God, who did it all! His love never quits!

PSALM 136:23-26 MSG

NOTES & PRAYERS ....

....

....

....

WHEN COMPARED TO THE HUMBLE PERFECTION OF YOUR LORD JESUS CHRIST, SELF REVEALS ITS EGOTISTICAL GOAL – RIDICULOUS VAINGLORY.

Do nothing out of selfish ambition or vain conceit. Rather, in humility value others above yourselves, not looking to your own interests but each of you to the interests of others.

PHILIPPIANS 2:3-4 NIV

Lord Jesus, thank you for using the apostle, Paul, to teach me that boasting about anything except gratitude for the opportunity to be lowly before Jesus is empty clatter talk. Self is nothing but puffed-up air and will never be anything else. I pray in your name, Savior and Master, remind me to elevate and glorify my Heavenly Father, never self. Amen.

Think of yourselves the way Christ Jesus thought of himself. He had equal status with God but didn't think so much of himself that he had to cling to the advantages of that status no matter what. Not at all. When the time came, he set aside the privileges of deity and took on the status of a slave, became human! Having become human, he stayed human. It was an incredibly humbling process. He didn't claim special privileges. Instead, he lived a selfless, obedient life and then died a selfless, obedient death, and the worst kind of death at that – crucifixion.

PHILIPPIANS 2:5-8 MSG

NOTES & PRAYERS ....

....

....

....

JESUS IS THE FRAGRANT ESSENCE OF GOD'S PERFECTION.

Pour out the perfume of Jesus' name in your every word and deed, before everyone you meet, everywhere you go. He has given you the tools to act as his commissioned ambassador, which are his teachings and exemplary life revealed in Scripture. With the Holy Spirit as your guide, broadcast the Good News of Jesus, God's healing balm for the whole world – salvation!

How pleasing is your fragrance;
your name is like the spreading fragrance of scented oils.
Song of Solomon 1:3a NLT

Jesus, thank you for commissioning me as your ambassador. I have no strength, knowledge, wisdom, or courage, nothing of my own, yet you promised that your Spirit Word would reveal God's Truth to me, and the Spirit himelf would empower me to share the Good News of your saving grace. In your name, I pray to be your perfume of divine love, communicating news of your Gospel to everyone I meet. Let me be your fragrance, Lord. Let me be your messenger. Amen.

Walk in love, as Christ loved us and gave himself up for us,
a fragrant offering and sacrifice to God.
Ephesians 5:1b ESV

NOTES & PRAYERS ....

....

....

....

GOD'S GIFT TO YOU IN JESUS IS THE CONSTANT COMPANIONSHIP OF HIS SPIRIT. YOU CAN DEPEND ON THE HOLY SPIRIT TO BE YOUR FAITHFUL GUIDE, COMFORTER, COUNSELOR, AND PROVIDER OF WISDOM.

After Jesus died for sinners and rose again, the Spirit of God in Jesus – the Holy Spirit – came to earth to abide with believers. If, therefore, you are a believer, the Spirit of God in Jesus dwells in your heart. You can relax in the presence of your Heavenly Father, whose Spirit bears witness to your spirit that you are saved for eternity through Jesus, the Son.

Father God, thank you the Holy Spirit brings forth good fruit in my life I could never produce on my own – love, joy, peace, patience, kindness, goodness, faithfulness, gentleness, and self-control. I pray in Jesus' name as I yield to the guidance of the Spirit that he will use me to share his fruit with others – your own good fruit, Father, in your Son and my Savior, Messiah Jesus. Amen.

[Jesus] Abide in me, and I in you. As the branch cannot bear fruit of itself, except it abide in the vine; no more can ye, except ye abide in me. I am the vine, ye are the branches: He that abideth in me, and I in him, the same bringeth forth much fruit: for without me ye can do nothing.

JOHN 15:4-5 KJV

NOTES & PRAYERS ....

....

....

....

FOREVER IS YOUR HEAVENLY FATHER'S EVERLASTING TO EVERLASTING. PAST, PRESENT, AND FUTURE BELONG TO HIM.

God gave you eternity with him when he saved you from sin and death through Jesus. He can accomplish that, because time unto infinity is his to give. Praise him in his awesome power.

Before the mountains were born or you brought forth the whole world, from everlasting to everlasting, you are God.
PSALM 90:2 NIV

[Jesus about believers] I give them eternal life, and they shall never perish.
JOHN 10:27A NIV

Lord Jesus, help me remember, the constraints of time I feel so strongly are never yours, for you have no constraints. Give me faith to put aside worries I may run out of time before getting everything done. I claim your promise my future in you stretches into the farthest beyond. In your name, I pray all gratitude for your certain promise of eternal life in your presence. Thank you, High Priest Savior, for welcoming me into your everlasting Kingdom. All time is yours, for you are Sovereign of every dimension. Amen.

But because Jesus lives forever, he has a permanent priesthood.
HEBREWS 7:24-26 NIV

NOTES & PRAYERS ....

....

....

....

GOD'S DIVINE STRENGTH OVERCOMES YOUR HUMAN WEAKNESS. HE IS YOUR GENEROUS PORTION NOW AND FOREVER.

He gives strength to the weary and increases the power of the weak.
ISAIAH 40:29 NIV

Jesus, my Lord and Savior, you have assured me in your Word your strength never fails. Sometimes I fret I will not have enough energy to meet life's demands, but then I remember you are my loving Savior, source of all energy. When my strength runs out, you lift me up. When I falter, you catch me. When I grow weak, you support me. In your name, thank you for allowing me to rest in your power. It is a comforting blessing to know when I am weak in the natural, you are strong in the supernatural. I praise your name, Jesus, with humblest gratitude for reminding me to draw strength from you. Amen.

But he (God) said to me (Paul), "My grace is sufficient for you, for my power is made perfect in weakness." Therefore, I will boast all the more gladly about my weaknesses, so that Christ's power may rest on me. That is why, for Christ's sake, I delight in weaknesses, insults, hardships, persecutions, and difficulties. When I am weak, I am strong.
2 CORINTHIANS 12:9-10 NIV

NOTES & PRAYERS ....
....
....
....

YOUR FRIEND STATUS WITH JESUS, THAT HE ASSIGNED TO YOU THROUGH HIS MERCY, GRACE, FORGIVENESS, AND GIFT OF FAITH, IS GUARANTEED AND UNCHANGING. JESUS IS YOUR ULTIMATE FRIEND AND MIGHTY SAVIOR.

If you ask God's Son to be your model for being a friend,
your friendships with others will bloom with delightful vitality.
But if you let self take over as your model,
your friendships will wither and die.

*[Jesus] I no longer call you servants, because a servant does not know his
master's business. Instead, I have called you friends, for everything
I learned from my Father I have made known to you.*

JOHN 15:15 NIV

Lord Jesus, I aspire to be as good a friend to you and to those around me as you are to me, which is impossible in my human weakness. And yet, I still try, knowing if I manage to be a decent friend, it will not be me doing that good thing. It will be your Spirit working through me. In your name, I ask for opportunities to befriend others on your behalf. Amen.

Most of all, love each other as if your life depended on it.

1 PETER 4:8A MSG

NOTES & PRAYERS ....

....

....

....

WHEN JESUS SAVED YOU, HE SEALED YOU BY THE HOLY SPIRIT AS A CHILD OF GOD.

At the moment of your salvation by God's grace and gift of faith, he gave you the indwelling presence and comfort of the Holy Spirit, who is the down payment and foretaste of what your life will be like with God throughout eternity, beginning when Jesus returns to earth and transforms your decaying body into your immortal body.

Blessed assurance, Jesus is mine! Oh, what a foretaste of glory divine!
(Hymn lyrics by Fanny Crosby)

And he (Jesus) has also set his seal upon us, and has put his Spirit into our hearts as a pledge and foretaste of future blessing.
2 Corinthians 1:22 WEY

Thank you, God, in the name of Jesus, for the Holy Spirit's present preview into the fullness of your timeless Kingdom, sweet anticipation of praising and worshiping my Savior forever. Glorify the Father, Son, and Holy Spirit. Amen.

When you believed, you were marked in him with a seal, the promised Holy Spirit, who is a deposit guaranteeing our inheritance until the redemption of those who are God's possession – to the praise of his glory.
Ephesians 1:13b-14 NIV

NOTES & PRAYERS ....

....

....

....

YOUR DIVINE HOME-SWEET-HOME
IS YOUR DIVINE HOME-SWEET-SAVIOR.
JESUS WELCOMES YOU HOME IN HIM.

If you feel homesick for God's eternal Kingdom, call out to Jesus. His Spirit will invite you into the sanctuary of his wondrous love.

My people will live in peaceful dwelling places, in secure homes, in undisturbed places of rest.

ISAIAH 32:18 NIV

King Jesus, you and you alone are my longed-for homecoming, for I reside in the loving shelter of your righteous heart and sure salvation. Holy Spirit, thank you in Jesus' name for abiding with me now as a pledge of my future home in God's Holy City. I am coming home to you, Father. Look! I am on my way! Amen.

[John] Then I saw a new heaven and a new earth, for the first heaven and the first earth had passed away, and there was no longer any sea. I saw the Holy City, the new Jerusalem, coming down out of heaven from God, prepared as a bride beautifully dressed for her husband. And I heard a loud voice from the throne saying, "Look! God's dwelling place is now among the people, and he will dwell with them. They will be his people, and God himself will be with them and be their God.

REVELATION 21:1-3 NIV

NOTES & PRAYERS ....
....
....
....

YOUR HEAVENLY FATHER'S PEACEABLE KINGDOM IS YOUR FUTURE HOME WITH HIM.

In the fullness of time, you as a believer in Jesus will see God's Peaceable Kingdom replace all evil chaos that characterizes today's world. For Satan is already defeated in your Master's divine future with his saved children.

Loving Jesus, thank you for every assurance in your Word of the peaceful dwelling place my future holds with you. I look forward to living in your pristine Peaceable Kingdom, praising and worshiping you, everlasting to everlasting. In your name, I pray all gratitude for your gift of joyful anticipation of being welcomed home by you. Peace! Amen.

[God's Peaceable Kingdom] The wolf shall dwell with the lamb, and the leopard shall lie down with the young goat, and the calf and the lion and the fattened calf together; and a little child shall lead them. The cow and the bear shall graze; their young shall lie down together; and the lion shall eat straw like the ox. The nursing child shall play over the hole of the cobra, and the weaned child shall put his hand on the adder's den. They shall not hurt or destroy in all my holy mountain; for the earth shall be full of the knowledge of the Lord as the waters cover the sea. In that day the root of Jesse (Jesus), who shall stand as a signal for the peoples – of him shall the nations inquire, and his resting place shall be glorious.

ISAIAH 11:6-10 ESV

NOTES & PRAYERS ....

....

....

....

JESUS IS GOD'S FRAGRANT FLOWER OF SACRED TRUTH. HE IS THE DIVINE ROSE E'RE BLOOMING IN YOUR HEART. BREATHE IN HIS DIVINE SPIRIT TO EXPERIENCE GOD'S EXQUISITE PURITY, FOR JESUS' NAME IS THE PERFUMED ESSENCE OF YOUR HEAVENLY FATHER'S HOLY RIGHTEOUSNESS.

The wilderness and the solitary place shall be glad for them;
and the desert shall rejoice, and blossom as the rose.

ISAIAH 35:1 KJV

Father, your Word, Jesus, fills my life with the fragrance of Truth. When I first believed, you quickened the desert of my heart by your Spirit's power. It burst forth into newness of life. I no longer wander in a wilderness of separation from you – lost! In your name, thank you for saving me to thrive in your garden. I grow and bloom with vigor in you. Amen.

[Foreshadowing Jesus] I am a rose of Sharon, a lily of the valleys.

SONG OF SONGS 2:1 ESV

But because of his great love for us, God, who is rich in mercy,
made us alive with Christ even when we were dead in transgressions –
it is by grace you have been saved.

EPHESIANS 2:4-5 NIV

NOTES & PRAYERS ....
....
....
....

BY LOVING AND SEEKING YOU WITH GOD'S HOLY AGAPE LOVE, JESUS EMBUED YOU WITH HIS PERSONAL AND PERFECT VALUE. YOU BECAME HIS GREAT TREASURE.

You thought you were seeking God when he saved you in Jesus. Then you discovered it was God in Jesus seeking you all along.

For the Son of Man (Jesus) came to seek and to save the lost.
LUKE 19:10 NIV

[Jesus] Here I am! I stand at the door and knock.
If anyone hears my voice and opens the door,
I will come in and eat with that person, and they with me.
REVELATION 3:20 NIV

How lovely to discover in your Word, Savior, you sought and bought me. In your name, I pray my gratitude for your presence and gift of salvation. I love you for seeking and saving me and for your promise never to forsake me. Lead me now to share with others the Good News you are seeking them, too. Thank you, Jesus, for drawing lost ones who need you so desperately into your Kingdom, even me. I seek you, Lord, with a grateful heart. Amen.

You, God, are my God. Earnestly, I seek you.
PSALM 63:1A NIV

NOTES & PRAYERS ....

....

....

....

WHO IS GOD'S WORD? JESUS IS GOD'S WORD!

It was Jesus' office as God's perfect Word, his sacred Truth
and wholly God himself, that made him worthy
and able to save you. Glorify the Word!

In the beginning was the Word (Jesus),
and the Word was with God, and the Word was God.
JOHN 1:1 NIV

Lord Jesus, my Savior, I am grateful John, your cherished
disciple, recorded his eyewitness testimony of your identity
– *Messiah and fully God, beloved Son in the Trinity.* And to
assure me further, this same John, quoted another John –
John the Baptist – who cried out in the wilderness announc-
ing your arrival: *John 1:15b NLT "This is the one (Jesus) I was
talking about when I said, 'Someone is coming after me who
is far greater than I am, for he existed long before me.'"* Thank
you, Savior, God's Word, for coming to earth to testify to
your divine Light, so that all may believe in your mightiness
to save. In your name, Lord, thank you for being the Word.
I am so grateful to be saved in you. Amen.

The Word became flesh and made his dwelling among us.
We have seen his glory, the glory of the one and only Son,
who came from the Father, full of grace and truth.
JOHN 1:14 NIV

NOTES & PRAYERS ....

....

....

....

JESUS, GOD'S PERFECT LAMB, GAVE HIS LIFE BLOOD AND ROSE AGAIN TO SAVE YOUR SOUL.

But if we walk in the light, as he (God) is in the light, we have fellowship with one another, and the blood of Jesus, his Son, purifies us from all sin.
1 JOHN 1:7 NIV

[Jesus] For this is my blood of the New Testament, which is shed for many for the remission of sins.
MATTHEW 26:28 KJV

Heavenly Father, I go back often in memory to the great hymn we sang in my childhood church – *There is pow'r, pow'r, wonder working pow'r in the precious blood of the Lamb.* Thank you, Jesus, for letting your blood flow down the wood of that old rugged cross to save me from sin and death. Your sacrifice washed me clean, and your resurrection assured the world of your power to forgive sin and conquer death. You are God's Messiah. In your name, Lord, I pray my gratefulness you were willing to cover me with your purity, when I had no purity of my own. I am redeemed by your blood, Christ Jesus. Forgiven. Cleansed. Regenerated. Saved! Amen.

Without the shedding of blood, there is no forgiveness.
HEBREWS 9:22b NIV

NOTES & PRAYERS ....

....

....

....

DO YOU EVER GET CONFUSED AS YOU TRY TO FIND THE RIGHT THING TO DO? THEN STOP SEARCHING ON YOUR OWN AND LOOK TO GOD. YOU WILL NEVER FIND THE RIGHT THING WITHOUT HIS WISDOM.

Tune your ears to wisdom and concentrate on understanding. Cry out for insight and ask for understanding. Search for them as you would for silver; seek them like hidden treasures. Then you will understand what it means to fear the Lord, and you will gain knowledge of God. For the Lord grants wisdom! From his mouth come knowledge and understanding.

PROVERBS 2:2-6 NLT

Father, I cry out in prayer in the name of Jesus. Lead me to right things and help me do them by your wisdom. In Jesus' name, give me a pure heart and a discerning mind. Thank you, God, for helping me find your right things. Amen.

He (God) grants a treasure of common sense to the honest. He is a shield to those who walk with integrity. He guards the paths of the just and protects those who are faithful to him. Then you will understand what is right, just, and fair, and you will find the right way to go. For wisdom will enter your heart, and knowledge will fill you with joy.

PROVERBS 2:7-10 NLT

NOTES & PRAYERS ....

....

....

....

YOU ARE CALLED TO BE BEAUTIFUL IN WAYS GOD COUNTS AS BEAUTIFUL.

Charm can mislead and beauty soon fades. The woman to be admired and praised is the woman who lives in the fear-of-God. Give her everything she deserves! Festoon her life with praises!

PROVERBS 31:30-31 MSG

Thank you, Heavenly Father, that on the day you saved me through the purity of Jesus and in his name, you made my inner heart beautiful in your sight, if not in the world's sight. Give me the desire, God, to be obedient, so that I can shine Jesus' matchless beauty on others as commanded in *Philippians 2:14-16a NIV. Do everything without grumbling or arguing, so that you may become blameless and pure, "children of God without fault in a warped and crooked generation." Then you will shine among them like stars in the sky as you hold firmly to the word of life.* Amen.

But the Lord said to Samuel, "Do not look on his appearance or on the height of his stature, because I have rejected him. For the Lord sees not as man sees: man looks on the outward appearance, but the Lord looks on the heart."

1 SAMUEL 16:7 ESV

NOTES & PRAYERS

YOU WERE – AND STILL ARE – AN INTEGRAL PART OF YOUR HEAVENLY FATHER'S ETERNAL PLAN. PRAISE JESUS, WHO IS THE HEART OF GOD'S HOLY DESIGN.

Long before he (God) laid down earth's foundations, he had us in mind, had settled on us as the focus of his love, to be made whole and holy by his love. Long, long ago he decided to adopt us into his family through Jesus Christ. (What pleasure he took in planning this!) He wanted us to enter into the celebration of his lavish gift-giving by the hand of his beloved son.

EPHESIANS 1:4-6 MSG

I am grateful, Jesus, that no matter what troubles befall me in the present, you have overcome evil in your grand plan into eternity. I am grateful to be claimed and sealed by the Holy Spirit as a citizen of your infinite Kingdom. In your name, Savior, I pray all gratitude you made me a part of your awesome creation. Thank you for including me. Amen.

He (God) thought of everything, provided for everything we could possibly need, letting us in on the plans he took such delight in making. He set it all out before us in Christ, a long-range plan in which everything would be brought together and summed up in him, everything in deepest heaven, everything on planet earth.

EPHESIANS 1:8-10 MSG

NOTES & PRAYERS ....

....

....

....

October

MAKE NO MISTAKE, SATAN AND HIS MINIONS ARE CONTINUALLY SEEKING OPPORTUNITIES TO ATTACK BELIEVERS (INCLUDING YOU).

For we do not wrestle against flesh and blood, but against the rulers, against the authorities, against the cosmic powers over this present darkness, against the spiritual forces of evil in the heavenly places.

EPHESIANS 6:12 ESV

Jesus, Son of God, my Lord and Savior, if Satan brazenly attacked you with temptations for forty days in the wilderness after you were baptized, what will he do to me? And not just Satan, but also his dreadful minions. If I were not living in victory through you, Lord, I would be fearful of satanic attacks. But with you as my protector, Satan can wage war on me and get nothing but defeat for all his efforts. In your name, Jesus, I pray for skill in the use of your sacred armor to resist evil attacks. Thank you for protecting me. Amen.

Stand therefore, having fastened on the belt of truth, and having put on the breastplate of righteousness, and, as shoes for your feet, having put on the readiness given by the gospel of peace. In all circumstances take up the shield of faith, with which you can extinguish all the flaming darts of the evil one; and take the helmet of salvation, and the sword of the Spirit, which is the Word of God, praying at all times in the Spirit.

EPHESIANS 6:14-18A ESV

NOTES & PRAYERS ....
....
....
....

IS IT POSSIBLE FOR CLIQUES TO DEVELOP WITHIN YOUR CHURCH? OR WORSE, CAN A WHOLE CHURCH BECOME A CLIQUE THAT JUDGES UNSCRIPTURALLY WHO WILL AND WILL NOT FIT IN?

When Jesus was eating supper at Matthew's house (Jesus' disciple and former tax collector) with his followers, disreputable characters came and joined them. When the Pharisees saw him keeping this kind of company, they had a fit, and lit into Jesus' followers. "What kind of example is this from your Teacher, acting cozy with crooks and riffraff?"
Jesus, overhearing, shot back, "Who needs a doctor: the healthy or the sick? Think on what this Scripture means: 'I'm after mercy, not religion.' I'm here for outsiders, not to coddle insiders."

MATTHEW 9:10-13 MSG

Lord Jesus, I understand that your purpose in cultivating close relationships with your disciples was to train them in God's loving outreach, which is inclusive, not exclusive. In your name, I pray for sharper focus on your mission – shining your Light (YOU!) on one and all in need of salvation, always including, not excluding, in the same way you included me, the neediest lost sheep of your flock. Amen.

But if you favor some people over others, you are committing a sin.

JAMES 2:9A NLT

NOTES & PRAYERS ....

....

....

....

JESUS, A MAN OF SORROWS HIMSELF, HAS EMPATHY FOR YOU IN SEASONS OF SADNESS. HE WILL HELP YOU THROUGH. JUST ASK HIM.

When life is heavy and hard to take, go off by yourself. Enter the silence. Bow in prayer. Don't ask questions. Wait for hope to appear. Don't run from trouble. Take it full-face. The "worst" is never the worst. Why? Because the Master won't ever walk out and fail to return.

LAMENTATIONS 3:28-31 MSG

Oh, Lord Jesus, it seems sadness in my life can last such a long time. It often leaves me with nothing except my comitment-to-commitment, a phrase that sounds odd even to my own ears, though I know you understand. I have decided, no matter how easy or hard the challenges I encounter, I will remain committed to the faith you have given me. And when I find myself weeping and mourning in human despair, I will take comfort in going back to my decision to accept you as my divine Savior, the most important commitment to which I cling. In your name, help me remain committed, Lord, no matter my situation or feelings. Thank you for your love and compassion. Praise you, Jesus. Amen.

The Lord is close to the broken-hearted; he rescues those whose spirits are crushed.

PSALM 34:18 NLT

NOTES & PRAYERS

DO YOU HEAR GOD CALLING YOU TO REMAIN SET APART IN YOUR CHRISTIAN WALK? ARE YOU WILLING TO ACCEPT HIS CALL?

You have been set apart as holy to the Lord your God, and he has chosen you from all the nations of the earth to be his own special treasure.
DEUTERONOMY 14:2 NLT

Take your everyday, ordinary life – your sleeping, eating, going-to-work, and walking around life – and place it before God as an offering. Embracing what God does for you is the best thing you can do for him. Don't become so well-adjusted to your culture that you fit into it without even thinking. Instead, fix your attention on God. You'll be changed from the inside out.
ROMANS 12:1B-2 MSG

Savior Jesus, left to my own devices, I would go down some wrong road every other minute (and still often do). In your divine name, I pray you will keep reminding me that my calling is to be like you, set apart, Christ-like. Amen.

Summing up: Be agreeable, be sympathetic, be loving, be compassionate, be humble. That goes for all of you, no exceptions. No retaliation. No sharp-tongued sarcasm. Instead, bless – that's your job, to bless. You'll be a blessing and also get a blessing.
1 PETER 3:8-12 MSG

NOTES & PRAYERS ....

....

....

....

WHICH KIND OF COMMITMENT DOES YOUR HEAVENLY FATHER EXPECT, INSINCERE RELIGIOSITY OR SINCERE RELATIONSHIP?

What can we bring to the Lord? Should we bring him burnt offerings?
Should we bow before God Most High with offerings of yearling calves?
Should we offer him thousands of rams and ten thousand rivers of olive
oil? Should we sacrifice our firstborn children to pay for our sins?
No, oh people, the Lord has told you what is good, and this is what
he requires of you: to do what is right, love mercy,
and walk humbly with your God.

MICAH 6:6-8 NLT

Holy God, I stand before you in humility and amazement that you love me and want me near you. I know you do. You blessed me with a personal relationship with you in the Holy Spirit through Jesus' salvation. In your Son's name, accept my gratitude for your Spirit closeness and for the blessing of personal prayer. Praise you, Father, Son, and Spirit in the Holy Trinity. I am glad to be one with you. Amen

---

The Spirit of God, who raised Jesus from the dead, lives in you.
And just as God raised Christ Jesus from the dead, he will give life to
your mortal bodies by this same Spirit living within you.

ROMANS 8:11 NLT

NOTES & PRAYERS ....

....

....

....

DO YOU EVER FEEL FLUTTERS OF RESENTMENT AGAINST GOD ABOUT THINGS YOU SUSPECT YOU ARE MISSING IN LIFE, OR WORSE, ABOUT SOME UNFAIR SITUATION YOU THINK GOD MAY BE CAUSING YOU TO ENDURE? IF SO, FIND COMFORT BY PRAYING THE WAY JESUS PRAYED IN THE GARDEN OF GETHSEMANE JUST HOURS BEFORE HE WAS CRUCIFIED. PRAY IN FAITH AND UTTER SUBMISSION.

[Jesus] Father, if you are willing, take this cup from me;
yet not my will, but yours be done.
LUKE 22:42 NIV

Father, I ask you to expose Satan's deceitfulness every time he attacks my mind with hateful suggestions you do not want the best for me. It is perverse the way he implies you are the one with cruel intentions, even as he and his minions attack me at every turn. In Jesus' name, I pray for wisdom to embrace your Truth and reject Satan's lies. You are my loving protector, Father. Thank you! Praise you! Amen.

And we know that God causes everything to work together for the good
of those who love God and are called according to his purpose for them.
ROMANS 8:28 NLT

NOTES & PRAYERS ....
....
....
....

JOB'S TRUST IN GOD'S GOODNESS IS A SHINING EXAMPLE OF STEADFAST FAITH. YOUR HEAVENLY FATHER IS WILLING AND ABLE TO HEAL YOU IN TIMES OF TROUBLE. YOU CAN HOPE IN HIM WITH CONFIDENCE, KNOWING JESUS AND THE HOLY SPIRIT EMPOWER YOUR HOPE BY GOD'S LOVE.

[Job, speaking about God] Though he slay me, yet will I hope in him.
JOB 13:15A NIV

Father, I pray for faith in you as fully formed as Job's faith. Satan took everything from Job – children, wealth, home, and health – yet he remained faithful. Job never knew why he was suffering. He just endured and trusted in your judgment concerning his circumstances. Bless me, Jesus, with unshakable faith and hope like Job's. Let me find solace in you when I cannot see beyond trials. Remind me, if I remain in you, your Light is on the other side of my difficulties, even within my difficulties. I pray in your name, rock of salvation, steadfast hope, faithful deliverer, object of my faith. I trust in you, Savior. You are my lively hope. Amen.

God blessed Job's later life even more than his earlier life.
JOB 42:12A MSG

NOTES & PRAYERS ....

....

....

....

IF YOU ARE NOT AFFLUENT, BE HAPPY. AFFLUENCE CAN FOOL YOU INTO THINKING YOU ARE SELF-SUFFICIENT AND DO NOT NEED GOD. OR, JUST AS SAD, AFFLUENCE CAN MAKE YOU LAZY IN YOUR CHRISTIAN WALK. CONVERSELY, IF YOU ARE AFFLUENT, DO NOT LIVE IN FEAR THAT AFFLUENCE WILL MAKE IT IMPOSSIBLE FOR YOU TO HEED GOD'S WORD AND REMAIN FAITHFUL, FOR ALL THINGS ARE POSSIBLE WITH GOD.

*As for the rich in this present age, charge them not to be haughty,
nor to set their hopes on the uncertainty of riches, but on God, who richly
provides us with everything to enjoy. They are to do good, to be rich
in good works, to be generous and ready to share, thus storing up
treasure for themselves as a good foundation for the future,
so that they may take hold of that which is truly life.*

1 TIMOTHY 6:17-19 ESV

Jesus, help me remember, just as you are faithful to meet my needs, I am responsible to meet others' needs. In your name, thank you for your faithfulness. Make me faithful in you. Amen.

[Jesus] When someone has been given much, much will be required.

LUKE 12:48B NLT

NOTES & PRAYERS ....

....

....

....

JESUS, WHOLLY GOD HIMSELF, HOLDS THE KEYS TO HEAVEN AND HELL. GIVE THANKS THAT WHEN HE SAVED YOU, HE SET ABOUT PREPARING A PLACE FOR YOU IN HIS KINGDOM AND MADE HIMSELF THE DIVINE KEY TO YOUR HEAVENLY HOME.

What he opens no one can shut, and what he shuts no one can open.
REVELATION 3:7B NIV

Thank you, Jesus, your Gospel-Good-News holds the key to your shining power as fully God. You have the authority to open the door of heaven to sinners like me, even as you lock evil behind the gates of hell. In your name, thank you, Jesus. You are God's key. Amen.

Simon Peter said, "You're the Christ, the Messiah, the Son of the living God." Jesus came back, "God bless you, Simon, son of Jonah! You didn't get that answer out of books or from teachers. My Father in heaven, God himself, let you in on this secret of who I really am (Son of God). And now I'm going to tell you who you are, really are. You are Peter, a rock. This is the rock on which I will put together my church, a church so expansive with energy that not even the gates of hell will be able to keep it out. And that's not all. You will have complete and free access to God's kingdom, keys to open any and every door."
MATTHEW 16:16-19A MSG

NOTES & PRAYERS ....

....

....

....

WHAT ARE YOUR THOUGHTS ON GOING TOO CASUAL BEFORE MIGHTY GOD?

Therefore, let us be grateful for receiving a Kingdom that cannot be shaken, and thus let us offer to God acceptable worship, with reverence and awe, for our God is a consuming fire.

HEBREWS 12:28-29 ESV

Father, thank you with all honor and respect for the blessing of personal prayer directly with you, made possible by the death and resurrection of Jesus. I am grateful his restoration and abiding Holy Spirit, who prays for me and with me continually as he comforts me. Savior Jesus, help me remember all you sacrificed to give me nearness to God. I stand in awe of your divinity as I surrender my entire being to you in humble gratitude. You are deserving of reverent worship, for you are God, just as the Father and Holy Spirit are God. I praise you, Savior, with a humble heart. In your name, let me worship your Holy Trinity in quiet reverence – Father, Son, and Holy Spirit. Hear my prayer. Amen.

During the days of Jesus' life on earth, he offered up prayers and petitions with fervent cries and tears to the one who could save him from death, and he was heard because of his reverent submission.

HEBREWS 5:7 NIV

NOTES & PRAYERS ....

....

....

....

MERRIAM-WEBSTER DICTIONARY'S THIRD OFFICIAL DEFINITION OF FEAR READS: "TO HAVE A REVERENTIAL AWE OF GOD; PROFOUND REVERENCE AND AWE, ESPECIALLY TOWARD GOD." FOR YOUR LIFE TO BE GREATLY BLESSED, CLAIM WEBSTER'S FORMAL DEFINITION OF FEAR AS YOUR LIVING/WORKING/ AMAZING/PERSONAL DEFINITION; THAT IS, PROFOUND REVERENCE FOR MIGHTY GOD.

Let all the earth fear the Lord;
let all the inhabitants of the world stand in awe of him!
PSALM 33:8 ESV

Heavenly Father, now that I know your divine definition of fear, let me live in your presence forever in utter fear. In your name, thank you for fulfilling every promise in Scripture reserved for those who fear you by giving them wisdom, rescue, mercy, blessings, and more. I fear you, God. Amen.

The fear of the Lord is the beginning of wisdom,
and knowledge of the Holy One is understanding.
PROVERBS 9:10 NIV

NOTES & PRAYERS ....
....
....
....

OFFER GRATITUDE TO JESUS FOR CLEANSING YOU OF SIN AND SAVING YOUR SOUL. LOVE HIM. WORSHIP HIM. PRAISE HIM. HE IS YOUR SALVATION!

Jesus said to him (Peter), "The one who has bathed does not need to wash, except for his feet, but is completely clean, and you are clean."
JOHN 13:10 ESV

Lord Jesus, you always model what you expect of me. During your last supper with your disciples, in the upper room, you took on the role of servant and washed their feet to remind them to stay clean from sin. I often picture in my mind what you must have looked like, moving around that room in humility and servitude, washing the feet of each man. Thank you for washing my feet, loving Savior, whenever I need forgiveness. I pray in your name for opportunities to do the same for others on your behalf. Bless me with your forgiving heart that emanates the perfumed fragrance of your mercy. Praise you, Son of God. Amen.

Now that I (Jesus), your Lord and teacher, have washed your feet, you also should wash one another's feet. I have set for you an example that you should do as I have done for you.
JOHN 13:14-15 NIV

NOTES & PRAYERS ....
....
....
....

DO YOU PRAISE GOD WHEN HE SAYS NO TO A PRAYER REQUEST, EVEN ONE YOU HAVE CONVINCED YOURSELF IS A WORTHY APPEAL?

[David] It was my desire to build a temple where the ark of the Lord's covenant, God's footstool, could rest permanently. I made the necessary preparations for building it, but God said to me, You must not build a temple to honor my name. You are a warrior and have shed much blood.
1 Chronicles 28:2b-3 NLT

[David] He (God) said to me, Your son Solomon will build my temple.
1 Chronicles 28:6b NLT

Father God, I pray in Jesus' name to be like King David. He wanted to build your temple, yet you said no. And though David was disappointed, he responded by praising and worshiping you with a genuine heart. Help me glorify you as David did, no matter your plan for my life. I trust you, even when you answer prayers differently than my human desires. Accept my grateful praise, Omnipotent God. Amen.

David praised the Lord in the presence of the whole assembly, saying, "Praise be to you, Lord, the God of our father Israel from everlasting to everlasting."
1 Chronicles 29:10 NIV

NOTES & PRAYERS ....

....

....

....

SCHADENFREUDE IS THE GERMAN TERM FOR FEELING GLAD ABOUT THE MISFORTUNE OF SOMEONE YOU THINK DESERVES IT. SCHADENFREUDE IS NOT CHRIST-LIKE. IT IS SATAN-LIKE.

[Jesus] This is what God does. He gives his best – the sun to warm and the rain to nourish – to everyone, regardless: the good and bad, the nice and nasty. If all you do is love the lovable, do you expect a bonus? Anybody can do that. If you simply say hello to those who greet you, do you expect a medal? Any run-of-the-mill sinner does that. In a word, what I'm saying is, grow up. You're Kingdom subjects. Now live like it.
MATTHEW 5:45B-47 MSG

Jesus, help me overcome my immature tendency to enjoy seeing someone experience bad circumstances, even if they appear to deserve it. Teach me to be like you, Savior, which is to respond to someone's destructive behavior with energies of prayer. If I can do that with your help, I will have no time for schadenfreude. In your name, remind me to reject schadenfreude. Merciful Jesus, let me be like you, compassionate toward those around me who are facing difficulties. Use me to comfort them in their need. Amen.

Live generously and graciously toward others, as God lives toward you.
MATTHEW 5:48B MSG

NOTES & PRAYERS

EVEN THOUGH YOU ARE SAVED, DO YOU SOMETIMES FIND YOURSELF WANDERING BACK INTO THE ARID WILDERNESS OF SIN? THEN, STOP. GO BACK TO WHERE YOU BELONG. BY HIS GRACE OF SALVATION, GOD CALLED YOU OUT OF SIN'S WASTELAND TO ABIDE FOREVER IN JESUS' MERCY GARDEN.

The Lord will guide you continually, giving you water when you are dry and restoring your strength. You will be like a well-watered garden, like an ever-flowing spring.

Isaiah 58:11-12 NLT

Savior Jesus, I did not know the Wilderness of Sin was the actual geographical place through which the Israelites wandered during their forty-year sojourn in the desert. Some scholars theorize the word Sin in this instance does not mean sinfulness, but is the name of an idol, Sin (Moon), worshiped by local unbelievers. Scholars may be correct about the idol's name, but to me, sin is still detestable sin. In your name, thank you for the garden of merciful salvation you planted for me. Praise you, forgiving Savior. Amen.

The Lord is my shepherd; I shall not want. He maketh me to lie down in green pastures: He leadeth me beside still waters. He restoreth my soul.

Psalm 23:1-3a KJV

NOTES & PRAYERS ....

....

....

....

IF YOU SENSE THE DEVIL IS BULLYING YOU, TALK IT OVER WITH YOUR HEAVENLY FATHER. HE WILL PROTECT YOU BY HIS SON IN THE SPIRIT FROM THAT AGGRESSIVE DRAGON.

*But the Lord is faithful, and he will strengthen you
and protect you from the evil one.*

2 THESSALONIANS 3:3 NIV

Thank you, Jesus, Son of God, for strengthening my faith as I read the Word to renew my mind. In your name, I pray my gratitude for assurance by the Spirit in Scripture that you have conquered sin and death, and in the process, conquered Satan and his minions. Thank you, Savior, for delivering me from evil. I am no longer afraid. Amen.

---

*Submit yourselves, then, to God. Resist the devil,
and he will flee from you.*

JAMES 4:7 NIV

*Because God's children are human beings – made of flesh and blood –
the Son also became flesh and blood. For only as a human being could
he die, and only by dying could he break the power of the devil,
who had the power of death.*

HEBREWS 2:14 NLT

NOTES & PRAYERS ....

....

....

....

DO YOU EVER FEEL LIKE A SMOLDERING CANDLE THAT HAS LOST ITS FLAME? DO NOT LOSE HEART. JESUS GOES OUT OF HIS WAY TO SHINE HIS TENDER, LOVING, HEALING LIGHT ON YOU AT YOUR WEAKEST MOMENT.

[Isaiah's prophecy of Jesus' compassion for the weak] A bruised reed he will not break, and a smoldering wick he will not snuff out, till he has brought justice through to victory.

MATTHEW 12:20 NIV

[Isaiah] The people who sat in darkness have seen a great light (Jesus).

MATTHEW 4:16A NLT

Thank you, God, for your mercy toward me, your lowliest child. I pray in Jesus' name that through me, you will be merciful toward other weak ones who need restoration. You shared your divine radiance with me when I needed it most. Help me follow your example out of love and gratitude that you freshened and healed me by your Light. Use me, compassionate Savior, to shine your Light on others. Amen.

[Jesus] I am the light of the world. If you follow me, you won't have to walk in darkness, because you have the light that leads to life.

JOHN 8:12B NLT

NOTES & PRAYERS ....

....

....

....

HAVE YOU EVER FELT RESENTFUL WHEN SOMETHING GOOD HAPPENS TO ANOTHER? THAT FEELING, KNOWN AS GLUCKSCHMERZ, IS AN ATTACK BY THE DEVIL ON YOUR HEART AND MIND. PRAISE YOUR SAVIOR, JESUS, FOR HELPING YOU DEFEAT GLUCKSCHMERZ THROUGH THE SON'S SPIRIT POWER. BE GLAD IN HIM FOR THE GOOD FORTUNE OF OTHERS, NOT BITTER IN SELF.

For jealousy and selfishness are not God's kind of wisdom.
Such things are earthly, unspiritual, and demonic.
JAMES 3:15 NLT

Generous Jesus, thank you for pricking my heart with understanding that gluckschmerz is based in jealousy and covetousness. I recognize the sin of gluckschmerz, even as I feel it invade my being. Only you, Lord, can lift me out of that dark pit. I pray in your name you will rid my heart of gluckschmerz by replacing jealousy with your gladness about good things happening to others. Kind Savior, fill my heart with your unselfish joy in others' good fortune. Amen.

A relaxed attitude lengthens a man's life; jealousy rots it away.
PROVERBS 14:30 TLB

NOTES & PRAYERS ....

....

....

....

IF YOUR HEART FEELS FRAGMENTED, ASK JESUS TO SETTLE YOUR SOUL. HE WILL HEAL YOU BY BRINGING TO YOUR REMEMBRANCE HIS DIVINE UNITY. YOU ARE ONE IN HIM, ONE IN FATHER GOD, ONE IN THE HOLY SPIRIT, AND ONE IN OTHER BELIEVERS.

I (self) have been crucified with Christ and I no longer live, but Christ lives in me. The life I now live in the body, I live by faith in the Son of God, who loved me and gave himself for me.

GALATIANS 2:20 NIV

Thank you, Jesus, for your beautiful prayer for believers in John's Gospel. How reassuring it is you asked Father God to make us all one in you. I am grateful you rendered my heart whole again by your grace. In your name, Savior, I pray to remain one with you in the Holy Trinity and other believers, unified forever and always. Amen.

[Jesus] My prayer is not for them (disciples) alone. I pray also for those (us!) who will believe in me through their message, that all of them may be one, Father, just as you are in me and I am in you. May they also be in us so that the world may believe you have sent me.

JOHN 17:20-23 MSG

NOTES & PRAYERS ....

....

....

....

ITCHING EARS WANT TO HEAR WHOMEVER OR WHATEVER PLEASES THEM. WHAT DO YOUR EARS WANT TO HEAR – GOD'S DIVINE TRUTH OR SELF'S HUMAN LIES.

Dear friends, do not believe everyone who claims to speak by the Spirit. You must test them to see if the spirit they have comes from God. For there are many false prophets in the world. This is how we know if they have the Spirit of God: If a person claiming to be a prophet acknowledges that Jesus Christ came in a real body, that person has the Spirit of God.

1 JOHN 4:1-3A NLT

Father, thank you for Truth in your Word, and not just Truth of yourself, but Truth of Jesus and the Holy Spirit. In your name, Jesus, and with the aid of the Spirit, I pray for discernment among teachers and teachings, for I believe with absolute certainty your Truth is the only Truth. Amen.

For a time is coming when people will no longer listen to sound and wholesome teaching. They will follow their own desires and look for teachers who will tell them whatever their itching ears want to hear. They will reject the truth and chase after myths. But you should keep a clear mind in every situation.

2 TIMOTHY 4:3-5 NLT

NOTES & PRAYERS ....

....

....

....

YOUR STATUS AS A NEW CREATURE IN CHRIST, REGENERATED BY THE HOLY SPIRIT, IS YOUR NEW-NORMAL. PUT AWAY SELF'S DEAD EXISTENCE, YOUR OLD-NORMAL. ABIDE FOREVER IN YOUR LIFE-GIVING SAVIOR.

[Jesus] The seed that fell among thorns represents those who hear God's word, but all too quickly the message is crowded out by the worries of this life and the lure of wealth, so no fruit is produced.

MATTHEW 13:22 NLT

Jesus, renew my faith when the deadness of self, my old-normal, tugs at me. Remind me to be thankful for my regenerated life in you, my new-normal. I am now alive eternally in the Spirit of God's Messiah (You, Jesus!). In your name, let me live in everlasting gratitude you paid for my salvation with your blood and resurrection. Thank you, Worthy Savior. Your gift of life is my new-normal forever. Amen.

Since you have heard about Jesus and have learned the truth that comes from him, throw off your old sinful nature and your former way of life, which is corrupted by lust and deception. Instead, let the Spirit renew your thoughts and attitudes. Put on your new nature, created to be like God – truly righteous and holy.

EPHESIANS 4:21-24 NLT

NOTES & PRAYERS ....

....

....

....

JESUS CAME TO MINISTER TO THOSE RELEGATED TO THE SIDELINES OF SOCIETY; THEREFORE, BE THANKFUL TO BE AN INHABITANT OF SOCIETY'S OUTER EDGES.

Take a good look, friends, at who you were when you got called into this life. I don't see many of "the brightest and the best" among you, not many influential, not many from high-society families. Isn't it obvious that God deliberately chose men and women the culture overlooks and exploits and abuses, chose these nobodies to expose the hollow pretensions of the somebodies? That makes it quite clear that none of you can get by with blowing your own horn before God.

1 Corinthians 1:26-29 MSG

Savior Jesus, thank you for loving insignificant, lowly me. I am grateful for your assurance you want me with you forever, though I deserve nothing. In your name, Lord, teach me to love the unlovable, as you do. After all, you love unworthy me. Now it is my turn to love others. Amen.

When the Pharisees saw him (Jesus) keeping this kind of company (Matthew's disreputable acquaintances), they had a fit, and lit into Jesus' followers. What kind of example is this from your Teacher, acting cozy with crooks and riffraff? (Jesus responded to them.) I'm after mercy, not religion. I'm here to invite outsiders, not coddle insiders.

Matthew 9:10-12; 13b MSG

NOTES & PRAYERS ....

....

....

....

JESUS HAS NO NEED TO BE A STRIVING PERFECTIONIST, FOR HE IS ALREADY GOD'S PERFECT SON, WHOLLY GOD HIMSELF. PRAISE YOU, SAVIOR, GOD'S MESSIAH.

For in Christ lives all the fullness of God in a human body.
COLOSSIANS 2:9 NLT

For God made Christ, who never sinned, to be the offering for our sin, so that we could be made right with God through Christ.
2 CORINTHIANS 5:21 NLT

Jesus, in your sinlesss righteousness, you are the worthy Son of Mighty God. Thank you for covering me with your purity. In your faultness name, I pray my gratitude for new life in you, my eternal salvation. Meet me, Lord, when I come home to you in Gloryland. Praise you. Worship you. Amen.

While he lived on earth, anticipating death, Jesus cried out in pain and wept in sorrow as he offered up priestly prayers to God. Because he honored God, God answered him. Though he was God's Son, he learned trusting-obedience by what he suffered, just as we do. Then, having arrived at the full stature of his maturity and having been announced by God as high priest in the order of Melchizedek, he became the source of eternal salvation to all who believingly obey him.
HEBREWS 5:7-9 MSG

NOTES & PRAYERS ....

....

....

....

IF YOU ARE DRAWN TO DOWN-TO-EARTH TALK RATHER THAN FANCY RHETORIC, IT IS NO WONDER YOU LOVE JESUS. HE IS GENUINE – GOD'S SON, GOD'S TRUTH, GOD'S WORD, GOD'S CHRIST, QUINTESSENCE OF THE SPIRIT OF GOD, YOUR SAVIOR AND DELIVERER, AND WHOLLY GOD. HEED HIS PERFECTLY DEFINED MESSAGE OF SALVATION.

[Paul] Watch out for people who try to dazzle you with big words and intellectual double-talk. They want to drag you off into endless arguments that never amount to anything. They spread their ideas through the empty traditions of human beings and empty superstitions of spirit beings. But that's not the way of Christ. Everything of God gets expressed in him, so you can see and hear him clearly.

COLOSSIANS 2:8-10 MSG

Jesus, I am grateful for your plain-spoken Scriptural instruction as the divine standard against which all other instruction must be measured. In your name, thank you. Amen.

[Paul] You'll remember, friends, that when I first came to you to let you in on God's master stroke, I didn't try to impress you with polished speeches and the latest philosophy. I deliberately kept it plain and simple: first Jesus and who he is; then Jesus and what he did – Jesus crucified.

1 CORINTHIANS 2:1-2 MSG

NOTES & PRAYERS ....

....

....

....

IF YOU EVER FEEL BULLIED OR HELD HOSTAGE BY "RELIGIOUS" LEGALISTS OR TRADITIONALISTS, JUST STOP THEM. JESUS' GIFT TO YOU IS DIVINE FREEDOM, NOT HUMAN BONDAGE.

Don't tolerate people who try to run your life, ordering you to bow and scrape, insisting that you join their obsession with angels and that you seek out visions. They're a lot of hot air, that's all they are. They're completely out of touch with the Source of life, Christ, who puts us together in one piece, whose very breath and blood flow through us.

COLOSSIANS 2:18-19 MSG

Jesus, remind me to focus on your Truth when discussions arise (even arguments) among believers on practices and personal tastes concerning worship or individual ideas on theological questions, rather than the bedrock of our faith – You, Jesus! In your name, thank you for the amazing freedom you provide your church. We look to you alone, Master and Savior, in the Spirit of the Word for sound instruction. Praise God for his Truth. Amen.

So don't put up with anyone pressuring you in details of diet, worship services, or holy days. All those things are mere shadows cast before what was to come; the substance is Christ.

COLOSSIANS 2:16-17 MSG

NOTES & PRAYERS ....

....

....

....

BY THE DIVINE GIFT OF YOUR FAITH IN JESUS, GIVEN TO YOU BY YOUR HEAVENLY FATHER, YOU HAVE CHOSEN TO DWELL WITH GOD IN HIS PROMISED KINGFOM OF ETERNAL LIFE, INSTEAD OF WITH SATAN IN HIS WILDERNESS OF SIN, SUFFERING, MISERY, AND DEATH.

For all creation is waiting eagerly for that future day when God will reveal who his children really are. Against its will, all creation was subjected to God's curse. but with eager hope, creation looks forward to the day when it will join God's children in glorious freedom from death and decay.

ROMANS 8:19-21 NLT

I am grateful, God, you gave me the privilege of living with you eternally in your Promised Land. In Jesus' name, thank you for inviting me home. I accept your invitation. Amen.

[John the Revelator] Then I saw a new heaven and a new earth, for the first heaven and the first earth had passed away, and the sea was no more. And I saw the holy city, new Jerusalem, coming down out of heaven from God, prepared as a bride adorned for her husband. And I heard a loud voice from the throne saying, "Behold, the dwelling place of God is with man. He will dwell with them, and they will be his people, and God will be with them as their God."

REVELATION 21:1-3 ESV

NOTES & PRAYERS ....

....

....

....

AS PLANTS LEAN AND GROW TOWARD PHYSICAL LIGHT, YOU, AS A BELIEVER, LEAN AND GROW TOWARD GOD'S SPIRITUAL LIGHT. THANK YOU, JESUS, FOR SALVATION LIGHT.

When Jesus spoke again to the people, he said, "I am the light of the world. Whoever follows me will never walk in darkness, but will have the light of life."

JOHN 8:12 NIV

Thank you, Jesus, for drawing me as naturally as the sun draws plants. Without you, I would droop and wither, *But you, Lord, are a shield around me, my glory, the One who lifts my head high. Psalm 3:3 NIV.* In your name, Savior, I pray my thankfulness for your assurance to believers in *Matthew 5:14a ESV "You are the light of the world."* My Lord and Master, I am honored to receive your celestial Light and to glow with its mercy and grace. Thank you, Jesus, for the amazing privilege of shining your Light on others. You are the one-and-only radiant Jesus, God's Holy Light of the world. Make me a useful pinpoint of Light in service. Amen.

For God, who said, "Let light shine out of darkness," made his light shine in our hearts to give us the light of the knowledge of God's glory displayed in the face of Christ.

2 CORINTHIANS 4:6 NIV

NOTES & PRAYERS ....

....

....

....

DO YOU KNOW THE LOCATION OF YOUR HEAVENLY FATHER'S DWELLING PLACE? WHAT ABOUT JESUS, THE SON – WHERE DOES HE LIVE? AND THE HOLY SPIRIT – WHERE IS HE?

I am grateful, Mighty God, that in your Holy Trinity, you are local and everywhere at the same time. Thank you in the name of Jesus for your – and his! – loving presence and personal companionship of the Holy Spirit inside my heart. Father God, you are omnipresent throughout creation, and also in heaven with Jesus. Let me be your temple dwelling place here on earth in the Spirit. Amen.

Now the main point of what we are saying is this: We do have such a High Priest (Jesus), who sat down at the right hand of the throne of the Majesty (God, the Father) in heaven, and who serves in the sanctuary, the true tabernacle set up by the Lord, not by a mere human being.

HEBREWS 8:1-2 NIV

Do you (believers) not know that you are God's temple and that God's Spirit dwells in you?

1 CORINTHIANS 3:16 ESV

The Spirit of God, who raised Jesus from the dead, lives in you.

ROMANS 8:11A NLT

NOTES & PRAYERS ....

....

....

....

HAVE YOU CONSIDERED IT MIGHT BE POSSIBLE TO SPEAK OUT THE TRUTH OF THE GOSPEL WITH SO LITTLE GRACE IT MAY BE RECEIVED AS A JUDGMENTAL REPROACH? GRACE AND TRUTH COMPLEMENT EACH OTHER. SHARE JESUS' TRUTH GRACEFULLY IN THE LOVING WAY HE SHARED WITH YOU.

And the Word (Jesus) became flesh and dwelt among us, and we have seen his glory, glory as of the Son from the Father, full of grace and truth. (John the Baptist bore witness about him, and cried out, "This was he of whom I said, 'He who comes after me ranks before me, because he was before me.'") For from his fullness we have all received grace upon grace. The law was given through Moses; grace and truth came through Christ.

JOHN 1:14; 16-17 ESV

Father, give me your compassion for the lost. Help me live for Jesus in a way that lets others know he is Good News, not bad news. *For God did not send his Son into the world to condemn the world, but to save the world through him. John 3:17 NIV.* In your name, Jesus, thank you for grace and Truth uniquely You! Help me share your Truth with others gracefully with tender love, for you embody love. Amen.

God is sheer mercy and grace; not easily angered, he is rich in love.

PSALM 103:8 MSG

NOTES & PRAYERS ....

....

....

....

HAVE YOU EVER PONDERED YOUR HEAVENLY FATHER'S COMPASSION TOWARD LOST ONES, THOSE WHO DO NOT HAVE JESUS? IF SO, YOU HAVE A BETTER UNDERSTANDING OF HIS LOVING FEELINGS TOWARD YOU.

*But God showed his great love for us by sending Christ
to die for us while we were still sinners.*

ROMANS 5:8 NLT

Father, thank you for loving lost sinners with such devotion. When I think of your love for me – even when I was not returning your love – my heart overflows with gratitude. I do not know why it took me so long to understand that your expectation of me is to love others, especially the lost, in the same generous manner you love me. You did not save me to serve my self-centered purposes. You saved me to serve you – alongside the Holy Spirit – by sharing your Gospel of Good News with those around me. Prompt me to do your will, not just talk, talk, talk, while doing nothing. In Jesus' name, thank you for the Spirit's witness. Amen.

---

*[Jesus] Just so, I tell you, there will be more joy in heaven over
one sinner who repents than over ninety-nine
righteous persons who need no repentance.*

LUKE 15:7 ESV

NOTES & PRAYERS ....

....

....

....

IF YOU WOULD LIKE TO KNOW HOW DEEPLY YOUR HEAVENLY FATHER LOVES YOU, CONSIDER HOW JESUS EXPRESSED IT IN THE PARABLE OF THE PRODIGAL SON. THEN BE GLAD WHEN GOD LOVES ANOTHER SINNER AS MUCH AS HE LOVES YOU.

Father, in Jesus' name, give me your heart for believers who have strayed and then repented and changed, as well as for lost ones who have never believed. Let me rejoice with you and the angels when any sinner comes home to you. Amen.

[Jesus] "Now his older son was in the field, and as he came and drew near to the house, he heard music and dancing. And he called one of the servants and asked what these things meant. And he said to him, 'Your brother has come home, and your father has killed the fattened calf, because he has received him back safe and sound.' But he was angry and refused to go in. His father came out and entreated him, but he answered his father, 'Look, these many years I have served you, and I never disobeyed your command, yet you never gave me a young goat, that I might celebrate with my friends. But when this son of yours came, who has devoured your property with prostitutes, you killed the fattened calf for him!' And he said to him, 'Son, you are always with me, and all that is mine is yours. It was fitting to celebrate and be glad, for this your brother was dead, and is alive; he was lost, and is found.'"

LUKE 15:25-32 ESV

NOTES & PRAYERS ....

....

....

....

November

DO YOU ACCEPT LIFE AND ITS ROLLING SEASONS GRACEFULLY OR AWKWARDLY? TRY BEING GRACEFUL BY BEING GRATEFUL. THANK YOUR HEAVENLY FATHER FOR FAIR AND STORMY DAYS ALIKE. NEVER FORGET, GOD IS IN CONTROL OF EVERY DETAIL OF YOUR EXISTENCE.

[God] Behold, I have engraved you on the palms of my hands;
your walls are continually before me.

ISAIAH 49:16 ESV

Father, thank you in Jesus' name for whatever you have for me in life. Teach me to lean on you in my weakness during trials. Some seasons are so difficult I find myself wondering what good they are to your Kingdom. Help me during those hard times to choose submission and obedience, not idle questioning, for you alone know the good intentions and purposes in your decisions. You are my Maker whom I trust, Mighty Father. I pray with faith in the name of your Son, Jesus, fully God himself. Amen.

Your eyes saw my unformed substance; in your book were written,
every one, the days that were formed for me,
when yet there were none of them.

PSALM 139:16 ESV

NOTES & PRAYERS ....

....

....

....

TAKE COMFORT YOUR HEAVENLY FATHER IS GOD OF THE LIVING, NOT THE DEAD, INCLUDING ALL SOULS OF FAITHFUL ONES IN CHRIST WHO HAVE ALREADY PASSED FROM EARTH TO HEAVEN, AND ALSO THOSE STILL LIVING ON EARTH.

[Jesus] And as for the resurrection of the dead, have you not read what was said to you by God: "I am the God of Abraham, and the God of Isaac, and the God of Jacob." He is not God of the dead, but of the living.

MATTHEW 22:31-32 ESV

Father, thank you that when I and all other believers die, our souls will enter heaven, where we will see Jesus in his place of honor at your right hand. And though our physical bodies will continue in the grave until you resurrect them, our living souls will abide with you in paradise. In Jesus' name, thank you, God, for ordering our lives eternally. Amen.

But Stephen, full of the Holy Spirit, gazed steadily into heaven (as he was being stoned to death) and saw the glory of God, and he saw Jesus standing in the place of honor at God's right hand. And he told them, "Look, I see the heavens opened and the Son of Man (Jesus) standing in the place of honor at God's right hand!"

ACTS 7:55-56 NLT

NOTES & PRAYERS ....

....

....

....

VICTORY IN JESUS IS YOURS FOR ONE REASON: YOUR SAVIOR JESUS SHARED HIS DESERVED VICTORY WITH UNDESERVING YOU.

Jesus makes his victory over sin and death your victory.
Without him, you lose, but with him, you conquer.

"Where O death, is your victory? Where O death, is your sting?"
The sting of death is sin, and the power of sin is the law. But thanks be
to God! He gives us the victory through our Lord Jesus Christ.
1 CORINTHIANS 15:55-57 NIV

Jesus, I sing aloud in a glad voice E.M. Bartlett's powerful refrain: *O victory in Jesus, my Savior, forever. He sought me and bought me with His redeeming blood; He loved me ere I knew Him, and all my love is due Him. He plunged me to victory, beneath the cleansing flood.* Thank you, Savior, for securing my eternal future victoriously. Your triumph over evil is past tense – done, achieved, finished, completed. The victory is yours, Lord, yet you shared it with undeserving me. In your conquering name, thank you, Jesus, God's ultimate victor. Amen.

For everyone born of God overcomes the world. This is the victory
that has overcome the world, even our faith. Who is it that overcomes
the world? Only the one who believes that Jesus is the Son of God.
1 JOHN 5:4-5 NIV

NOTES & PRAYERS ....

....

....

....

BE GLAD IN THE KNOWLEDGE YOU CAN PRAY TO ALL THREE MEMBERS OF THE HOLY TRINITY – FATHER GOD, SON JESUS, AND THE HOLY SPIRIT. WHICH MEANS MIGHTY GOD, THE GREAT THREE-IN-ONE, IS AVAILABLE TO YOU FAITHFULLY.

Whatever you ask in my name (Jesus), this I will do that the Father may be glorified in the Son. If you ask me anything in my name, I will do it.
JOHN 14:14 ESV

Heavenly Father, thank you for encouraging me to pray without ceasing day and night. It is reassuring to know you allow me to call on you in your Holy Trinity. Which I do with love, gratitude, respect, and reverence for who you are – Mighty God! In Jesus' name and with the aid of the Spirit, I pray to you, loving Father, constantly and reverently. Amen.

And pray in the Spirit on all occasions with all kinds of prayers and requests. With this in mind, be alert and always keep on praying for all the Lord's people.
EPHESIANS 6:18 NIV

NOTES & PRAYERS ....

....

....

....

PASSIONATE FIRE FOR JESUS IS AN IMPORTANT GIFT FROM GOD. KEEP YOUR FLAME FOR YOUR SAVIOR BURNING BRIGHTLY THROUGH PRAYER, STUDY, SERVICE, SURRENDER, AND OBEDIENCE.

Don't burn out; keep yourselves fueled and aflame. Be alert servants of the Master, cheerfully expectant. Don't quit in hard times; pray all the harder. Help needy Christians; be inventive in hospitality. Bless your enemies; no cursing under your breath. Laugh with your happy friends when they're happy; share tears when they're down. Get along with each other; don't be stuck-up. Make friends with nobodies; don't be the great somebody.

ROMANS 12:11-16 MSG

Savior, you spent time plodding along a roadway with Cleopas and his companion not long after your crucifixion and resurrection, opening Scriptures for them concerning yourself. And now you spend time with me, plodding along the roadway of my life, opening Scriptures for me, as well. In your name, I pray you will keep my fire for service to you blazing with grateful obedience. Praise you, Jesus! Amen.

Didn't we (Cleopas and another believer) feel on fire as he (Jesus) conversed with us on the road, as he opened up the scriptures for us?

LUKE 24:32B MSG

NOTES & PRAYERS ....

....

....

....

OPEN GOD'S WORD – JESUS, THE WORD! – BY IMMERSING YOURSELVES IN SCRIPTURE AND PRAYER. HIS SPIRIT WILL SHINE GOD'S LIGHT INTO YOUR HEART.

By your words (God's words) I can see where I'm going;
they throw a beam of light on my dark path.
PSALM 119:105 MSG

This, in essence, is the message we heard from Christ and are passing
on to you: God is light, pure light; there's not a trace of darkness in him.
1 JOHN 1:5 MSG

Heavenly Father, thank you for using your Word (Jesus), plus your Word (Holy Scripture) to impart your Truth and Light to me through the power of the Spirit who dwells within me. In the name of your Son – Jesus! Truth! Light of the World! – I pray my gratitude for his divine radiance that he shines on me so graciously. Remind me, God, to share his Light with others as I keep myself grounded in his Good News Gospel through prayer and Scripture. Amen.

The unfolding of your words (God's words) gives light;
it imparts understanding to the simple.
PSALM 119:130 ESV

NOTES & PRAYERS ....

....

....

....

WOULD YOU LIKE TO LIVE IN GOD'S KINGDOM WITH NO SHARP EDGES INTERFERING WITH YOUR FIT? THEN ASK JESUS IN PRAYER TO MOLD YOUR IMPERFECT SHAPE INTO HIS PERFECT SHAPE.

You learned Christ! My assumption is that you have paid careful attention to him, been well instructed in the truth precisely as we have it in Jesus. Since, then, we do not have the excuse of ignorance, everything – and I mean everything – connected with that old way of life has to go. It's rotten through and through. Get rid of it! And then take on an entirely new way of life, a God-fashioned life, a life renewed from the inside and working itself into your conduct as God accurately reproduces his character in you.

EPHESIANS 4:20B-24 MSG

Savior Jesus, I am grateful for the Spirit's regeneration work in my heart. When you saved me, a common sinner, you transformed me into a shape that slipped with perfect ease through the narrow gate to your Kingdom. In your name, I beg you to continue molding me toward your righteous image, since I have no righteousness of my own. Amen.

I appeal to you, therefore, brothers, by the mercies of God, to present your bodies as a living sacrifice, holy and acceptable to God.

ROMANS 12:1A ESV

NOTES & PRAYERS ....

....

....

....

YOU ARE NOT GOD. YOU ARE DEPENDENT ON GOD. HE CREATED YOU TO NEED SLEEP, FOOD, EXERCISE, WORK, AND LOVING RELATIONSHIPS IN OBSERVERANCE OF SENSIBLE HABITS CONDUCIVE TO HEALTH AND STRENGTH, ALL TO SERVE HIM. SO THEN, LET YOURSELF BE NEEDY AND HUMAN, AND LET GOD BE UNNEEDY AND DIVINE. FOR YOU ARE NOT GOD. YOU ARE DEPENDENT ON GOD.

Trust God from the bottom of your heart; don't try to figure out everything on your own. Listen for God's voice in everything you do, everywhere you go; he's the one who will keep you on track.
PROVERBS 3:5-6 MSG

Father, you are in charge of my life. When I strive to control things, it is all for naught, for my dependence is on you, not self. In Jesus' name, I am grateful you made your Son my divine destiny, unearned and undeserved. Thank you, Father, Son, and Holy Spirit. I am overjoyed to be dependent on you in the splendor of your Holy Trinity Godhead. Amen.

It's useless to rise early and go to bed late and work your worried fingers to the bone. Don't you know he (God) enjoys giving rest to those he loves?
PSALM 127:2 MSG

NOTES & PRAYERS ....

....

....

....

GOD GAVE YOU A CHOICE BETWEEN JESUS OF COMPLETION OR SATAN OF DEPLETION. PRAISE YOUR HEAVENLY FATHER! YOU CHOSE COMPLETION IN JESUS.

Keep your eyes on Jesus, who both began and finished this race we're in. Study how he did it. Because he never lost sight of where he was headed – that exhilarating finish in and with God – he could put up with anything along the way: cross, shame, whatever. And now he's there, in the place of honor, right alongside God. When you find yourselves flagging in your faith, go over that story again, item by item, that long litany of hostility he plowed through. That will shoot adrenaline into your souls!
HEBREWS 12:2-3 MSG

Lord Jesus, I am grateful you have already defeated Satan's efforts to destroy your children. You have vanquished him in his quest to be worshiped. In your name, thank you that no matter what Satan and his minions do to deplete me, your Spirit is there to complete me. Praise you, Jesus, author and finisher of my faith. I am whole in you. Amen.

Jesus (from the cross), seeing that everything had been completed so that the Scripture record might also be complete, then said, "I'm thirsty." A jug of sour wine was standing by. Someone put a sponge soaked with the wine on a javelin and lifted it to his mouth. After he took the wine, Jesus said, "It's done...complete." Bowing his head, he offered up his spirit.
JOHN 19:28-30 MSG

NOTES & PRAYERS ....

....

....

....

GOD WANTS TO HAVE A REVITALIZING EFFECT ON YOUR LIFE. HOW BLESSED YOU ARE HE LOVES YOU ENOUGH TO RESTORE YOU BY HIS MERCY AND FORGIVENESS, IN ADDITION TO HEALING YOU WITH JESUS' GRACE-GIFTS OF FAITH AND SALVATION.

I want you to share your food with the hungry and to provide shelter for homeless, oppressed people. When you see someone naked, clothe him! Don't turn your back on your own flesh and blood! Then your light will shine like the sunrise; your restoration will quickly arrive.

ISAIAH 58:7-8A NET

Thank you, Jesus, for restoring me from death in sin to life in you. You have convicted me that I am to restore others and heal their hurts by the power of your Holy Spirit. Yet, I stumble in self's weakness as I try to serve. In your name, Lord, I pray you will draw others to your restoration through my witness in the Spirit, for alone I have no power or grace to restore anyone, not even myself. Amen.

It was God [personally present] in Christ, reconciling and restoring the world to favor with Himself, not counting up and holding against [men] their trespasses [but cancelling them], and committing to us the message of reconciliation (of the restoration to favor).

2 CORINTHIANS 5:19 AMPC

NOTES & PRAYERS ....

....

....

....

IF YOU ARE A BELIEVER IN JESUS, SHOUT HALLELUJAH! YOUR SAVIOR LOVED, FORGAVE, ADOPTED, SAVED, AND TRANSFORMED YOU. HE ALSO JUSTIFIED YOU AND IS NOW SANCTIFYING YOU UNTO HIMSELF. PRAISE HIM, GOD'S WORTHY MESSIAH.

For you are all children of God through faith in Christ Jesus.
GALATIANS 3:26 NLT

Savior Jesus, thank you for making it possible for me to be born again into the Kingdom of God through salvation provided by you, Son of God, and through regeneration by your Holy Spirit. When I professed my faith, you made me a legally adopted heir to salvation with eternal life in you as a citizen of your Kingdom. In your name, I pray my everlasting gratitude it pleased you to adopt me. Amen.

How blessed is God! And what a blessing he is! He's the Father of our Master, Jesus Christ, and takes us to the high places of blessing in him. Long before he laid down earth's foundations, he had us in mind, had settled on us as the focus of his love, to be made whole and holy by his love. Long, long ago he decided to adopt us into his family through Jesus Christ. (What pleasure he took in planning this!) He wanted us to enter into the celebration of his lavish gift-giving by the hand of his Son.
EPHESIANS 1:3-6 MSG

NOTES & PRAYERS ....

....

....

....

HOW OFTEN DO YOU RESORT TO SELF'S CRAFTINESS, INSTEAD OF GOD'S WISDOM, TO GET WHAT YOU NEED OR WANT?

He (God) thwarts the plans of the crafty. Their hands achieve no success.
JOB 5:12 NIV

Jesus, I admit it. Every time I try to outsmart someone, I end up outsmarting myself, and not in a good way. I blame my tendency toward duality and cunning on my worst enemy – self! – that same old sly sinful nature within me still trying to regain control of the new creature your salvation Spirit transformed me to be. Who is crafty? Satan is crafty. Who is wise? God is wise. Who is transparent? Jesus is transparent, which says all that needs saying about whom I should be emulating. Dear God, in the name of Jesus, I beg you to empty Satan's craftiness out of my heart and fill it to overflowing with Jesus' wisdom. Thank you, Father, for answering my prayer. I reject craftiness. Amen.

Don't be misled: No one makes a fool of God. What a person plants, he will harvest. The person who plants selfishness, ignoring the needs of others – ignoring God! – harvests weeds. All he'll have to show for his life is weeds! But the one who plants in response to God, letting God's Spirit do the growth work in him, harvests a crop of real life, eternal life.
GALATIANS 6:7-8 MSG

NOTES & PRAYERS ....

....

....

....

ARE YOU EVER GUILTY OF ASPIRING TO BE DISHONESTLY HOLIER-THAN-THOU BEFORE MAN, RATHER THAN HONESTLY HUMBLE-AND-SUBMISSIVE BEFORE GOD?

[Jesus] Be especially careful when you are trying to be good so that you don't make a performance out of it. It might be good theater, but the God who made you won't be applauding.

MATTHEW 6:1 MSG

Jesus, can believers be guilty of competing for who is more Spiritual, knowledgeable, wise, humble, loving, caring, giving, self-sacrificing, mission-minded, good, faithful, pure, wholesome, generous, gentle, kind, patient, joyful, tenderhearted, forgiving, and more? Help me, Savior. Make my question be, "How can I be more like Jesus?" Not, "Why can't people I am trying to serve be more like me?" In your name, Son of God, thank you for covering me with your virtue, for I can accomplish nothing pure without your worthiness. Only God is good, and you are God. Amen.

[Jesus] Beware of the scribes, who like to walk around in long robes, and love greetings in the marketplaces and the best seats in the synagogues and the places of honor at feasts, who devour widows' houses and for a pretense make long prayers. They will receive the greater condemnation.

LUKE 20:46-47 ESV

NOTES & PRAYERS ....

....

....

....

JESUS DIED FOR YOU ON THE CROSS. WILL YOU LIVE FOR HIM?

You'll remember, friends, that when I first came to you to let you in on God's master stroke, I didn't try to impress you with polished speeches and the latest philosophy. I deliberately kept it plain and simple: first Jesus and who he is; then Jesus and what he did – Jesus crucified.

1 CORINTHIANS 2:1-2 MSG

Lord, I am overwhelmed by your work on the cross. You were willing to sacrifice your life and rise again to empower God's Gospel Truth. For without the crucible of your crucifixion and resurrection – those deciding events establishing your worthiness to lead me, the unworthy, into the very throne room of God in personal prayer – there would be no salvation for sinners like me. In your name, Jesus, I pray my humblest gratitude for your love in salvation. Amen.

For Christ also suffered once for sins, the righteous for the unrighteous, to bring you to God. He was put to death in the body but made alive in the Spirit.

1 PETER 3:18 NIV

He personally carried our sins in his body on the cross so that we can be dead to sin and live for what is right. By his wounds you are healed.

1 PETER 2:24 NLT

NOTES & PRAYERS ....

....

....

....

QUESTION: WHY IS YOUR SAVIOR'S GOSPEL SUCH GOOD NEWS? ANSWER: HE, MESSIAH JESUS, SON OF GOD, CONQUERED AND CANCELLED ALL BAD NEWS OF SIN, DEATH, EVIL, SATAN, AND HELL.

What we believe is this: If we get included in Christ's sin-conquering death, we also get included in his life-saving resurrection. We know that when Jesus was raised from the dead, it was a signal of the end of death-as-the-end. Never again will death have the last word. When Jesus died, he took sin down with him, but alive he brings God down to us. From now on, think of it this way: Sin speaks a dead language that means nothing to you; God speaks your mother tongue, and you hang on every word. You are dead to sin and alive to God. That's what Jesus did.

ROMANS 6:8-11 MSG

My Savior Jesus, you overcame the lethal realities of sin, death, and hell, once and for all, by dying on the cross and rising again. In your triumphant name, I thank you for salvation. You in your worthiness loved, forgave, redeemed, saved, and changed me. I will remain your grateful servant forever. Praise you, Savior Deliverer. Amen.

Could it be any clearer? Our old way of life was nailed to the cross with Christ, a decisive end to that sin-miserable life.

ROMANS 6:6 MSG

NOTES & PRAYERS ....

....

....

....

IS YOUR LIFE AS A BELIEVER ORGANIC OR STATIC? WHICH KIND OF LIFE DOES JESUS WANT YOU TO LEAD?

*God wants us to grow up, to know the whole truth and tell it in love –
like Christ did in everything. We take our lead from Christ,
who is the source of everything we do. He keeps us in step with each other.
His very breath and blood flow through us, nourishing us so that
we will grow up healthy in God, robust in love.*

EPHESIANS 4:15-16 MSG

Lord Jesus, you have taught me in your Word – *He is not
the God of the dead, but of the living, for to him all are alive.
Luke 20:38 NIV.* And since I know living things are organic
– either growing or withering – my life needs to be organic,
as well, growing toward the likeness of you, not remaining
a still-shot of my salvation day. In your living name, Savior
Jesus, I ask you to grow me as your faithful follower who
produces lively fruit of your Spirit, flourishing divinely for
the benefit of others – love, joy, peace, patience, kindness,
goodness, faithfulness, gentleness, and self-control. Let me
be a branch off your one True Vine, Jesus, my Savior. Amen.

---

*But grow in the grace and knowledge of our Lord and Savior Jesus Christ.
To him be glory both now and forever! Amen.*

2 PETER 3:18 NIV

NOTES & PRAYERS ....
....
....
....

JESUS' BLOOD IS GOD'S MOST PRECIOUS PERFUME POURED OUT FOR YOU.

[Jesus] And he took a cup, and when he had given thanks, he gave it to them (disciples during the Lord's supper in the upper room), saying, "Drink of it, all of you, for this is my blood of the covenant, which is poured out for many for the forgiveness of sins."

MATTHEW 26:27-28 ESV

Father, I am grateful you replaced the repetitive Old Testament blood sacrifices of animals for the atonement of sin with the single New Testament blood sacrifice of Jesus. In the name of the Son, I pray to be cleansed by his blood and covered with the fragrance of his righteousness, even as I am unrighteous in my human weakness. Thank you, Jesus, that God reconciled himself to his beloved children through you, Worthy Savior. Amen.

But when the Messiah (Jesus) arrived, High Priest of the superior things of this new covenant, he bypassed the old tent (tabernacle) and its trappings in this created world and went straight into heaven's "tent" – the true Holy Place – once and for all. He also bypassed the sacrifices consisting of goat and calf blood, instead using his own blood as the price to set us free, once and for all.

HEBREWS 9:11-15 MSG

NOTES & PRAYERS ....

....

....

....

HAS ANYONE EVER TRIED TO MAKE YOU FEEL ASHAMED OF BEING A BELIEVER IN JESUS AS YOUR SAVIOR? IF SO, YOU ARE NOT ALONE. SATAN HAS BEEN SHAMING BELIEVERS FOR THEIR FAITH IN GOD SINCE ADAM AND EVE.

Anyone who believes in him (Jesus) will never be put to shame.
ROMANS 10:11B NIV

Father God, my problem of occasionally feeling embarrassed about being a believer is a miserable weakness of my impoverished heart. In Jesus' name, I ask you to deliver me from diluted faith, which is never diluted by you, but by self's ingratitude. Thank you for your grace of faithfulness and forbearance. You always forgive and restore me. I am grateful and glad to know you, God. I pray you will allow me to absorb enough of your character in Jesus to make you glad to know me. Amen.

For I am not ashamed of the gospel, because it is the power of God that brings salvation to everyone who believes: first to the Jew, then to the Gentile. For in the gospel the righteousness of God is revealed – a righteousness that is by faith from first to last, just as it is written: "The righteous will live by faith."
ROMANS 1:16-17 NIV

NOTES & PRAYERS ....

....

....

....

AS YOU PONDER JESUS CHRIST, YOU ARE PONDERING GOD'S GREATEST BLESSING, HIS ULTIMATE GIFT TO THE WORLD.

Receiving a gift is like getting a rare gemstone;
any way you look at it, you see beauty refracted.

PROVERBS 17:8 MSG

Now may our Lord Jesus Christ himself and God our Father, who loved
us and by his grace gave us eternal comfort and a wonderful hope,
comfort you and strengthen you in every good thing you do and say.

2 THESSALONIANS 2:16 NLT

Heavenly Father, I am grateful for every gift you have ever given me (too many to count), but I am most grateful for your grace-gift of Jesus, who, by his completed work on the cross and subsequent resurrection, provided me direct access to you though personal prayer and placed me in the constant presence of the Holy Spirit. In the name of Jesus, your Son, Source of salvation, thank you for your gift of my multi-faceted relationship with your Holy Trinity – Father, Son, and Holy Spirit. Praise! Honor! Worship! Amen.

For by grace you have been saved through faith. And this is not your own
doing; it is the gift of God, not a result of works, so that no one may boast.

EPHESIANS 2:8 ESV

NOTES & PRAYERS ....

....

....

....

GOD DOES NOT WANT YOU TO STOP AT RECEIVING HIS OUTPOURING OF UNDESERVED GRACE. HE WANTS YOU TO SHARE HIS GRACE WITH OTHERS.

He (God) has told you, O man, what is good; and what does the Lord require of you but to do justice, and to love kindness, and to walk humbly with your God?

MICAH 6:8 ESV

Thank you, Father, for not forsaking me, as I have struggled with extending to others the same forgiving grace you extended to me. I was overjoyed to accept your grace of forgiveness for my sins on the day you saved me, and also on the many occasions since my initial salvation that I have had to come to you in confession and repentance for new sins, knowing I deserved nothing in the way of forgiveness. Jesus, transform my hard human heart into your tender forgiving heart, grace-filled and loving. You forgave me mercifully. In your name, I pray for help in forgiving those around me just as mercifully. Savior, your grace is undeserved favor, which increases as it is shared. Let me share your grace of forgiveness. Amen.

Forgive others, and you will be forgiven.

LUKE 6:37B NLT

NOTES & PRAYERS ....

....

....

....

YES, GOD FORGAVE YOUR SINS AND SAVED YOUR SOUL BY HIS GIFTS OF GRACE, FORGIVENESS, AND FAITH, NOT BY YOUR WORKS. EVEN SO, WHY NOT MAKE AN EFFORT TO PLEASE GOD BY OBEYING HIM IN LOVING GRATITUDE? HE WILL BE FAITHFUL TO BLESS YOUR OBEDIENCE.

And this is love: that we walk in obedience to his (God's) commands.

2 JOHN 1:6A NIV

Father God, in Jesus' name, I am grateful for your Word that instructs me how to please you by obeying your precepts. And thank you for Jesus' life model of obedience. Holy Spirit, help me to be obedient by following my Savior's example. Let me choose submission. Let me choose obedience. Let me choose Christ! Amen.

Dear friends, do you think you'll get anywhere in this if you learn all the right words but never do anything? Does merely talking about faith indicate that a person really has it? For instance, you come upon an old friend dressed in rags and half-starved and say, "Good morning, friend! Be clothed in Christ! Be filled with the Holy Spirit!" And then walk off without providing so much as a coat or a cup of soup – where does that get you? It is obvious God-talk without God-acts is outrageous nonsense?

JAMES 2:14-17 MSG

NOTES & PRAYERS ....

....

....

....

IS YOUR CONSCIENCE A TASKMASTER WHO DECLARES YOU GUILTY AT EVERY TURN? IF SO, CONFESS EVERYTHING BEFORE GOD, REPENT, AND ASK HIS FORGIVENESS. FOR THE ONLY WAY TO RID YOURSELF OF THE MISERY OF A GUILTY CONSCIENCE IS TO CLEAR IT WITH CONFESSION, REPENTANCE, AND A CHANGED LIFE BEFORE MERCIFUL GOD.

If we confess our sins, he is faithful and just and will forgive us our sins and purify us from all unrighteousness.

1 JOHN 1:9 NIV

Thank you, God, in the name of Jesus, for clearing my conscience with forgiveness and declaring me not guilty. Amen.

Oh, what joy for those whose disobedience is forgiven, whose sin is put out of sight! Yes, what joy for those whose record the Lord has cleared of guilt, whose lives are lived in complete honesty! When I refused to confess my sin, my body wasted away, and I groaned all day long. Day and night your hand of discipline was heavy on me. My strength evaporated like water in the summer heat. Finally, I confessed all my sins to you and stopped trying to hide my guilt. I said to myself, "I will confess my rebellion to the Lord." And you forgave me! All my guilt is gone.

PSALM 32:1-5 NLT

NOTES & PRAYERS

IF YOU ALLOW JESUS TO BE YOUR TUNING FORK FOR LOVE, YOU WILL MAKE BEAUTIFUL, HARMONIC MUSIC WITH OTHER BELIEVERS IN YOUR INTERRELATED LIVES. OTHERWISE, YOU WILL BE NO MORE THAN A CLANGING CYMBAL, OUT OF TUNE WITH GOD.

How good and pleasant it is when God's people live together in unity!
PSALM 133:1 NIV

Lord Jesus, tune my life as a believer to your perfect A-note. I am counting on you to blot out the dissonance of self's sour chords as you play my heart in harmony with your Truth. You are not relative in pitch when it comes to righteousness, my Savior and Lord. You are perfect in righteous pitch – flawlessly, divinely, absolutely perfect. You are the exquisite keynote of God himself, the beloved Son, who always was and will always be the one Heavenly note to which all creation is tuned. In your name, Master, I pray everything I think, say, and do will be forever in tune with you. Amen.

Be filled with the Spirit, addressing one another in psalms and hymns and spiritual songs, singing and making melody to the Lord with your heart, giving thanks always and for everything to God the Father in the name of our Lord Jesus Christ.

EPHESIANS 5:18B-20A ESV

NOTES & PRAYERS

GOD'S HOLY SPIRIT SHARES HIS KNOWLEDGE WTIH YOU IN THE WORD CONCERNING REDEMPTION. HE TEACHES JESUS' SPILLED BLOOD AND RESURRECTION. HEED HIM!

In whom (Jesus) we have redemption through his blood,
even the remission of sins.

COLOSSIANS 1:14 KJV

Thank you, Father, for using the Old Testament system of sacrifice and shed blood of animals to foreshadow the sacrifice and shed blood of Jesus for the remission of sins. King David, by faith, participated in the Mosaic sacrifice system – the blood of animals for atonement – an imperfect system you perfected once and for all in the New Testament with the sacrifice, spilled blood, and resurrection of Jesus. In our Savior's name, thank you for redemption made possible by your one-and-only perfect Son, worthy to save. Amen.

But when the Messiah (Jesus) arrived, high priest of the superior things
of this new covenant, he bypassed the old tent (tabernacle) and its
trappings in this created world and went straight into heaven's
"tent" – the true Holy Place – once and for all. He also bypassed the
sacrifices consisting of goat and calf blood, instead using his
own blood as the price to set us free once and for all.

HEBREWS 9:11-15 MSG

NOTES & PRAYERS ....

....

....

....

IF YOU ACCEPT JESUS AS MESSIAH, BE ASSURED BY GOD'S PROMISE THAT SATAN WILL BE UNSUCCESSFUL AT PRONOUNCING YOU GUILTY OF SIN. FOR GOD, THROUGH JESUS' DEATH AND RESURRECTION, HAS PRONOUNCED YOU NOT GUILTY.

But now God has shown us a different way to heaven – not by "being good enough" and trying to keep his laws, but by a new way (though not new, really, for the Scriptures told about it long ago). Now God says he will accept and acquit us – declare us "not guilty" if we trust Jesus Christ to take away our sins. And we all can be saved in this same way, by coming to Christ, no matter who we are or what we have been like.

ROMANS 3:21-22 TLB

Thank you, Jesus, for exposing subtle lies of Satan. He is correct in alleging I am guilty of sin in self. But he leaves out the Truth that Jesus, through his own goodness, has rendered me not guilty before my Father God. In your name, Savior, thank you for freedom from guilt in salvation. Amen.

[John] Then I heard a loud voice in heaven say: "Now have come the salvation and the power and the kingdom of our God, and the authority of his Messiah (Jesus). For the accuser (Satan) of our brothers and sisters, who accuses them before our God day and night, has been hurled down.

REVELATION 12:10 NIV

NOTES & PRAYERS ....

....

....

....

IF YOU ARE KIND TO SOMEONE WHO DESERVES IT, THAT MAY BE OF YOU. BUT IF YOU ARE KIND TO SOMEONE WHO DOES NOT DESERVE IT, THAT IS GRACE-KINDNESS, WHICH IS OF JESUS WITHIN YOU.

If you love only those who love you, what reward is there for that?
Even corrupt tax collectors do that much. If you are kind only to your
friends, how are you different from anyone else? Even pagans do that.
But you are to be perfect, even as your Father in heaven is perfect.
MATTHEW 5:46-48 NLT

Father God, remind me that true acts of grace-kindness on my part reflect your Son's loving attitude in the Holy Spirit. Thank you, Jesus, for healing me by grace at my salvation. I pray in your name you will give me even more grace-kindness to share with others, knowing it is your grace, not my own, that I will be sharing. I am grateful. Amen.

[Jesus] You have heard the law that says, love your neighbor
and hate your enemy. But I say, love your enemies!
Pray for those who persecute you! In that way,
you will be acting as true children of your Father in heaven.
MATTHEW 5:43-45 NLT

NOTES & PRAYERS

IN GOD'S ECONOMY, YOU WILL FIND YOURSELF REFRESHED BY YOUR HEAVENLY FATHER WHEN YOU REFRESH OTHERS, AND BLESSED BY YOUR HEAVENLY FATHER WHEN YOU BLESS OTHERS.

The generous will prosper; those who refresh will themselves be refreshed.
PROVERBS 11:25 NLT

Thank you, God, in Jesus' name, for your divine economic principle of giving. You bless cheerful givers bounteously. Make me cheerful in giving on your behalf, Lord. Amen.

[Jesus] Give away your life; you'll find life given back, but not merely given back – given back with bonus and blessing.
Giving, not getting, is the way. Generosity begets generosity.
LUKE 6:38 MSG

[Jedus] Mus gii ta oda people. Den God esef gwine gii to oona. E gwine gii ya plenty, jes like wen people full op a basket wid sompin an dey mash um down. Dey shakum bout an pile um op til e ron oba de top of de basket. So if ya gii plenty, God gwine gii ya plenty. Ef ya ain gii plenty, God ain gwine gii ya plenty.
LUKE 6:38 GULLAH TRANSLATION, DE GOOD NYEWS BOUT JEDUS WA LUKE WRITE

NOTES & PRAYERS ....

....

....

....

JESUS' WORTHINESS AS YOUR SAVIOR OPENS THE ENTRANCE – FOR YOU! – TO GOD'S HOLY OF HOLIES IN PERSONAL PRAYER.

We have a great High Priest (Jesus) who rules over God's house. Let us go right into the presence of God with sincere hearts fully trusting him.
HEBREWS 10:21-22A NLT

Jesus, you are worthy High Priest of my salvation as I pray in your name to Holy God. I need no other Savior. Amen.

[Old Covenant] Only the high priest entered the inner room (Holy of Holies), once a year, and never without blood (of animals), which he offered for himself and the sins the people had committed in ignorance.
HEBREWS 9:7 NIV

[New Covenant] And Jesus cried out again with a loud voice and yielded up his spirit (from the cross). And behold, the curtain of the temple was torn in two, from top to bottom.
MATTHEW 27:50-51A ESV

[New Covenant] Dear brothers and sisters, we can boldly enter heaven's Most Holy Place because of the blood of Jesus. By his death, Jesus opened a new and life-giving way through the curtain in the Most Holy Place.
HEBREWS 10:19-20 NLT

NOTES & PRAYERS ....

....

....

....

GOD WILL BLESS YOUR WORK, PLAY, AND INTERESTS, EVEN YOUR HOBBIES, IF YOU PURSUE THEM TO HIS GLORY. PRAISE THE FATHER! PRAISE JESUS! PRAISE THE SPIRIT!

And whatever you do, whether in word or deed, do it all in the name of the Lord Jesus, giving thanks to God the Father through him.

COLOSSIANS 3:17 NIV

Father, your Word teaches that Jesus was not only our Savior, he knew how to work with his hands as a carpenter – a sinless carpenter. I am grateful carpentry, and every other constructive activity, are all acceptable in your sight if pursued to your glory. In the name of the divine carpenter from Nazareth – your Son – thank you, God, for the many wholesome activities you have provided believers to glorify you. Amen.

---

*Whether you eat or drink or whatever you do,
do it all for the glory of God.*

1 CORINTHIANS 10:31 NIV

Work willingly at whatever you do, as though you were working for the Lord rather than for people. Remember the Lord will give you an inheritance as your reward, and that the Master you are serving is Christ.

COLOSSIANS 3:23-24 NLT

NOTES & PRAYERS ....

....

....

....

SELF IS THE CORRUPT AND UNMERCIFUL JUDGE LURKING INSIDE YOU WHO LIKES TO PLAY AT BEING GOD BY POINTING OUT THE FAULTS OF OTHERS, VERBALLY AND/OR MENTALLY. NEXT TIME SELF JUDGES SOMEONE ELSE, WALK STRAIGHT TO A MIRROR AND HAVE SELF TAKE A LONG LOOK AT ITS OWN FAULT-RIDDLED REFLECTION.

[Jesus] Don't pick on people, jump on their failures, criticize their faults – unless, of course, you want the same treatment. That critical spirit has a way of boomeranging.

MATTHEW 7:1-2 MSG

Thank you, Jesus, for your grace and mercy in covering my faults with your righteousness, a blessing I do not deserve. Your willingness to purify me with your virtue convicts me I need to offer grace and mercy to others, even as they, also, are undeserving. In your name, Savior, grow me in your grace and forgiveness toward those around me, no matter how much my judgmental self resists. Amen.

Don't bad-mouth each other, friends. It's God's Word, his Message, his Royal Rule, that takes a beating in that kind of talk. You're supposed to be honoring the Message, not writing graffiti all over it.

JAMES 4:11 MSG

NOTES & PRAYERS

December

INVITE JESUS TO BE YOUR MOST ESTEEMED GUEST IN YOUR LIFE PRESENTLY AND ETERNALLY, NOT JUST AN AFTERTHOUGHT AT YOUR FUNERAL. THEN REJOICE ON RECEIVING HIS RSVP OF DELIGHTED ACCEPTANCE FOR EVERY MOMENT.

[Jesus] Behold, I stand at the door and knock. If anyone hears my voice and opens the door, I will come in to him and eat with him, and he with me. The one who conquers, I will grant him to sit with me on my throne, as I also conquered and sat down with my Father on his throne.

REVELATION 3:20 ESV

Lord Jesus, when I answered your knock at the door of my heart, you entered in Spirit with the full portion of grace and forgiveness you prepared for me before I was ever born. In your divine name, Jesus, thank you for seeking, finding, forgiving, saving, and transforming me. You are my beloved Savior. I am grateful for the blessing of new life in your presence now and forever. Amen.

My response is to get down on my knees before the Father, this magnificent Father who parcels out all heaven and earth. I ask him to strengthen you by his Spirit – not brute strength, but inner strength – that Jesus will live in you as you open the door and invite him in.

EPHESIANS 3:14-17 MSG

NOTES & PRAYERS ....

....

....

....

IF YOU LOOK TO GOD FOR HELP IN DETERMINING YOUR PURPOSE IN LIFE, EVEN THE SMALLEST DETAILS WILL WORK OUT BETTER. TO BE SUCCESSFUL IN GOD'S WAY, MAKE HIS PURPOSE YOUR PURPOSE.

He (God) has saved us and called us to a holy life – not because of anything we have done, but because of his own purpose and grace.

2 TIMOTHY 1:9 NIV

Thank you, God, for your Spirit of Truth. He is my indwelling Comforter, Friend, Guide, and Wise Counselor, who shows me my human purpose within the context of your divine purpose. In your name, Jesus, I pray you will close the door to self's shadowy plots and fling open the door to your bright plans for my eternal future. *The Lord is my shepherd; I shall not want. He maketh me to lie down in green pastures: he leadeth me beside the still waters. He restoreth my soul: he leadeth me in the paths of righteousness for his name's sake. Psalm 23:1-3 KJV.* Amen.

[Jesus] But when the Friend comes, the Spirit of Truth, he will take you by the hand and guide you into all the truth there is. He won't draw attention to himself, but will make sense out of what is about to happen and, indeed, out of all that I have done and said.

JOHN 16:13A MSG

NOTES & PRAYERS ....

....

....

....

IMMUTABLE, PERFECT, ETERNAL – HOLY GOD HAS NO NEED OF CHANGE OR IMPROVEMENT. YET, HE IS WILLING THROUGH HIS FAULTLESS SON TO CHANGE AND IMPROVE NEEDY YOU.

Since you have heard about Jesus and have learned the truth that comes from him, throw off your old sinful nature and your former way of life, which is corrupted by lust and deception.
Instead, let the Spirit renew your thoughts and attitudes.
Put on your new nature, created to be like God – truly righteous and holy.
EPHESIANS 4:21-24 NLT

In Jesus' unchangeable name, thank you, God, for changing me into a new creature acceptable to you. Praise! Amen.

Listen, I tell you a mystery: We will not all sleep, but we will all be changed – in a flash, in the twinkling of an eye, at the last trumpet. For the trumpet will sound, the dead will be raised imperishable, and we will all be changed. For the perishable must clothe itself with the imperishable, and the mortal with immortality. When the perishable has been clothed with the imperishable, and the mortal with immortality, then the saying that is written will come true: "Death has been swallowed in victory." The sting of death is sin, and the power of sin is the law. Thanks be to God! He gives us the victory through our Lord Jesus Christ.
1 CORINTHIANS 15:51-54; 56 NIV

NOTES & PRAYERS ....

....

....

....

YOUR SALVATION IN JESUS MEANS YOU WILL NO LONGER BE ESTRANGED FROM GOD, FOR HE RECONCILED HIMSELF TO YOU THROUGH THE DEATH AND RESURRECTION OF JESUS, HIS BELOVED SON.

For God was in Christ, reconciling the world to himself, no longer counting people's sins against them. And he gave us this wonderful message of reconciliation. So we are Christ's ambassadors; God is making his appeal through us. We speak for Christ when we plead, "Come back to God!" For God made Christ, who never sinned, to be the offering for our sin, so that we could be made right with God through Christ.

2 CORINTHIANS 5:19-21 NLT

Loving Father, I am grateful for your tender love, your compassionate reason for reconciling yourself to me through the blood of Jesus. In Jesus' name, thank you, Father, for divine reconciliation. Help me share with others your message of Truth and love that you want to reconcile with them, as well – through Jesus! Praise the Son. Amen.

And all of this is a gift from God, who brought us back to himself through Christ. And God has given us this task of reconciling people to him.

2 CORINTHIANS 5:18 NLT

NOTES & PRAYERS ....
....
....
....

CONFORMING TO GOD IN JESUS IS THE BRIGHT WAY. CONTORTING TO FLESH IN SELF IS THE DARK WAY. REJECT DARKNESS. GO BRIGHT. BURN BRILLIANTLY IN YOUR SAVIOR.

But the path of the righteous is like the light of dawn,
which shines brighter and brighter until full day. The way of the
wicked is like deep darkness; they do not know over what they stumble.
PROVERBS 4:18-19 ESV

Lord Jesus, thank you for calling and naming me as one of your people, a sheep of your pasture, a citizen of your Kingdom. In your name, I pray my life will shine brightly with your healing Light, for you are *the radiance of the glory of God and the exact imprint of his nature. Hebrews 1:3a ESV*. Amen.

It started when God said, "Light up the darkness!" and our lives filled up
with light as we saw and understood God in the face of Christ,
all bright and beautiful.
2 CORINTHIANS 4:6 MSG

Then the righteous will shine like the sun
in the kingdom of their Father.
MATTHEW 13:43 ESV

NOTES & PRAYERS ....
....
....
....

ARE YOU THANKFUL FOR GOD'S GIFT OF LAUGHTER? SHARE THE FAVOR WITH A GENEROUS HEART, FOR YOUR HEAVENLY FATHER'S BLESSING OF HEALTHY LAUGHTER IS A DIVINE TONIC FOR BODY AND SOUL.

A cheerful heart brings a smile to your face; a sad heart makes it hard to get through the day. A miserable heart means a miserable life; a cheerful heart fills the day with song.

PROVERBS 15:13; 15 MSG

He (God) will yet fill your mouth with laughter and your lips with shouts of joy.

JOB 8:21 NIV

Father, only you could have created the enjoyable wonder of laughter to code into your human creations. What a sweet indicator of how much you love us, for laughter as a response to good clean humor is a blessing that refreshes the soul and heals the body. In Jesus' name, thank you for innocent laughter that expresses my grateful joy in him. Amen.

Our mouths were filled with laughter, our tongues with songs of joy. Then it was said among the nations, "The Lord has done great things for them." The Lord has done great things for us, and we are filled with joy.

PSALM 126:2 NIV

NOTES & PRAYERS ....

....

....

....

WHOSE DIRECTION DO YOU SEEK DAILY, GOD'S OR SELF'S? AS YOU CHOOSE, DO NOT FORGET: GOD'S WAY LEADS TO WONDROUS SPIRITUAL PROMISES (THAT HE ALWAYS KEEPS), AND SELF'S WAY LEADS TO DEATH AND DESTRUCTION (A GRIM CERTAINTY).

*God's word warns us of danger and directs us
to hidden treasure. Otherwise, how will we find our way?*
PSALM 19:11B MSG

Your (God's) word is a lamp to guide my feet and a light for my path.
PSALM 119:105 NLT

Thank you, God, that prayer and your Word thwart self and lead me to you. I pray in Jesus' name for Spirit guidance toward your important Truth that if I seek and find your goodness, your goodness will seek and find me. *Surely goodness and mercy will follow me all the days of my life: and I will dwell in the house of the Lord forever. Psalm 23: KJV.* Thank you, Father, for keeping your loving promises of guidance, direction, goodness, and mercy, all for me. Amen.

---

*[Jesus] Whoever follows me will not walk in darkness,
but will have the light of life.*
JOHN 8:12B ESV

NOTES & PRAYERS ....

....

....

....

JESUS WANTS TO TRANSFORM YOUR FLAWED CHARACTER INTO HIS PERFECT CHARACTER. THE QUESTION IS: WHAT DO YOU WANT – CURSES OF FLAWED SELF, OR BLESSINGS OF FLAWLESS JESUS?

Since you have heard about Jesus and have learned the truth that comes from him, throw off your old sinful nature and your former way of life, which is corrupted by lust and deception. Instead, let the Spirit renew your thoughts and attitudes. Put on your new nature, created to be like God – truly righteous and holy.

EPHESIANS 4:21-24 NLT

Jesus, I pray in your name you will make good progress as the Spirit transforms imperfect self into your perfection. Out of gratitude for forgiveness and salvation, I pray you will turn my character into your character. Move your divine excellence to the forefront and my human worthlessness to the background. Let me be like you, Lord. Amen.

Therefore, since we are surrounded by such a huge crowd of witnesses to the life of faith, let us strip off every weight that slows us down, especially the sin that so easily trips us up. And let us run with endurance the race God has set before us. We do this by keeping our eyes on Jesus, the champion who initiates and perfects our faith.

HEBREWS 12:1-2A NLT

NOTES & PRAYERS ....

....

....

....

NOT LONG BEFORE JESUS ASCENDED TO HEAVEN, HE PROMISED BELIEVERS THE ABIDING PRESENCE OF THE HOLY SPIRIT. YOU ARE NEVER ALONE.

[Jesus] If you love me, show it by doing what I've told you. I will talk to the Father, and he'll provide you another friend so that you will always have someone with you. This friend is the Spirit of Truth. The godless world can't take him in because it doesn't have eyes to see him, doesn't know what to look for. But you know him already because he has been staying with you, and will even be in you! I will not leave you orphaned. I'm coming back.

JOHN 14:15-18 MSG

I am grateful to you, Jesus, for reminding me when I feel lonely, the Holy Spirit is my constant comfort, just as you promised. I am grateful you banished painful solitude from my life. Isolation flees from me. The Holy Spirit is my divine consolation. He never leaves, nor forsakes, nor fails me. I know him and rest in his comfort until your return, Jesus. Thank you for your Spirit's company while I wait. Amen.

[Jesus] The person who knows my commandments and keeps them, that's who loves me. And the person who loves me will be loved by my Father, and I will love him and make myself plain to him.

JOHN 14:21 MSG

NOTES & PRAYERS

DEBILITATING TIREDNESS COMES FROM TRYING TO DO EVERYTHING IN YOUR OWN STRENGTH, RATHER THAN ADMITTING YOUR NEED FOR GOD. PLACE YOUR WEARINESS AT THE FOOT OF THE CROSS, WHERE YOU WILL BE GIVEN AN OVERABUNDANCE OF ENERGY TO LIVE FOR JESUS.

It's useless to rise early and go to bed late and work your worried fingers to the bone. Don't you know God enjoys giving rest to those he loves?
PSALM 127:1-2 MSG

Father, in Jesus' name, I pray for deliverance from my tendency to wear myself out working, even as I forget that any worthwhile work is yours, not mine. And you are capable of doing it on your own, no matter if I exhaust myself tasking in pitiful human efforts to help you. Lord, remind me to count my tiredness as a blessing that underscores my need for you. Thank you for refreshing me in your love. Amen.

[Jesus] Come to me, all who labor and are heavy laden, and I will give you rest. Take my yoke upon you, and learn from me,
for I am gentle and lowly in heart, and you will find rest for your souls.
For my yoke is easy, and my burden is light.
MATTHEW 11:28-30 ESV

NOTES & PRAYERS ....

....

....

....

YOU HAVE LEARNED FROM SCRIPTURE YOUR HEAVENLY FATHER BLESSES THOSE WHO SHARE, ESPECIALLY THOSE WHO SHARE THE GOOD NEWS OF JESUS.

The one who blesses others is abundantly blessed;
those who help others are helped.

PROVERBS 11:25 MSG

Father God, the destitute widow who shared the last of her flour and oil with Elijah saw in her own life the faithfulness of God in taking care of those who give, even out of their want. *For the jar of flour was not used up and the jug of oil did not run dry, in keeping with the word of the Lord spoken by Elijah. 1 Kings 17:16 NIV.* In your name, remind me, Jesus, Christian sharing points to sharing your Gospel, not just material things. You said, *Man shall not live by bread alone, but by every word that comes from the mouth of God. Matthew 4:4b ESV.* Savior, prompt me to share your Gospel of Good News with others, as you shared with me. Amen.

Let's not allow ourselves to get fatigued doing good. At the right time
we will harvest a good crop if we don't give up, or quit. Right now,
therefore, every time we get the chance, let us work for the benefit of all,
starting with the people closest to us in the community of faith.

GALATIANS 6:9-10 MSG

NOTES & PRAYERS ....

....

....

....

IF YOU ARE GOD'S CHILD, YOUR REPUTATION IS NO LONGER JUST YOUR OWN. IT COULD IMPACT THE WAY PEOPLE AROUND YOU VIEW GOD, WHICH IS THE MAIN REASON FOR KEEPING YOUR REPUTATION ABOVE REPROACH. WHEN YOU CONSIDER ALL GOD HAS DONE FOR YOU, MINDING YOUR REPUTATION ON HIS BEHALF IS THE LEAST YOU CAN DO FOR HIM.

God's reputation is twenty-four-carat gold, with a lifetime guarantee.
PSALM 19:9A MSG

Heavenly Father, I pray in Jesus' spotless name for help guarding my reputation to the purpose of becoming a better ambassador for you. Let me be your witness who shines forth your pure Light before others. Amen.

We're being shown how to turn our backs on a godless, indulgent life, and how to take on a God-filled, God-honoring life. This new life is starting right now and is whetting our appetites for the glorious day when our great God and Savior, Jesus Christ, appears. He offered himself as a sacrifice to free us from a dark, rebellious life into this good, pure life, making us a people he can be proud of, energetic in goodness.
TITUS 2:12-14 MSG

NOTES & PRAYERS ....
....
....
....

DO YOU POSSESS MATERIAL THINGS, OR DO MATERIAL THINGS POSSESS YOU? REMINDER: EVERYTHING BELONGS TO GOD. YOU ARE SIMPLY HIS STEWARD OF A FEW SMALL POSSESSIONS FOR A LITTLE WHILE, ALL OF WHICH HE WANTS YOU TO USE TO FURTHER HIS KINGDOM.

Tell those who are rich not to be proud and not to trust in their money, which will soon be gone, but their pride and trust should be in the living God who always richly gives us all we need for our enjoyment. Tell them to use their money to do good. They should be rich in good works and should give happily to those in need, always being ready to share with others whatever God has given them.

1 TIMOTHY 6:17-18 TLB

Heavenly Father, thank you for the freedom that comes with knowing everything I have belongs to you, even life itself. In Jesus' name, help me be a good steward. Give me Jesus' heart for generosity. Stop self from clamoring for more things I do not need. Let me be an honest steward out of gratitude for your love and mercy, my Father God. Amen.

But if anyone has the world's goods and sees his brother in need, yet closes his heart against him, how does God's love abide in him?

1 JOHN 3:17 ESV

NOTES & PRAYERS ....

....

....

....

GOD WANTS TO COMFORT YOU IN YOUR GRIEF, THAT OPPRESSIVE GLOOMY COMPANION WHO ACCOMPANIES LOSS OF EVERY SORT, LARGE OR SMALL, LONG OR SHORT, EXPECTED OR UNEXPECTED. GOD IN JESUS WILL HOLD YOU UP EVERY DAY OF YOUR MOURNING, NO MATTER HOW LONG IT LASTS, EVEN A LIFETIME.

Praise be to the God and Father of our Lord Jesus Christ, the Father of compassion and the God of all comfort, who comforts us in all our troubles, so that we can comfort those in any trouble with the comfort we ourselves receive from God.

2 CORINTHIANS 1:3-4 NIV

Father, you were with Jesus in the Garden of Gethsemane as he grieved over the prospect of being separated from you, even for a short time. In my own seasons of grief, inspire me to be willing, as Jesus was willing, to accept whatever suffering or joy you have for me. Thank you, God, that no matter what I find myself going through, the Holy Spirit is right there with me. In Jesus' name, out of gratitude, I pray to console others, as I have been so lovingly consoled. Amen.

If your heart is broken, you'll find God right there.

PSALM 34:18A MSG

NOTES & PRAYERS ....

....

....

....

THERE IS NO SUCH THING AS WHOLESOME GOSSIP, NO MATTER IF IT IS TRUE AND NOT JUST RUMOR. GOSSIP IS A NEGATIVE AND WICKED ACTIVITY, MORE DESTRUCTIVE FOR THE GOSSIPER THAN THE GOSSIPEE.

Listening to gossip is like eating cheap candy;
do you really want junk like that in your belly?
PROVERBS 18:8 MSG

Don't criticize and speak evil about each other, dear brothers. If you do,
you will be fighting against God's law of loving one another.
JAMES 4:11-12 TLB

Heavenly Father, I pray in Jesus' name to speak well of people, not evil. Help me model my speech after the upright speech of Jesus. Remind me to look to him as my guide. Give me the conviction of your loving Son to control my tongue. God, teach me to avoid common gossip. Give me the power of Jesus in the Holy Spirit to root out this malevolent stronghold. Let me love others as you love me. Amen.

Mean people spread mean gossip; their words smart and burn.
Troublemakers start fights; gossips break up friendships.
PROVERBS 16:27-28 MSG

NOTES & PRAYERS ....
....
....
....

AS YOU BEGIN THE HEALING PROCESS OF FORGIVING SOMEONE WITH THE HELP OF GOD'S SON, EXPECT YOUR SAVIOR TO REMIND YOU OF AN INSTANCE OR TWO WHEN YOU BETRAYED AND HURT ANOTHER AND NEEDED FORGIVENESS YOURSELF. ALLOW JESUS TO DO THIS WORK IN YOU, SO THAT YOU WILL FINALLY UNDERSTAND THE CRUSHED FEELINGS OF THE ONES YOU INJURED.

Jesus knows everything there is to know about betrayal and hurt at the hands of others. His own betrayors sent him to the cross.

[Jesus] For if you forgive other people when they sin against you, your Heavenly Father will also forgive you. But if you do not forgive others their sins, your Father will not forgive your sins.
MATTHEW 6:14 NIV

In Jesus' name, remind me, Father, to be thankful for hurts that come my way, for only hurts give me valid opportunities to forgive others and be forgiven by you. Teach me, Jesus, to forgive as you forgive, in healing love. Amen.

[Jesus] In everything, do to others what you would have them do to you.
MATTHEW 7:12a NIV

NOTES & PRAYERS ....
....
....
....

HAVE YOU EVER ABUSED THE BLESSING OF PRAYER TO QUESTION YOUR HEAVENLY FATHER? THEN, STOP! GOD IS GOD – ALWAYS SOVEREIGN, GOOD, AND IN CONTROL. YOU AND I ARE MERELY HIS CREATIONS AND IN NO POSITION TO QUESTION HIM, ONLY TO WORSHIP, OBEY, THANK, PRAISE, AND GLORIFY HIM.

Remember your proper place in relation to God, that of humble gratitude and obedience, never arrogant interrogation.

Who in the world do you think you are to second-guess God? Do you for one moment suppose any of us know enough to call God into question?
ROMANS 9:20 MSG

Heavenly Father, you are my God. You do not answer to me. I answer to you. In the name of Jesus, who never questioned you, thank you for being my Father on whom I can depend. I question nothing you ever decide. As your servant in Christ, I live to glorify you. Amen.

[God] For as the heavens are higher than the earth, so are my ways higher than your ways and my thoughts than your thoughts.
ISAIAH 55:9 ESV

NOTES & PRAYERS ....

....

....

....

SUBMIT TO GOD, AND HE WILL PRUNE YOU INTO THE EXACT FORM YOU NEED TO BECOME A FLOURISHING, FRUITFUL BRANCH OF HIS ONE TRUE VINE. AND SINCE GOD IS THE ALL-WISE MASTER GARDENER, YOU ARE GOING TO LOVE EVERY OUTCOME OF HIS PRUNING DECISIONS. HE WILL MAKE YOUR LIFE A PART OF HIS HOLY GARDEN.

[Jesus] I am the true vine, and my Father is the vinedresser.
Every branch in me that does not bear fruit he takes away, and every
branch that does bear fruit he prunes, that it may bear more fruit.

JOHN 15:1-2 ESV

Father God, since pruning promotes healthy growth, prune my life into the divine contours of Jesus, your beautiful Son-form pleasing to you. You have given me faith your decisions will bring me far more joy than any decision self would ever make. Prune me, then, to the proper shape to thrive as a grafted branch into your One True Vine. In Jesus' name, thank you, God. Amen.

But the fruit of the Spirit is love, joy, peace, patience, kindness, goodness,
faithfulness, gentleness, self-control; against such things there is no law.

GALATIANS 5:22-23 ESV

NOTES & PRAYERS ....

....

....

....

SATAN LIKES TO SOW DOUBT IN YOUR HEART WITH DEADLY DOUBLESPEAK. BUT IF YOU STOP HIM WITH GOD'S TRUTH IN PRAYER, SCRIPTURE, AND FAITH, SATAN WILL FLEE FROM YOU AND TAKE DOUBT WITH HIM. ENTER TRUTH. EXIT DOUBT. ENTER FAITH. EXIT SATAN.

For whatever God says to us is full of living power.
HEBREWS 4:12A TLB

Father God, I am grateful for the amazing privilege of entering your throne room of grace in prayer, where faith is the norm and doubt nonexistent. I believe with all my heart Jesus made this possible through his worthiness embued to me. Any sly seed of doubt Satan tries to plant in my heart is nothing compared to individual access to you. In your Son's name, I pray freely as a believer with the aid of the Spirit. Thank you for hearing and answering my prayers. In Messiah's name, thank you for personal prayer to you in the Spirit, for with Jesus as my High Priest and advocate before you, I am made worthy and doubtless in him. Amen.

So it is with prayer – keep asking and you will keep getting; keep looking and you will keep finding; knock and the door will be opened.
LUKE 11:9 TLB

NOTES & PRAYERS ....

....

....

....

WHICH DO YOU WANT – CONTENTMENT IN JESUS OR DISCONTENTMENT IN SELF? MORE IMPORTANTLY, WHICH DOES GOD WANT FOR YOU?

Godliness with contentment is great gain.

1 TIMOTHY 6:6 ESV

Thank you, Father, for convicting me of my habit of infantile self-talk and self-centered prayers – "If only I get this-or-that, I'll finally be happy." Forgive me for taking so long to learn your Truth that so many things I have convinced myself I just-have-to-have will turn to ashes in my mouth, if they are not to your glory. You have made your own list of what I just-have-to-have to experience contentment in your will. In Jesus' name, give me wisdom to make your list my list. For I have learned the hard way you lead to peace, while self leads to turmoil. Thank you, God, for making the perfect life-list for me and bringing it to completion. Amen.

If you get rid of unfair practices, quit blaming victims, quit gossiping about other people's sins, and if you are generous with the hungry and start giving yourselves to the down-and-out, your lives will begin to glow in the darkness. Your shadowed lives will be bathed in sunlight.

ISAIAH 58:9-10 MSG

NOTES & PRAYERS ....

....

....

....

WHEN GOD LISTENS TO YOUR PRAYERS, WHAT DOES HE HEAR ON DEEP LEVELS, RATHER THAN SURFACE LEVELS – MORE CONCERN FOR OTHERS, INCLUDING GOD? OR MORE CONCERN FOR SELF, EXCLUDING GOD?

[God] But this is the one to whom I will look:
he who is humble and contrite in Spirit and trembles at my word.

ISAIAH 66:2B ESV

Commit your way to the Lord; trust in him, and he will act.

PSALM 37:5 ESV

In Jesus' name, Heavenly Father, I ask the Holy Spirit to ground my prayers in upright motives pleasing to you. Remind me to put you first, not last. I believe if I get that part right – you first – all good things will flow from it into the lives of those for whom I pray, even my life. Thank you, Father, for being worthy of all glory. You are first. Amen.

[Jesus] "So do not worry, saying, 'What shall we eat?' or 'What shall we drink?' or 'What shall we wear?' For the pagans run after these things, and your Father knows you need them. But seek first his Kingdom and righteousness, and all these things will be given to you, as well."

MATTHEW 6:31-33 NIV

NOTES & PRAYERS ....

....

....

....

IN WHICH CONSTANT CONDITION HAVE YOU CHOSEN TO LIVE YOUR LIFE – WOEFUL IN SELF OR WONDERFUL IN JESUS?

For a child (Jesus) will be born to us, a Son will be given to us;
and the government will rest on his shoulders; and his name will be called
Wonderful Counselor, Mighty God, Eternal Father, Prince of Peace.

ISAIAH 9:6 NASB

Lord Jesus, one of your names is Wonderful, which in Hebrew can mean miraculous – and miraculous is what you are, my Savior. In your wonderful and miraculous name, thank you for rescuing me from hopeless woe. Guide me now toward sharing with others the miracle of your extraordinary love. Jesus, you are Light, Love, and Wonder. Amen.

By awesome and wondrous (miraculous) things, you answer us in
righteousness, O God of our salvation. You who are the trust and hope
of all the ends of the earth and of the farthest sea; Who creates the
mountain by His strength, Being clothed with power, Who stills the
roaring of the seas, The roaring of their waves, And the tumult of the
peoples, So they who dwell at the ends of the earth stand in
awe of Your signs [the evidence of Your presence].
You make the dawn and the sunset shout for joy.

PSALM 65:5-8 AMP

NOTES & PRAYERS ....
....
....
....

GABRIEL, GOD'S ANGEL, INFORMED MARY THAT AS A VIRGIN, SHE WOULD GIVE BIRTH TO GOD'S SON.

Thank you, Father, in the name of Jesus, for Mary's humble willingness to embrace your divine plan for her life. Amen.

And in the sixth month (of the pregnancy of Elisabeth with John the Baptist – Elisabeth being Mary's cousin) the angel Gabriel was sent from God unto a city of Galilee, named Nazareth, to a virgin espoused to a man whose name was Joseph, of the house of David; and the virgin's name was Mary. And the angel came in unto her, and said, Hail, thou that art highly favoured, the Lord is with thee: blessed art thou among women. And when she saw him, she was troubled at his saying, and cast in her mind what manner of salutation this should be. And the angel said unto her, Fear not, Mary: for thou hast found favour with God. And, behold, thou shalt conceive in thy womb, and bring forth a son, and shalt call his name Jesus. He shall be great, and shall be called the Son of the Highest: and the Lord God shall give unto him the throne of his father David: And he shall reign over the house of Jacob forever; and of his kingdom there shall be no end. Then said Mary unto the angel, How shall this be, seeing I know not a man? And the angel answered and said unto her, The Holy Ghost shall come upon thee, and the power of the Highest shall overshadow thee: therefore, also that holy thing which shall be born of thee shall be called the Son of God. And Mary said, Behold the handmaid of the Lord; be it unto me according to thy word.

LUKE 1:26-35; 38A KJV

NOTES & PRAYERS ....

....

....

....

AN ANGEL OF THE LORD CAME TO JOSEPH IN A DREAM TO INFORM HIM THE BABY IN MARY'S WOMB WAS OF THE HOLY GHOST.

In Jesus' name, thank you, God, for sending an angel to assure Joseph the unborn baby of his future wife, Mary, was of the Holy Ghost, and that he (Joseph) would be doing the right thing to marry her, take care of her, and serve as earthly father to her heavenly child. And Joseph did! Amen.

Now the birth of Jesus Christ was on this wise: When as his mother Mary was espoused to Joseph, before they came together, she was found with child of the Holy Ghost. Then Joseph her husband, being a just man, and not willing to make her a public example, was minded to put her away privily. But while he thought on these things, behold, the angel of the Lord appeared unto him in a dream, saying, Joseph, thou son of David, fear not to take unto thee Mary thy wife: for that which is conceived in her is of the Holy Ghost. And she shall bring forth a son, and thou shalt call his name Jesus: for he shall save his people from their sins. Now all this was done, that it might be fulfilled which was spoken of the Lord by the prophet, saying, Behold, a virgin shall be with child, and shall bring forth a son, and they shall call his name Emmanuel, which being interpreted is, God with us. Then Joseph being raised from sleep did as the angel of the Lord had bidden him, and took unto him his wife: And knew her not till she had brought forth her firstborn son: and he called his name Jesus.

MATTHEW 1:18-25 KJV

NOTES & PRAYERS ....
....
....
....

JESUS HAS ARRIVED, BRINGING SALVATION!

And it came to pass in those days, that there went out a decree from Caesar Augustus that all the world should be taxed. And all went to be taxed, every one into his own city. And Joseph also went up from Galilee, out of the city of Nazareth, into Judaea, unto the city of David, which is called Bethlehem; (because he was of the house and lineage of David:) To be taxed with Mary his espoused wife, being great with child. And so it was, that, while they were there, the days were accomplished that she should be delivered. And she brought forth her firstborn son, and wrapped him in swaddling clothes, and laid him in a manger; because there was no room for them in the inn. And there were in the same country shepherds abiding in the field, keeping watch over their flock by night. And, lo, the angel of the Lord came upon them, and the glory of the Lord shone round about them: and they were sore afraid. And the angel said unto them, Fear not: for behold, I bring you good tidings of great joy, which shall be to all people. For unto you is born this day in the city of David a Saviour, which is Christ the Lord. And this shall be a sign unto you; Ye shall find the baby wrapped in swaddling clothes, lying in a manger. And suddenly there was with the angel a multitude of the heavenly host praising God, and saying, Glory to God in the highest, and on earth peace, good will toward men. And it came to pass, as the angels were gone away from them into heaven, the shepherds said one to another, Let us now go even unto Bethlehem, and see this thing which is come to pass, which the Lord hath made known unto us. And they came with haste, and found Mary, and Joseph, and the babe lying in a manger. And when they had seen it, they made known abroad the saying which was told them concerning this child. And all they that heard it wondered at those things, which were told them by the shepherds. But Mary kept all these things, and pondered them in her heart.

L U K E 2:1; 2-19 KJV

NOTES & PRAYERS ....

....

....

....

IF YOU NEED A LIFT, LIFT UP YOUR EYES. LIFT UP YOUR EYES AND PRAISE GOD IN SPIRIT AND TRUTH FOR WHAT YOU SEE IN HIS GLORY IN THE SKY. LIFT UP YOUR EYES TOWARD HEAVEN AND BE HUMBLED BY THE CREATIVE POWER OF THE HEAVENLY FATHER, SON, AND SPIRIT. LIFT UP YOUR EYES AND OBSERVE GOD'S GLORIOUS CREATION.

The heavens declare the glory of God; the skies proclaim the work of his hands. Day after day they pour forth speech; night after night they reveal knowledge. They have no speech; they use no words; no sound is heard from them. Yet their voice goes out into all the earth, their words to the ends of the world.

PSALM 19:1-4A NIV

In Jesus' name, thank you, Father, for prompting me to behold the expansive evidence of your majesty in the sky. Your creation reveals the beauty of you, my Heavenly Father – breathtaking, majestic, resplendent, magnificent, glorious, and holy. Praise you, Father, Son, and Holy Spirit. Amen.

[God] You, Lord (Jesus), laid the foundation of the earth in the beginning, and the heavens are the work of your hands.

HEBREWS 1:10 ESV

NOTES & PRAYERS ....
....
....
....

IF YOU BELONG TO GOD, EXPECT TO BE BLESSED BY HIS DISCIPLINE. GOD IS WISE. HE KNOWS THAT DIVINE DISCIPLINE IN THE SHORT TERM MAKES FOR A BETTER LIFE IN THE LONG TERM. THANK GOD FOR USING DISCIPLINE TO PREPARE YOU FOR YOUR GLORIOUS ETERNITY IN HIM.

[Jesus] The people I love, I call to account – prod and correct and guide so they'll live at their best. Up on your feet, then! About face! Run after God!

REVELATION 3:19 MSG

Father, I trust your judgment and accept whatever discipline you have for me. Thank you in Jesus' name for being my most excellent and loving Creator. Amen.

My son, do not make light of the Lord's discipline, and do not lose heart when he rebukes you, because the Lord disciplines the one he loves, and he chastens everyone he accepts as his son.

HEBREWS 12:5B-6 NIV

Know then in your heart that as a man disciplines his son, so the Lord your God disciplines you. Observe the commands of the Lord your God, walking in obedience to him and revering him.

DEUTERONOMY 8:5-6 NIV

NOTES & PRAYERS ....

....

....

....

TO BE RESPONSIBLE IN OBEDIENCE TO GOD IS TO BE A BELIEVER WHO REAPS ETERNAL BENEFITS. GREAT IS GOD'S FAITHFULNESS TO BLESS HIS CHILDREN.

So we make it our goal to please him (Jesus), whether we are at home in the body or away from it. For we must all appear before the judgment seat of Christ, so that each of us may receive what is due us for the things done while in the body, whether good or bad.

2 CORINTHIANS 5:9-10 NIV

Heavenly Father, guide me toward maturity in your ways. It is no use pretending I do not know what your ways are. I cannot hide behind ignorance. You know very well I am aware of your Word. I ask you to prompt me, Father – remind me – to pay attention to your commands and precepts. Teach me to engage in responsible obedience that springs from a heart overflowing with love and gratitude for all you have done for me. In Jesus' name, help me remain loving, grateful, obedient, true, and constant in you. Make me faithful to obey you, God. Bless my efforts. Amen.

Whatever you do, work at it with all your heart, as working for the Lord, not human masters, since you know that you will receive an inheritance from the Lord as a reward. It is the Lord Christ you are serving.

COLOSSIANS 3:23-24 NIV

NOTES & PRAYERS ....

....

....

....

GOOD MORNING, FATHER. GOOD DAY, SON. GOODNIGHT, HOLY SPIRIT. GOOD EVERY-MOMENT-OF-EVERY-HOUR-OF-EVERY-DAY, HEAVENLY FATHER AND CREATOR.

This is too glorious, too wonderful to believe! I can never be lost to your Spirit! I can never get away from my God! If I go up to heaven, you are there; if I go down to the place of the dead, you are there. If I ride the morning winds to the farthest oceans, even there your hand will guide me, your strength will support me. If I try to hide in the darkness, night becomes light around me. For even darkness cannot hide from God.

PSALM 139:6-11 TLB

I am grateful, Father, for your loyal Spirit presence in your Son. Thank you, Jesus, for standing before God, my Father, constantly advocating for me. Thank you, Holy Spirit – Comforter, Counselor, and Teacher – for indwelling my heart and never leaving me alone. In Jesus' name, I pray for wisdom to conduct myself with keen awareness that you, Father, in your Holy Trininty, Divine Three-In-One, are always with me. Thank you, Mighty God. Amen.

Am I a God at hand, declares the Lord, and not a God far away? Can a man hide himself in secret places so that I cannot see him? declares the Lord. Do I not fill heaven and earth?

JEREMIAH 23:23-24a ESV

NOTES & PRAYERS ....

....

....

....

YOU ARE CHOSEN BY YOUR HEAVENLY FATHER TO BE HIS CHILD. PRAISE HIM! THANK HIM!

Dear friends, God the Father chose you long ago and knew you would become his children. And the Holy Spirit has been at work in your hearts, cleansing you with the blood of Jesus Christ, making you to please him.

1 PETER 1:2A TLB

In your Son's name, thank you, Father, for choosing, loving, forgiving, saving, and transforming me from dark to light. I am grateful for salvation in Jesus. Glory to God. Amen.

But you are the ones chosen by God, chosen for the high calling of priestly work, chosen to be a holy people, God's instruments to do his work and speak out for him, to tell others of the night-and-day difference he made for you – from nothing to something, from rejected to accepted.

1 PETER 2:9-10 MSG

Long ago, even before he made the world, God chose us to be his very own through what Christ would do for us; he decided then to make us holy in his eyes, without a single fault – we who stand before him covered with his love. His unchanging plan has always been to adopt us into his own family by sending Jesus Christ to die for us. And he did this because he wanted to!

EPHESIANS 1:4-5 TLB

NOTES & PRAYERS ....

....

....

....

YOU CONFESSED YOUR SINS BEFORE GOD, REPENTED, CHANGED, ASKED FORGIVENESS, AND PROFESSED YOUR BELIEF IN JESUS AS HIS SON. WHICH WAS THE MOMENT GOD SAVED YOU THROUGH THE BLOOD SACRIFICE AND RESURRECTION OF YOUR SAVIOR. THEN THE HOLY SPIRIT RECREATED AND SEALED YOU AS A CITIZEN OF HIS KINGDOM. PRAISE GOD, GRANTOR OF DIVINE CITIZENSHIP.

Now you are no longer strangers to God and foreigners to heaven, but you are members of God's very own family, citizens of God's country, and you belong in God's household with every other Christian. What a foundation you stand on now: the apostles and the prophets; and the cornerstone of the building is Jesus Christ himself! We who believe are carefully joined together with Christ as part of a beautiful, constantly growing temple for God. And you also are joined with him and with each other by the Spirit and are part of the dwelling place of God.

EPHESIANS 2:19-20 TLB

Thank you, Father, in my Savior's name that he sealed my citizenship in the Kingdom of Heaven forever. Amen.

Friends, this world is not your home, so don't make yourselves cozy in it. Don't indulge your ego at the expense of your soul.

1 PETER 2:11 MSG

NOTES & PRAYERS ....

....

....

....

Look for Terry Ward Tucker's book,
Radiance ~ Daily Devotions.

Please enjoy the following sample.

AS YOU BEGIN THE NEW YEAR, WALK IN THE RADIANCE OF JESUS, GOD'S GLORY. HE WILL LIGHT YOUR PATH.

For Jesus is God's "flow'r, whose fragrance, tender with sweetness, fills the air, and dispels with glorious splendor the darkness everywhere."

LO, HOW A ROSE E'ER BLOOMING, FRIEDRICH LAYRITZ

Thank you, Heavenly Father, for C.S. Lewis' inspired certainty that Jesus is, indeed, your Son, my Savior, and Light of the world. Lewis wrote: *"I believe in Christianity as I believe that the sun has risen: not only because I see it, but because by it I see everything else."* Mighty God, you gave Jesus – your own radiance – to save my soul. He is the illumination of your Holy Spirit by which I see how to live my life. In his name, thank you, Father, for the freedom you have given me in him, salvation's bright morning star. Let me live forever in his healing Light that is your glorious Light. Praise the Son, my Savior. Praise the Father. Praise the Holy Spirit. Praise God in his Holy Trinity. Amen.

The son is the radiance of God's glory and exact representation of his being, sustaining all things by his powerful word. After he had provided purification for sins, he sat down at the right hand of the Majesty.

HEBREWS 1:3A NIV

NOTES & PRAYERS ....

....

....

....

ABOUT THE AUTHOR

TERRY WARD TUCKER and her family are members of First Baptist Church of Charleston, South Carolina. She holds a PhD in Reading Education. Her first book, *Charleston's Elegant Sinners*, is set in the Lowcountry of South Carolina. Her second novel, *Moonlight and Mill Whistles*, received *ForeWord Magazine's* Silver Book of the Year Award. Winston Groom, author of Forrest Gump wrote, *"Terry Ward Tucker tells a lovely and captivating story in Moonlight and Mill Whistles. Her writing is a joy to read."* Terry's latest novel, *Moonbow Over Charleston*, is also set in the South. Pat Conroy wrote about *Moonbow*, *"Terry Ward Tucker paints a moonbow upon Charleston's night sky and gifts us all with its loveliness. Thank you, Terry!"* Tucker served as screenplay co-writer for faith-based movie, *Only God Can*, produced by Inspire You Entertainment, and sole screenplay writer for *Hate Won't Win*, a new film in development based on the shooting massacre at Mother Emanuel Church in Charleston. Tucker came to Christ at age eight in a revival meeting at First Baptist Church in Lancaster, South Carolina. She is thankful to be known as a born again Christian and hopes people all over the world will be as blessed by her daily devotions as she was by writing them.

Made in the USA
Columbia, SC
08 August 2020

15013097R00231